New Paths in
Muslim Evangelism

New Paths in Muslim Evangelism

Evangelical Approaches to Contextualization

Phil Parshall

Foreword by Warren W. Webster

BAKER BOOK HOUSE
Grand Rapids, Michigan 49506

ISBN: 0-8010-7056-2

First printing, January 1981
Second printing, November 1982
Third printing, August 1984
Fourth printing, August 1986

Printed in the United States of America

TO
JULIE and LINDY
My two best friends and intimate colleagues in the ministry

Acknowledgments

A book of this nature is a composite of a lifetime of ministry and experiences. Out of a varied mosaic of the spectacular and the mundane, the tears and the laughter, the valleys and the peaks, slowly emerges a set of beliefs—beliefs not embedded in concrete, but rather clothed in the errant nature of the human mind and heart. As these working postulates continue to be refined by involvement in real situations, along with helpful critiques from other believers, there emerges a broad consensus, reinforced by an inner conviction given by the Holy Spirit, that "this is the way; walk in it." As will be seen in this book, the sequence described above is "in process." It is dynamic rather than stationary.

To those who have assisted me in my sojourn to this point, I would like to express my heartfelt gratitude. Samuel Barkat, now vice-president of King's College, was the first to be used of the Lord to challenge me to give my life to Muslim evangelism. Operation Mobilization (O.M.) and a 1960 summer crusade in Mexico gave me spiritual direction which was absolutely crucial at that pivotal point in my life. George Verwer, founder of O.M., and a close friend for the past twenty years, has been a great source of challenge and inspiration. Our back-up team of churches and individuals, both in finances and in prayer, has been outstanding. Highland Park Baptist Church in Southfield, Michigan, our home church, epitomizes all that a missionary could possibly desire in areas of love, concern, and involvement.

At the risk of being trite and traditional, I publicly acknowledge the many hours my wife Julie has spent typing this manuscript. In addition to this, her incisive critiques have been invaluable.

And lastly, I "acknowledge" Jesus Christ, my Savior, my Lord, and my Master.

Trinity Evangelical Divinity School and the Fuller Seminary School of World Mission have contributed immeasurably to the concepts found in this book. My mind has been stretched and my heart enlarged by an in-depth exposure to the men of God who serve on the faculty of both schools. Special recognition is given to Charles Kraft, whose fertile mind has guided me through many of the foundational concepts found in this book. Paul Hiebert and Dean Gilliland were also extremely helpful in this process. Herbert Kane of Trinity, by personal example, first proved to me that an academic missiologist can be a humble, gracious man of God.

Foreword

Two major problems confront anyone endeavoring to communicate God's Good News in Christ to Muslim friends.

The first stems from a failure to separate the kernel of the gospel from the cultural shell in which it is conveyed. People should not have to become Westerners—or first-century Greeks —in order to become followers of Jesus.

A second problem arises from so thoroughly accommodating the gospel of Christ to the values, thought patterns, and cultural forms of Muslim society that a syncretistic religious mixture results which is really "another gospel" of the type that the apostle Paul condemned in his letter to the Galatians.

Phil Parshall has successfully avoided both difficulties. Having lived in the Muslim world for more than twenty-one years he is understandably impatient with traditional approaches which have too often proven ineffective in bringing communities of Muslims to follow Jesus Christ as Savior and Lord. In this creative and stimulating study the author calls for a new readiness to experiment with forms of cultural adaptation which are both biblical and workable in sharing with Muslims the great truth that "God was in Christ reconciling the world to Himself."

Eastern rather than Western patterns of worship are advocated so that the Muslim inquirer or convert feels at home in joining with other followers of Jesus. He is not made to embrace modes of religious expression that are totally foreign to his culture and upbringing. Shoes are removed before entering the place of worship, and all worshipers sit on the floor as they would in a mosque. Believers greet by embracing in Muslim fashion. During prayer, hands are lifted with palms toward heaven. Bibles are placed on folding stands such as are used for the Quran, and Scriptures are chanted in Quranic style. Hymns, if sung at all, are Eastern rather than Western tunes. No biblical truth or practice is compromised through these cultural adaptations. Initial response in various Muslim countries has been gratifying and encouraging.

This book aptly reminds us that identification and communication lie at the very heart of our incarnational faith—"the Word became flesh and dwelt among us" in the role of a Servant. Having met Him we are commissioned to go and tell others. That includes the household of Islam.

Warren W. Webster
General Director
Conservative Baptist Foreign Mission Society

Contents

11

PART III

Potential for Contextualization

Introduction

The world is coming alive to the presence of a religious community which for centuries has been basically ignored. Muslims stretch from Indonesia to Tunisia; there are vast numbers of them even in Russia. Almost every nation on earth has on its soil a community of dedicated "Sons of Ishmael." The political, religious, and economic clout of Islam has never been greater. People who ignore or belittle the Muslim power structure do so to their own peril. *Time* magazine devoted its April 16, 1979, cover story to this emerging and dynamic movement:

> Islam is the world's youngest universal faith, and second largest, with 750 million adherents, to about 985 million for Christianity. Across the eastern hemisphere but primarily in that strategic crescent that straddles the crossroads of three continents, Muslims are rediscovering their spiritual roots and reasserting the political power of the Islamic way of life. Repelled by the bitter fruits of modernization and fired by a zealous pride in its ancient heritage, the umma (world community) of Islam is stirring with revival.... The West can no longer afford to ignore or dismiss the living power of the Prophet's message.[1]

1. *Time*, 16 April 1979, pp. 40, 49.

Islam moved off the deserts of Arabia in the seventh century. From there, it quickly spread, mainly through conquest, to embrace the Middle East, all of North Africa, and large parts of Europe. For the next several hundred years, Islam developed a proud heritage of culture and art, and held varying degrees of power and influence. An all-time low was reached in Muslim-Christian relations when Crusaders in the late eleventh and twelfth century marched forth into Muslim-occupied lands with terrible, destroying vengeance. The Sons of Ishmael cringed before the powerful armies of the West. Cities were ransacked, homes burned, women were raped, and children enslaved.

The Crusaders were indeed a pious group. Their breastplates of armor blazed with the red brilliance of painted crosses. They marched on and on to the tune of war hymns. Only on Sunday did they cease their genocidal operations in order to devoutly worship God the Father and Jesus the Son. What spiritual goal prodded these zealots forth in their unrelenting conquests? Muslims were occupying the holy city of Jerusalem. At any cost, they must be driven from sacred Christian soil. The memories of this dark page of church history linger on with vivid reality in the minds and hearts of huge segments of Muslim people.

Much of Islam was under colonial domination in the nineteenth and first half of the twentieth century. A persuasive argument could be made regarding Muslim economic improvement during this period. But can a subjugated people who are denied full human rights be really happy? Even the relatively benign rule of the British in India was destined to come to an end. In the bosom of humans God has placed a natural and right desire to be free from domination by other human beings.

> The dedicated Christian at times finds it difficult to understand the thrust of nationalism that causes a "backward" people to be ungrateful for schools, hospitals, literacy programs, and other Christian achievements that have been such a blessing to literally millions of people in the Third World. A similar problem existed in the minds of the colonial rulers when they were being made to leave lands that they felt they

had governed in all fairness and justice. Laurens van der Post has written of a conversation he had with the Governor-General of Indonesia at the time the Dutch regime was rapidly breaking up. The Governor-General was totally perplexed. He cited the many improvements the Dutch had implemented in Indonesia. He referred to schools, hospitals, roads, and the inauguration of a fair and efficient judicial system. The discouraged Governor-General looked over at van der Post and said, "Can you tell me why this is happening?" The wise van der Post made an extremely pertinent reply. He said, "Yes, I believe I can tell you. It is because of the look in your eye when you were talking to them."[2]

This haughty look of the West has made a deep impression on the Muslim. Colonial empires fragmented in the months following the Second World War. Muslims were allowed to taste the clean, fresh air of freedom once again. How exhilarating! Poor, downtrodden, illiterate, but—free, yes, free to forge their own destiny. In this euphoric atmosphere a dynamic new force emerged which compelled the world to recognize and treat with proper respect the Islamic bloc of nations. Massive oil reserves have caused scores of the world's most prestigious diplomats to make respectful pilgrimages to Saudi Arabia and other Middle Eastern nations.

There is now an important process of authentication and rediscovery going on among Muslims. Islamic culture and religion are being portrayed as symbols of a positive self-identity. There is a strong flow of nationalism that is making Muslims proud to be Muslims. They can now make it in their own right. No longer is the West the all-powerful patron saint.

The factors we have just discussed, along with theological issues, have made the Muslim extremely resistant to the gospel of Jesus Christ. Only in Indonesia, where political issues have been heavily involved, has there been a significant turning to Christ.

2. Phil Parshall, *The Fortress and the Fire* (Bombay: Gospel Literature Service, 1976), p. 80.

The church's response has often been to turn away from the great
challenge of Islam and to seek out more "fruitful" fields of labor.

But what about Christian responsibility to this bloc of
unreached peoples? Ralph Winter has stated, "The Muslim group,
which is already immense, is growing at a biological rate almost
double that of the Chinese . . . if present rates continue, there will
be more Muslims than Chinese within about ten years."[3]

This book will cite illustrations of ministry among Muslims
around the world. Most of these ministries will not be specifically
identified. This policy has been adopted in order to protect Christian nationals and missionaries presently living and working in
sensitive areas of the world.

It is necessary to clearly state the theological perspective
from which I write. I first heard the gospel when I was a student at
Miami Senior High School. That same evening I placed my faith in
Jesus. Immediately, a transforming process began in my life that
continues to the present. It is with a deep-felt conviction that I affirm the authority of Scripture as well as my motivating belief that
there is no salvation apart from faith in Jesus Christ. I am happy to
be placed in the general category of an evangelical. I disavow,
however, the attitude of those who, while holding to evangelical
orthodoxy, feel it right to engage in accusing and attacking other
Christian brethren who may not hold to every jot and tittle of theology as they personally perceive it. Such action seems to lead to a
rigid pharisaism that knows little of grace and the love of the
cross. Infighting can only deter us from the great all-consuming
task of world evangelization.

Some of the things I say and/or the positions I take may trouble certain readers. Let me explain my thinking in four areas of
potential misunderstanding:

1. At places, this book raises provocative issues. This is not
done with any desire to be simply controversial. It is my conviction that the Christian church must look with a critical eye at the
whole subject of Muslim evangelism. There is a piercing urgency

    3. Ralph D. Winter, "The Highest Priority: Cross-Cultural Evangelism," in
Crucial Dimensions in World Evangelization, ed. Arthur F. Glasser (Pasadena: William
Carey Library, 1976), p. 122.

to our deliberations. The Great Commission provided for no exceptions. The imperative of proclamation is affirmed by the reality that thousands of Muslims die daily with no saving knowledge of Jesus Christ.

It is acknowledged that this book will be read and discussed by people from many varying backgrounds. Conclusions will differ greatly. That is not altogether bad. There is no ultimate methodology, only an ultimate message. The gospel should be allowed to flow in the most productive manner possible in each distinct situation.

2. Academicians might say that this book is calling for a "paradigm shift." That is, it seeks a move away from models of evangelistic technique that have proved barren and a shift toward experimental methodology that may result in a fruit-bearing experience among Muslims. "By this is My Father glorified, that you bear much fruit, and so prove to be My disciples" (John 15:8).

Readers are frequently on the defensive when encountering material that challenges their previous perspectives. Krister Stendahl has observed that "our vision is more obstructed by what we think we know than by our lack of knowledge."[4] Perhaps humility is the greatest need of all of us. Our previous approaches are not necessarily more scriptural just because they have been around longer. Nor dare I claim that my insights are more right simply because they are mine. But our presuppositional filters (whether conservative or innovative) do need to be recognized and compensated for as we consider that the Lord might be speaking to us in a new and fresh manner concerning the methods we use to communicate to Muslims His changeless love.

An evangelical leader involved in Muslim outreach has commented on the need for a possible new approach to Islam:

> And finally, a plea to *openness and experimentation*. I think we all are a little bit too timid there. We need to do much more experimentation. We have big million dollar studios and stations that we feel we immediately are jeopardizing, but

4. Krister Stendahl, *Paul Among Jews and Gentiles and Other Essays* (Philadelphia: Fortress Press, 1976), p. 7.

somewhere along the line I think we need to experiment much more.[5]

From the liberal wing of the church comes a rather startling proposal that "every mission board should put twenty percent of its total budget into experiments in mission."[6] Lesslie Newbigin, one of India's most respected missionary statesmen, reflects on his long career with some misgivings about his own attitudes and approaches:

> But like others who have spent long periods in foreign missionary service, I have to bear witness that the experience of living for most of four decades as part of an Indian Church has made me acutely aware of the cultural conditioning of the Christianity in which I was nurtured, and of the culture-bound character of many of the assumptions which are unquestioned by English Christians.[7]

As long as we do not engage in compromising the Bible, I feel we are no worse off proceeding with careful and sensitive experimentation than we are by remaining content with a methodology which has proven to be ineffective in bringing Muslims to our Lord. A new approach at least gives us hope of bringing some seed to fruition and then on to harvest.

3. The word *contextualization* has a negative ring to a certain segment of people. This often occurs due to a lack of understanding and definition of the concept. By some it is seen as synonymous with syncretism. My early chapters seek to reassure the reader that a proper usage of contextualization can maintain total fidelity to the Word of God. If this were not my absolute conviction, I would not be writing this book. My plea is for patience and discernment as the reader plows through to the last page. Only through such a process will my thoughts emerge with any degree of clarity.

5. *Conference on Media in Islamic Culture Report,* ed. C. Richard Shumaker (Marseilles: Evangelical Literature Overseas, 1974), p. 78.

6. Arden Almquist, *Missionary, Come Back!* (New York: World Publishing, 1970), p. 142.

7. Lesslie Newbigin, *The Open Secret* (London: S.P.C.K., 1978), p. 166.

4. The majority of books written on Islam deal with orthodox, intellectual Islam. Writers like W. Montgomery Watt and Kenneth Cragg typify this approach. Few writers have focused entirely on what is generally termed "popular Islam." This latter designation of Islam points to the practices and beliefs of the common man. It deals particularly with the significant amount of animistic belief resident in grassroots Islam. The study of popular Islam digs in at the local level and seeks to analyze thought processes behind common behavioral patterns that are widespread among the masses.

It is not wise, however, to completely dichotomize popular and intellectual Islam. They are very much interwoven with each other. The great apostle to Islam, Samuel Zwemer, did the best job of synthesizing the two emphases. Zwemer, a prolific and outstanding writer, always maintained his focus on the Islam he saw actually being worked out in the Middle East. Yet, he could see the influence of the orthodox creeds and Quranic injunctions on every community of Muslims.

This book is basically following the Zwemer approach, with the added dimension of exploring relatively untried and untested methodological options for communicating Christ in an Islamic cultural and religious milieu. My rather extensive reading of Zwemer indicates that he engaged in little experimentation or innovation in areas of methodology.

The target group under consideration in this book is the reasonably orthodox Muslim living in a rural area in a country which is predominantly Islamic. This should be constantly borne in mind. Others more qualified than myself will speak to issues like the urbanized Muslim, the cultic Muslim outside the mainstream of Islam, or the Muslim immigrant living in a major Western city. My focus, by design, is the great mass of Muslims living as simple, devout, unsophisticated people in more than a score of countries.

My visits to eleven Muslim countries lead me to conclude that, beneath surface-level similarities, there lie a large number of theological, structural, and cultural variations. The unity of Islam encompasses much diversity. Though what I say is intended to have value for those working in many parts of the Muslim mosaic, the fact that the majority of my experience and study has been specifically to but one country must be borne in mind. The reader with exposure to other Muslim countries will need to adjust for the differences between his situation and mine. Furthermore, many of my observations should be regarded as general. This book is presented as a painter presents the background of a picture. It is an overview. It is my hope that others will follow who are competent to fill in the painting with the necessary specifics and detail.

Any author keenly feels his own limitations. I experience these even more deeply now than I did five years ago when I wrote my first book, *The Fortress and the Fire*. But it seems to me that Christian commitment demands pushing forward to new frontiers. A beautiful picture of a ship on an ocean in the midst of a storm graces my bedroom wall. The inscription reads, "A ship in a harbor is safe, but that is not what ships are built for." The "safe haven" of easy, comfortable, serene Christianity seems to me quite antithetical to the whole spirit of what the Word of God is all about.

This is a book that is written in the spirit of breaking out of safe harbors. The task of conquering new frontiers demands reflection, decision, and, most importantly, engagement.

And now, on to the task. . . .

Lombaro Case Study

Examples of contextualized witness to Muslims are rare. The following is based on an ongoing experiment in one Muslim country. Certain nonessential details have been altered in order to protect the identity of missionaries and nationals who are engaged in this outreach. Many of the postulates of this book will be seen in a practical setting within this case study.

Lombaro is a nation of seventy million people. Approximately 80 percent of them are Muslim, while 20 percent are animist. Fewer than 1 percent are Christian. The government officially acknowledges its dependence on Allah and is quite Islamic in orientation.

Christians number some four hundred thousand—equally divided between Protestants and Catholics. Christian missionary outreach commenced in Lombaro in 1840. Pioneer missionaries soon began to see fruit from their preaching among the animists. As a result, the forms of church worship are predominantly those of Western Christianity combined with an animistic religious flavor. This admixture of harmless "form" syncretism works well in evangelistic efforts among the animists of Lombaro, but it is devastating in terms of Muslim evangelism.

The churches, then, are made up almost entirely of a small body of believers of animistic background. Administratively, there are some excellent men of God who give able leadership to the church. Financially, however, the various denominations are almost entirely dependent on assistance from Western Christians. This not only applies to church budgetary needs, but also extends to job opportunities in mission institutions and Western developmental organizations.

Thirty-five Protestant mission societies have fielded some four hundred missionaries throughout Lombaro. Most of these are working within the established church or are attached to mission-operated institutions. It is gratifying to note a definite trend to place more missionaries in full-time evangelistic outreach. There is a warm, cordial, and mutually appreciative interchange among missionaries.

Historical Development

The Whole World Mission (W.W.M.) entered the town of Gaziville in 1955. Since that time up to the present two to four missionary couples have always been resident in this town of some thirty thousand. Their goal was to evangelize using the traditional methodology of the church. Until 1975, the zealous efforts of these missionaries remained fruitless. No church was established and almost no one led to Christ. Gaziville appeared barren and resistant. W.W.M.'s field council determined it would be expedient to withdraw from the area unless a breakthrough occurred in the ensuing twelve months. Then—the miraculous began to unfold!

Presently, there are two worshiping groups of Muslim converts in the Gaziville area. One fellowship is made up of twenty converts while fifteen former Muslims comprise the other worshiping community. Almost all are male heads of families. The work is young and not fully tested. Only time will reveal the stability or instability of these newborn believers in Christ. What follows is the story of the past five years.

Description of Converts

Though geographically divided by some twenty miles, the two fellowships are quite similar. The majority are barely literate farmers. Economically they are self-supporting, and their families are close enough sociologically to intermarry. The most rapid spiritual growth has been experienced among those who were formerly *devout* Muslims. Almost all are reading the Bible (or having it read to them), are praying, and are meeting together informally in their homes for worship—without the presence of a foreign missionary. Witnessing to their neighbors and extended families commences from the day of conversion and has been the major cause of numerical increase. Up to now, the missionary has won very few of these men to the Lord. His role is basically to give spiritual encouragement and biblical teaching.

In evangelistic witness the following areas are stressed: (1) Old Testament stories which are found in the Quran; (2) the universality of sin; (3) the biblical teaching of atonement; and (4) the second coming of Christ.

None of the believers reside in Gaziville. All live in nearby villages. Most have suffered ridicule for their faith and some have been physically abused. Not one has left his village or asked for asylum. A few of the wives and children have accepted Christ, but progress in this area of evangelism is slow.

The believers have shown initiative and vision. After a study of I Corinthians 12, one of the groups, on their own, appointed an evangelist, an administrator, a prayer coordinator, and a pastor. In response to the lack of a church building, a national offered to deed a plot of his land to the church. It was then decided that one family would purchase a calf. A second family would feed it for six weeks and then pass it on to a third family. At the end of a year, after the transient calf had eaten the grass of several plots of land, it would be sold for the amount of money needed to construct an attractive worship center made of bamboo. This plan was later dropped in favor of continuing low-profile meetings in the homes of believers.

There has been an appreciation of the supernatural on a practical level. Visions and dreams of spiritual significance have been fairly frequent. There is a simple faith that prayer is an instrument of change. Crying out to God and fasting are utilized to effect release from difficulty as well as to bring healing to the afflicted.

Approach to the Fellowship of Muslim Converts

Financial Considerations

It has been mentioned that gifts and employment opportunities from the West have created a syndrome of dependence within the Lombaro Christian community composed of converts from animism. There is little motivation to give sacrificially or to pray about church needs when one is assured budgets will be met with foreign assistance. Christians are given preferential treatment at mission hospitals and schools. A select few are granted theological scholarships abroad.

The situation is somewhat different with respect to the fellowship of Muslim converts in the Gaziville area. The remainder of our case study will concentrate on the mission's approach to this group.

Missionary Adjustments

The mission possesses no compounds or property. This assures the missionaries of mobility as well as a lower financial profile. Missionaries adopt as simple a lifestyle as emotional and physical health permit. Most families reside in simple cement houses rented from Muslim landlords.

Financial Relationships with Nationals

It is the aim of the mission to preserve the financial autonomy of the convert in relationship to himself, his family, and his peers. Existing economic structures are retained. "Redemption and lift" occur, but at the initiative of the convert—not through the gifts of the "rich, foreign missionary."

Adaptations

The Missionary's Lifestyle

1. Missionary men wear the clothing of the target group, that is, the clothing of the village farmer. The wives wear the dress of village women, and at times have worn the veil covering, a practice which has been very much appreciated by the Muslim and convert community.

2. Several of the missionary men have full beards; this corresponds to the appearance of a Muslim religious man.

3. Lifestyles are simple.

4. Muslim dietary practices are adopted. No pork is eaten.

5. Time is regarded, not in absolute terms as in the West, but as event-oriented. Some missionaries have adopted the 8 p.m. suppertime of the Muslims and thus have entered into the pattern of social visitation which takes place each evening between 6 and 8 p.m.

6. Taking pictures of the converts and bringing a large number of foreign guests into the area to meet the new believers are discouraged.

Worship Practices Adopted for the Sake of Nationals

1. A place for washing before prayer is provided for optional use. It is explained that there is no merit attached to such ceremonial washing.

2. Shoes are removed before entering the worship center.

3. All worshipers sit on the floor.

4. Bibles are placed on folding stands such as are used for the Quran.

5. Occasionally, Greek and Hebrew Bibles are placed in a prominent position in front of the worshipers. Thus is demonstrated regard for the "original" Bible such as Muslims feel toward the Arabic Quran.

6. Hands are lifted up Muslim-style during prayer times. Prostration is frequently practiced. Some pray with their eyes open and wear the traditional prayer hats.

7. Muslim tunes with Christian words are utilized. Scripture is chanted, as are personal testimonies.

8. Worshipers embrace in Muslim fashion.

9. Days and times of worship are pragmatically regulated.

10. Fasting is an area of liberty, but is scripturally explained.

11. Instead of traditional Christian preparations, Muslim-type food is served at the training center.

12. The church of Muslim converts maintains a homogeneous rather than a heterogeneous character (that is, its members are strictly from a Muslim background; there are none from an animistic background).

13. Informal church organization is promoted, basically along the lines of the mosque.

14. The Muslim names of converts are retained.

15. The word *Christian* is avoided because of negative connotations. Presently, "Followers of *Isa* [Jesus]" is being used.

16. Bible study, prayer, and fasting are emphasized. A higher profile of religious observance is encouraged.

17. The converts choose their own leadership.

18. Propagation is centered along family and friendship lines.

Areas Under Consideration

Many questions have no easy black-and-white answers. The following is a list of problematic gray areas that the missionaries are seeking to understand more fully.

1. Should the wearing of prayer hats by converts and missionaries be encouraged?

2. How should the Muslim festivals and Christian observances (Christmas, Good Friday, Easter, the month of fasting, the celebration following Ramazan, the festival of sacrifice which relates to Abraham and Ishmael, etc.) be celebrated?

3. Should circumcision be practiced?

4. What marriage ceremony should be followed? What is to be the attitude if a Muslim convert desires to marry a girl from the Christian community which has an animistic background, thus affecting the homogeneity of the group?

5. Are there particular forms to follow at the time of a birth? What about funeral ritual?

6. How can converts be stimulated to give sacrificially to the Lord's work? Can they successfully follow the pattern of the mosque by placing a box by the door for freewill offerings?

7. What if another Christian group comes into the area and seeks to win over the converts through financial inducements?

8. How should convert churches relate to each other? Should they follow the loose autonomous relationship of the mosques? Would it be good to try to develop a Christian equivalent of the Muslim *pir* (teacher with a dedicated band of disciples)?

9. How would the converts stand up in case of serious persecution which might cost them their land and livelihood? In such an event, what is to be the role of the missionary?

10. What is a good Bible-teaching series for a church composed of Muslim converts? How can the Trinity and the incarnation best be explained?

11. How long should the missionary remain in an active role in one church? When should he totally withdraw?

12. How can the wives and daughters of the converts be reached with the gospel? What about the role of women in the church? (Muslim women do not actively participate in the mosque.)

13. Should missionaries seek to keep a low profile in the villages so as to minimize foreignness? If so, how can new areas be reached without paid national workers?

14. What is to be the missionaries' relationship to Muslim priests, that is, the *imams, maulvis,* and *pirs?*

15. How far should the missionary go in adapting to the lifestyle of his target audience—in regard to housing, eating habits, dress, and issues relating to his children?

This ministry is an evolving process. It is worthy of much prayer. Out of this experimentation may arise a contextualized model of evangelization applicable to other parts of the Muslim world.

PART I

Principles of Contextualization

CHAPTER 1

An Overview of Contextualization

Basic Issues

"Contextualization" is a word which has recently come into popular usage among evangelicals. The word itself directs our attention to "context." This includes the total matrix of society which embraces the social patterns of a people, their economic policies, politics, and a host of other integrative areas.

The gospel of Jesus Christ must be attractively presented into the context of any given group of people. This is a process which involves great sensitivity.

In the Bible we observe a wide array of approaches to people. The aim of the communicator was to maximize the impact of the gospel upon the receptor community. A basic principle was to start where the person was in his own orientation to life. The woman at the well was witnessed to in a very different manner than was Nicodemus. The rich young ruler heard a presentation of the gospel quite distinct from the presentation to blind Bartimaeus. In each case, Jesus was meeting people on their own unique level. The needs of the receptor group were uppermost at all times in His thinking.

31

This does not mean that Jesus presented a partial gospel. Neither was the message emasculated or syncretistic. Christ embraced a strategy that was contextually related, in initial witness, to felt needs. The receptor's attention was captured by a message that quickly entered into his world-view.

Liberal theologians have taken the concept of contextualization and utilized it in a way which is unacceptable to evangelicals. In their concern for avoiding religious offense, liberals have deleted certain passages of the Bible which they consider unacceptable to the receptor community. Other theological truths have been reinterpreted to the point of syncretism. Or the liberals have agreed to substitute some other "holy book" (such as the Quran or the Gitas) for the Bible as the basis for contextualized theology. Such approaches are not endorsed by evangelicals.

Charles Taber seeks to catch the true spirit of contextualization:

> Contextualization. . . is the effort to understand and take seriously the specific context of each human group and person on its own terms and in all its dimensions—cultural, religious, social, political, economic—and to discern what the Gospel says to people in that context. This requires a profound empirical analysis of the context in place of flip or *a priori* judgments. . . . Contextualization tries to discover in the Scriptures what God is saying to these people. In other words, contextualization takes very seriously the example of Jesus in the sensitive and careful way he offered each person a gospel tailored to his or her own context.[1]

The tensions of cross-cultural movement of the gospel are seen in the Jewish-Gentile, law-grace controversy in the early church. The emotional impact of moving across these cultural lines was shattering.

When a Christian from Jerusalem went down to Corinth, the

---

1. Charles R. Taber, "Contextualization: Indigenization and/or Transformation," in *The Gospel and Islam: A 1978 Compendium,* ed. Don M. McCurry (Monrovia, CA: MARC, 1979), p. 146.

shock must have been even more severe. The Corinthian in Jerusalem found himself in a society stiff, uncouth, severe, formal, pedantic. The Jewish Christian in Corinth must have thought the Church there given over to unbridled license. Uncircumcised Christians attended the feasts of their pagan friends in heathen temples. Every letter of the ceremonial law was apparently broken every day without rebuke. Even in the meetings of the Church, preachings and prayers were built on a strange system of thought which could hardly be called Christian, and there was a most undignified freedom of conduct.[2]

Acts 15 goes into significant detail on the clash between Jews and Gentiles. The issue had come to a crisis point. Paul and Barnabas made the trip from Antioch to Jerusalem to meet with James and the church elders. How could a compromise be effected? Each side was convinced of its own position. The Jews incorporated grace and salvation in Christ into their system of faithfully observing the laws of Moses. Paul was dealing with people who knew absolutely nothing of the law. He saw no reason to legislate that Gentiles must come to Christ through a Judaistic route. They were free to encounter Christ in a direct relationship of saving faith.

It can be concluded from Acts 15:28 that the council's decisions were Spirit-inspired. The Jewish believer was free to follow Jewish custom as long as he understood the grace of God as revealed in Christ. James spoke the council's decision concerning Gentiles: "It is my judgment that we do not trouble those who are turning to God from among the Gentiles" (v. 19). They would be free from Jewish law. However, James also made a cultural request: a letter was sent to the effect that the Gentiles should

abstain from things contaminated by idols and from fornication and from what is strangled and from blood. For Moses from ancient generations has in every city those who preach him, since he is read in the synagogues every Sabbath. (vv. 20–21)

2. Roland Allen, *Missionary Methods: St. Paul's or Ours?* (Grand Rapids: Wm. B. Eerdmans, 1962), p. 129.

The Jews would be onlookers to the development of Christianity. James requested a cultural accommodation when he urged Gentile converts not to eat food offered to idols and to abstain from whatever was strangled and from blood. This would be an exercise of restraint in the interest of not offending Jews. The council then adjourned in a beautiful, harmonious spirit.

The Gentiles in Antioch were very pleased with the results: "And when they had read [the letter], they rejoiced because of its encouragement" (v. 31). They were happy to avoid cultural offense—even though they were quite free in Christ to eat and drink as they pleased.

I Corinthians 8 discusses a related example of contextualization. The issue is food offered to idols. Paul is writing exclusively to Gentile Christians. Therefore, in dealing with this subject Paul makes no reference to the events of Acts 15, where it seems evident that the Gentile believers agreed that, in areas where Jewish Christians were present, they would abstain from eating food offered to idols. Now Paul takes up the subject in a different context—one in which no Jewish believers are resident.

Paul, with Gentiles in mind, makes no appeal to Old Testament texts. His teaching is based on two truths. First, the idol has no real existence (I Cor. 8:4); and second, food has no religious value (v. 8). Therefore, the Christian is free in Christ even to partake of food which has been offered to idols. Paul proceeds to deal with this issue in a contextual manner:

1. Christians should not eat in the temple (vv. 10–12). In Corinth this act would be equated with the worship of idols; therefore, it was prohibited.

2. Outside of the temple, eating meat offered to idols may or may not connote worship of the idol. Does the Christian believe it does? If so, he should abstain. Do others (Christians or non-Christians) regard such an act to be sin? If so, the believer will not eat the meat.

3. If there is no contextual offense involved, then the Christian is allowed to do as he pleases. This may lead him to eat privately in his own home away from the presence of others so that no one will be offended. There is no biblical issue involved as long as the context of the situation is properly considered.

Now rather than being a matter of inconsistency, which it superficially is, Paul's tactic gives us a clear indication of how to deal with contextual behavior. It is *meaning* which determines the acceptability or nonacceptability of cultural forms. If the *meaning* is intrinsically contrary to Christian truth, no Christian may participate. If, however, the practice is wrong only in the view of some people, then the Christian must abstain only in their presence.[3]

Shortly after the discussion of meat offered to idols, there is another passage which is very significant for an understanding of contextualization (I Cor. 9:19–23):

> For though I am free from all men, I have made myself a slave to all, that I might win the more. And to the Jews I became as a Jew, that I might win Jews; to those who are under the Law, as under the Law, though not being myself under the Law; to those who are without law, as without law, though not being without the law of God but under the law of Christ, that I might win those who are without law. To the weak I became weak, that I might win the weak; I have become all things to all men, that I may by all means save some. And I do all things for the sake of the gospel, that I may become a fellow-partaker of it.

Paul, in his earnest desire to win the multitudes to Christ, adopted five distinct contextual roles. This does not mean Paul suffered from theological schizophrenia. He maintained a steady fidelity to the authority of the Word of God. His loyalty to Jesus Christ was unassailable. In his driving passion to preach Christ, however, he realistically grappled with serious and complex contextual issues as he crossed the great divide which separated the Jewish and Gentile worlds.

1. *Servant.* In verse 19, Paul speaks of having made himself a slave to all people. This was an overarching humility. It allowed him, as a highly educated Jew, humbly to present Christ to a

---

3. Norman R. Ericson, "Implications from the New Testament for Contextualization," in *Theology and Mission*, ed. David J. Hesselgrave (Grand Rapids: Baker Book House, 1978), p. 76.

runaway slave whom he later came to regard as an intimate friend (Philem. 16). In the role of servant Paul endured afflictions, hardships, distresses, beatings, imprisonments, tumults, labors, sleeplessness, and hunger (II Cor. 6:4–5).

2. *Jew*. Paul, as a Jew, easily identified with the world-view as well as the religious yearnings of the Jewish race. He understood their political frustrations as well as their messianic hope. He loved the Jews. His first priority in evangelism in the cities he visited was a preaching stop at the local synagogue.

Paul did not see the Messiah as a destroyer of the law, but rather as the One who fulfilled it. Therefore, he saw no conflict when, in deference to local opinion, he took vows which were uniquely Jewish. Acts 18 and 21 record these instances. He felt free to take or not to take these vows. Freedom in Christ broke all cultural bondages. Paul was at liberty, depending on the context of the situation, to act in any way he felt would be useful in fulfilling his all-consuming desire to see Jews come to faith in the Messiah.

Some Christians have faulted Paul for "going back under the law." I will not engage in this controversy except to say that it is clear what motives prompted Paul to take the vows. There is no indication he ever felt he was in error in his action.

3. *Proselyte*. A large group of Gentiles had converted to Judaism. They were now "under the law." This group of people would be responsive to the gospel. They had already proven that they were open to change by the fact that they had embraced the Jewish faith. Paul could quite easily identify with this segment of society. In religious commitment they were as Jews. This was familiar ground to Paul.

4. *Gentile*. "To those who are without law, [Paul became] as without law." This embraces Paul's primary ministry, his mission among the Gentile peoples. It wasn't easy for him to move among idol worshipers. These were people who despised both Jews and their God. Yet, the Lord had called Paul to be the apostle to the Gentiles. With that calling came adequate grace and wisdom to successfully engage in church planting on the European continent.

On Mars' Hill Paul sought to communicate to a people who worshiped multiple gods (Acts 17). In his speech he felt free to quote a heathen poet (v. 28). This is one example of Paul's contextualizing his message so as to be a more effective communicator. The quote (which would in no way have weakened or harmed the Christian message) would have helped in establishing a rapport between speaker and audience.

5. *Weak.* Paul, though a dynamic leader, was still a sensitive Christian. He was very conscious of the weaker type of person. Just before his key section on contextualization Paul had written: "But take care lest this liberty of yours somehow become a stumbling block to the weak" (I Cor. 8:9). One can visualize Paul interacting with a weak, introspective person with great care and tact.

Paul saw the great gospel message as applicable to all men throughout the world. He longed to see Christianity take deep root in the soil of every culture. It was not to be just a foreign import. To attain this goal Paul became "all things to all men."

This good and proper concept can be abused. Recently, in a nationwide television special, an American evangelist introduced his Jewish guest as "brother" and then gave his name. A friend of mine was disturbed since the evangelist's words and manner of interacting with the Jewish comedian seemed to convey to the audience that the guest was an evangelical Christian. My friend then wrote to the evangelist, asking whether the Jew had become a believer. In a letter of response, the evangelist stated, "No, he has not become a Christian, but he is very favorable to Christian causes. I referred to him as 'brother' in my desire to be 'all things to all men.' "

This teaching of Paul is not license to be less than totally ethical. Also, it is not to be a cover for syncretism—a subject which will be dealt with in the next chapter.

Paul summed up his activities by stating his purpose: "that I may by all means save some" (I Cor. 9:22). Five times in this passage Paul refers to his motivation as being the salvation of the lost. Saving the lost was the heartthrob of this man of God.

Paul's ministry is a prime example of proper and successful contextualization of the gospel. Norman R. Ericson lists three basic criteria of such contextualization:

> (1) *Truth.* There is a body of truth which is assumed. This truth, whether implicit or explicit, forms the absolute standard by which everything must be evaluated.
>
> (2) *Meaning.* The Christian in society must so contextualize that the right meanings are delivered through the cultural forms and ideology. We must be continually aware that the meanings of actions or objects in Western society will not regularly have the same meanings in the Third World. The Christian must then be careful not to deliver the wrong meaning by his mode of behavior or cultural participation. The question must always be asked: What does this *mean* to the people?
>
> (3) *Communication.* At the verbal-ideological level, consistent attention must be given to effectiveness. How is our gospel communicated?. . . How are the people to know that God is love if there is no activity which in culturally meaningful ways demonstrates the love of God in the lives of the evangelizers?
>
> These three criteria form the basis for the evaluation of a contextualized gospel. It honors the Word of God, it respects culture as the natural product of God's creation, and it emphasizes the goal of the Word who came and lived among us—effective communication.[4]

Contextualization Illustrated

At this point it is appropriate to present several illustrations, some negative and some positive, which bear on the issue of contextualization.

Early European missionaries to Indonesia felt they should construct an appendage of ten "culturally relevant" laws to the Ten Commandments of the Old Testament.

4. Ibid., pp. 79–80.

1. Thou shalt have thy hair cut short.
2. Thou shalt not take off thy head-kerchief in church.
3. Thou shalt not listen to *gamelan* music.
4. Thou shalt not attend a *wayang* performance.
5. Thou shalt not be circumcised.
6. Thou shalt not attend a *slametan.*
7. Thou shalt not read Javanese verse.
8. Thou shalt not care for the graves of thy ancestors.
9. Thou shalt not decorate thy cemeteries with flowers and trees.
10. Thou shalt forbid thy children to play idle games.

One of these missionaries went on to say "even as the soldiers of the king all wear the same uniform, so all the soldiers of Christ in Java should wear: shoes on their feet, white trousers, a long black coat and a small cap on the head."[5]

The "culturally relevant" aspect of this missionary approach was related to only the European way of life. These highly ethnocentric missionaries were quite convinced that what was good for Europe was good for the world. The result was a ludicrous breed of Christian community that was a laughingstock of their own people.

A missionary couple in Zaire had difficulty in establishing rapport with one particular group of nationals. Finally, an old man took it upon himself to explain the problem to the missionaries:

"When you came, you brought your strange ways," he said. "You brought tins of food. On the outside of one was a picture of corn. When you opened it, inside was corn and you ate it. Outside another was a picture of meat, and inside was meat, and you ate it. And then when you had your baby, you brought small tins. On the outside was a picture of babies, and you opened it and fed the inside to your child."[6]

5. Philip Van Akkeren, *Sri and Christ: A Study of the Indigenous Church in East Java,* trans. Annebeth Mackie (London: Lutterworth Press, 1970), pp. 79-80.
6. Paul Hiebert, *Cultural Anthropology* (New York: J. B. Lippincott, 1976), p. 52.

Though we may chuckle at such a story, we can be assured it was an extremely serious issue to those bewildered nationals. How could an act of cannibalism square with the message of the missionaries?

In another part of Africa, a church service went on and on without regard to the lateness of the hour.[7] The missionary looked again and again at his watch as his level of irritation soared. The service continued on into the night as more people than usual wanted to testify of the work of God in their lives. When the African pastor stood to preach, it was nearly midnight. The missionary was so upset that he stormed out of the church and went to his home nearby. When the service showed no signs of ending, he switched off the main electricity supply, causing the church to plunge into immediate darkness. Usually the lights at the mission station were switched off at ten o'clock, so the missionary felt he had been more than reasonable. When the African pastor realized what had happened, he broke down and cried. The missionary was highly time-oriented in a Western sense, whereas the national church was event-oriented. They were enjoying themselves immensely and had planned to stay on, without regard to time, until the event ceased to be meaningful.

A Liberian became confused as to the real meaning of Christianity: "Bathing frequently, brushing one's teeth, abstaining from beer, tobacco, and betel nut, and refusing to eat clams or oysters have all been preached by various missionaries as symbols of the 'new life in Christ Jesus.' "[8] How difficult it can be for the national to try to work through these externals and still keep his focus on or even discover the message of redemption.

In a positive vein, Don Corbin relates measures which have been implemented with a view to contextualization:

We have begun to Africanize our music as much as possible; the organ and piano are out and the tom-toms have been

7. Pius Wakatama, *Independence for the Third World Church* (Downers Grove, IL: Inter-Varsity Press, 1976), p. 88.

8. Eugene Nida, *Message and Mission* (New York: Harper and Bros., 1954), p. 255.

brought in, much to the dislike of some of my missionary friends. We have begun moving away from European speakers to black speakers only. We moved away from a preaching kind to a conversational kind of format.[9]

This style of contextualization is highly commendable, communicating as it does a message that is more faithful to the essence of Christianity.

Another illustration comes from Stanley Mooneyham, president of World Vision.[10] Just prior to the fall of Cambodia into Communist hands, Mooneyham conducted several very successful evangelistic campaigns in the capital city of Phnom Penh. In his sermon research on topics that would effectively communicate to the people, Mooneyham came across a local legend that spoke of the end time in Cambodia. According to the legend, all the nations of the world will gather themselves in battle against Phnom Penh at the location where five rivers come together. The blood of the battle will be as deep as an elephant's thigh, and the Cambodians will be saved only when a deliverer riding a white horse comes on the scene. Mooneyham took Revelation 19 as his text and spoke of the great coming battle and the role of Jesus Christ as deliverer. This was powerful contextual communication. The people could relate intimately with a Bible story that had so many similarities to a legend which was widely known and highly regarded in their own culture.

The "etic-emic distinctions" have relevance to the issue of contextualization. Kenneth Pike coined these words from "phonetic" and "phonemic." The etic viewpoint observes behavior from a perspective external to a particular society. The emic approach studies behavior from inside the culture. Etic understandings are alien and often fail to adequately deal with issues that are crucial to insiders. Emic perspectives provide a view that is grap-

9. Don Corbin, "Attempts to Penetrate the Culture," in *Conference on Media in Islamic Culture Report*, ed. C. Richard Shumaker (Marseilles: Evangelical Literature Overseas, 1974), p. 40.

10. William A. Dyrness, "Contextualization and the Christian Communicator," *ACCF Journal* 1 (1978): 7.

pling for answers from within. Such an approach is vastly superior to a purely etic one.

Contextualization must be carried out with emic methodology. Theological formulations should be made after coming to grips with emic concepts. The following description of ethnotheology is worth thoughtful consideration:

> Christian ethnotheology is theology done from inside the system, rendering the supracultural Christian absolutes not only in the linguistic idiom but also within the particular forms that "system" takes within the system: concepts of priority, sequence, time, space; elements of order, customs of validation and assertion; styles of emphasis and expression.[11]

11. James O. Buswell, III, "Contextualization: Theory, Tradition and Method," in *Theology and Mission*, ed. David J. Hesselgrave (Grand Rapids: Baker Book House, 1978), p. 98.

Syncretism

Dynamics

It is our tendency to make syncretism a black-and-white issue. As Westerners we feel more comfortable with Neapolitan rather than strawberry-swirl ice cream. In a private discussion with me, Charles Kraft noted that Neapolitan ice cream has three distinct colors and flavors which are easily identifiable. They are like autonomous blocks. Even though attached, they are independently structured. Strawberry-swirl ice cream, on the other hand, is a mixture. The color of red is dominant, but it is intermixed with vanilla.

Is Christian expression in any society ever totally "pure"? Is it possible to have Neapolitan Christianity? Ralph Winter points a finger inward when he writes concerning Western "Christian" practices:

> I grew up without realizing that Easter sunrise services could easily revert to their original paganism if Christians attending them do not see and sense a Christian meaning in them. The very word *Easter* comes from a Teutonic spring goddess of fertility called Eostre. The same is true of Christmas. We have all fought to maintain Christ in Christmas, since Christmas is

also originally a pagan holiday that was taken over by the early church. Romans gave gifts to each other on December 25th long before Jesus was born, and for that matter, Jesus may have been born in June, not in December.[1]

Missionaries, out of fear of syncretism, often become overly denunciatory of local culture. Nationals are encouraged to become like the missionary. But this in itself creates syncretism. Beliefs and practices flow from the missionary and his own cultural background to the receptor. These beliefs and practices mix with those of the indigenous setting. Jacob Loewen illustrates the potential dangers in this process:

> The high regard of Scripture and the reverence that many missionaries show for the Word of God has in many circumstances become the basis for using the Bible as a magic object powerful in healing, divining, or even revenge killing. The author saw this in the Caribbean where people suddenly began buying a very poor translation of the Psalms in large numbers. A closer look revealed that the people were using the deprecatory Psalms as spells to kill neighbors' animals or even neighbors themselves when there was tension between families. Likewise, the missionary use of the promise box as a source of inspiration and guidance has frequently led to the validation of the use of the Scriptures for divining purposes. . . . In one South American culture the missionary's use of the two-way radio was interpreted as communication with the spirit world and this in turn became the validation for the continuation of the diviner's role even after the group became Christian. They had someone who would communicate with the spirit world even without the short-wave radio.[2]

1. Ralph D. Winter, "The Highest Priority: Cross-Cultural Evangelism," in *Crucial Dimensions in World Evangelization,* ed. Arthur F. Glasser (Pasadena: William Carey Library, 1976), p. 125.

2. Jacob A. Loewen, "Toward Contextualization—An Analysis of Factors Motivating or Inhibiting Syncretism" (unpublished paper, Emory University, 1979), p. 37.

Christianity in any society is in dynamic process. It is not stationary, rigid, or polarized. It may be, then, that certain practices
look quite syncretistic to an outsider, including Christians from
different cultures. Christian grace should lead the observer to first
investigate the meanings of the forms he is observing. If he is still
convinced syncretism exists, he should approach the situation
with tact and humility in recognition of the fact that his own practice of Christianity is similarly tainted (syncretistic) through the
mixing of his cultural values with those of Scripture. This fact
should humble us into patience and politeness. For we realize that
Christianity is always (for ourselves as well as others) a process in
which God works patiently with believers "who have not yet attained." Though we may often despair over the slowness of that
process (both in others and in ourselves), we must, with Kraft,
subscribe to

> a "high" view of the continual operation and effectiveness of
> the leading of God in the human arena. I see God as in con-
> stant, effective interaction with his people both individually
> and corporately to bring about ends that he and his people
> mutually agree upon.[3]

A number of theologians have attempted to define syncretism. Hendrik Kraemer writes that syncretism is "a systematic
attempt to combine, blend and reconcile inharmonious, even
often conflicting elements in a so-called synthesis."[4] The 1966
Wheaton Declaration states that syncretism is "the attempt to
unite or reconcile biblically revealed Christian truth with the
diverse or opposing tenets and practices of non-Christian religions
or other systems of thought that deny it."[5] Bruce Nicholls, a missionary theologian living and writing in the context of syncretistic
India, draws the controversy into focus:

3. Charles H. Kraft, *Christianity in Culture* (Maryknoll, NY: Orbis Books,
1979), p. 195.
4. Hendrik Kraemer, *Religion and the Christian Faith* (Philadelphia: Westminster Press, 1956), p. 392.
5. Harold Lindsell, ed., *The Church's Worldwide Mission* (Waco, TX: Word
Books, 1966), p. 222.

The central issue in the contemporary Asian theological debate is where do we draw the boundary between contextualization and syncretism. Assuming that contextualization is a right and necessary way of doing theology and syncretism a wrong and undesirable result of theologizing, what then constitutes the dividing line between them?[6]

Perhaps this query can be partially answered by the observation that "syncretism occurs when critical and basic elements of the Gospel are lost in the process of contextualization."[7] There is always some leakage of content in gospel transmission across cultures; the communicator must carefully monitor what is being lost. He should probe for an approach that faithfully expresses scriptural truth in a manner in which there is as little dilution of meaning as possible.

It is clear that, in the process of the translation and transmission of the gospel, there will be some measure of adaptation necessary in order to assure that what is said is both understood and relevant. The new shape and mold resulting from adaptation of the message should not be considered syncretism.

Paul Hiebert has sought to draw a comparison of syncretism and indigenization:

> Not only must we separate the Gospel from our own culture, we must seek to express it in terms of the culture to which we go. The people may sit on the floor, sing songs to native rhythms and melodies, and look at pictures of Christ who is Black or Chinese. The Church may reject democracy in favor of wise elders, or turn to drama to communicate its message.
>
> But, as we have seen, translation involves more than putting ideas into native forms, for these forms may not carry meanings suitable for expressing the Christian message. If we, then, translate it into native forms without thought to

    6. Bruce J. Nicholls, "A Living Theology for Asian Churches" (paper presented to the Asia Theological Association Consultation, Singapore, November 1978), p. 1.
    7. James O. Buswell, III, "Contextualization: Theory, Tradition and Method," in *Theology and Mission,* ed. David J. Hesselgrave (Grand Rapids: Baker Book House, 1978), p. 88.

preserving the meaning, we will end up with syncretism—the mixture of old meanings with the new so that
the essential nature of each is lost.

If we are careful to preserve the meaning of the Gospel even
as we express it in native forms we have indigenization. This
may involve introducing a new symbolic form, or it may involve reinterpreting a native symbol.[8]

Some of these concepts can perhaps be made clearer by a
concrete illustration. William Carey, the father of modern missions, arrived in India in the year 1793. Carey had two strategy
options before him. He could choose to center his work among
either Hindus or Muslims. To the best of my knowledge, the
population ratio was about equal. Early in his missionary career
Carey noted the great gulf that separated the two communities—
both socially and religiously. He was aware of the well-docu-
mented Muslim resistance to the gospel message. It was therefore
natural for his efforts to flow toward the Hindu population.

The present church in that geographical area is historically
linked with those early pioneering efforts of Carey and his colleagues. It emerged out of Hinduism. Very few Muslim converts
are to be found among the believers. Thus, there are almost no
forms in their worship which can be identified as having a Muslim
flavor. There are, however, a number of Western-style cultural accretions in their expression of Christianity. Church architecture is
Western; pulpits and pews are provided; liturgy and church
government follow the example of the parent denomination
abroad; and hymns are often direct translations of Sankey-type
songs.

More germane to this discussion are the Hindu elements
found in the church. Many of them are linguistic in nature:

1. The Hindu word *nomoskar* is a common form of greeting for
   Christians. (The Muslims use *a salam oalaikum.*)

---

8. Paul Hiebert, "Culture and Cross-Cultural Differences," in *Crucial Dimensions in World Evangelization*, ed. Arthur F. Glasser (Pasadena: William Carey
Library, 1976), p. 58.

2. *Iswar* is the Hindu and Christian term for God. (*Allah* is the word used by Muslims.)
3. *Boli dan* is the word of Hindu and Christian communities to denote offering of a sacrifice. (*Korbani* is used by Muslims.)
4. The Hindu word *babu* (rather than the Muslim *shaib*) is used by Christians as a title for a male.
5. The complete Christian vocabulary for relatives is Hindu.
6. Christian names are often taken directly from Hindu. Some Western and biblical names are used also.
7. The word *puja* is used by Hindus to denote the worship of their idols. This same word is frequently used by Christians in their songs and prayers to denote worship of God the Father and Jesus the Son.

Many Hindu practices are also found in the church:

1. The uniquely Hindu *dhuti* (five yards of material wrapped around the body) is worn by many village Christian men. (It is never worn by a Muslim.)
2. Very few Hindu and Christian males have beards. (Beards are common among Muslims.)
3. Christians, like Hindus, fold their hands in greetings. (Muslims salute.)
4. Christians and Hindus do not circumcise their sons. (Muslims do.)
5. The eating habits of Christians and Hindus are very similar. They both eat pork (which is repugnant to Muslims). Most Christians abstain from beef as do Hindus. Christians and Hindus eat their lentils and rice before their meat and vegetables. (Muslims eat their meat and vegetables first.)
6. *Annaprashan* is a celebration of feeding a child his first rice — a unique ceremony observed only by Hindus and Christians.
7. Drama and musicals are used by both Hindus and Christians to communicate religious teaching. (Muslims do not sing or have instruments in their mosque services.)

Is this historic church, founded by the highly revered William Carey, in reality just a deluded group of half-breeds (half Christian and half Hindu) who are engaging in a syncretism that is an abomination to a holy God? The Protestant wing of the church includes Baptists, Anglicans, Presbyterians, Lutherans, and members of the Assemblies of God. Basically, they all have adopted the above-mentioned linguistic elements and practices. Are they heretical?

My considered opinion is that these Christian-Hindu patterns are all healthy and valid expressions of contextualization. The church is not syncretistic. There are a number of reasons for this firm conclusion:

1. The Christians are completely orthodox in their understanding of the meanings of the Hindu words they use. They are not "thinking Hindu" when they use these words. All Hindu meanings have been transformed into solid biblical content. There is no compromise nor syncretism involved.

2. None of these practices are prohibited by Scripture. Christians, then, are free to engage in those practices which are culturally relevant.

3. These contextual adaptations make Christianity look good to the Hindu. It is true, the Hindu convert will gradually need to understand familiar theological terms in a new light, but the initial introduction to Christianity is generally a positive experience. He feels at home in the church, except in relation to the Western imports which affect him negatively.

The above adaptations have, however, made Christianity look extremely negative to the Muslim onlooker. The Muslim's first understanding of Christianity is that it is like Hinduism—and to him, that is abominable. There is nothing worse, from his point of view, than the worship of multiple gods and idols. Consequently, there must be a new type of outreach to the Muslim community. This approach must be at least as adaptive to Muslim language and culture as the present Christian tradition has been to Hindu language and culture.

Carey had at least four choices for the word *God*. He could have chosen the Muslim, the Hindu, the English, or the Hebrew word. Carey had made a choice to work among Hindus. He felt, therefore, that his best option was to use an imperfect Hindu word for God which was clearly understood by the people whom he wanted to reach with the gospel. I would conjecture that each time Carey used this word for God he made sure he explained it in biblical context. Gradually, the converts came to a scriptural understanding of words that had formerly possessed only Hindu meanings for them. The same process will need to be repeated over and over in order that former religious meanings are thoroughly purged from the heart of the convert. Anything less will, to a lesser or greater degree, involve syncretism.

Kraft gives us a graphic illustration of linguistic transformation:

> Some of the most striking examples of linguistic transformation have come from the introduction of the allegiance to Christianity into a culture. The Greek word "agapao" (and its derivatives), for example, was transformed from a word whose "etymology is uncertain, and its meaning weak and variable," a word which lacked "the power or magic of erao" and "the warmth of philein" and often meant no more than "to be satisfied with something" ["Agapao," in *Theological Dictionary of the New Testament*, ed. Gerhard Kittel and G. Friedrich, trans. G. W. Bromiley (Grand Rapids: Wm. B. Eerdmans, 1964), vol. I, p. 36], into the distinctively Christian word for love. This concept was to Paul "the only vital force which has a future in this aeon of death" [ibid., p. 51] and to John "the principle of the world of Christ which is being built up in the cosmic crisis of the present."[9]

Dangers

Every religion stands in danger of the effects of syncretism. Islam itself has been known to incorporate Hindu influences. Many Indian Hindus of artisan and other lower economic classes converted to Islam. They retained a great deal of their superstitions after conversion. This was particularly true in the village areas. In Bengal, during the first half of the nineteenth century,

9. Kraft, *Christianity in Culture*, p. 52.

Muslims of rural areas joined Hindus in certain worship ceremonies. They also consulted Brahmins for auspicious days for weddings and other special events. In this century, some Muslims have specialized in *bhashan gan*, the songs of praises directed to the Hindu deity Mansa. Other Muslims have been known to recite hymns in the honor of Lakshmi, the Hindu goddess of wealth.

This path of syncretism often can be confusing, as illustrated in Sierra Leone by the Temne Muslim house which had symbols of three religions on the lintel of the doorway: at the top was a printed Temne Christian text; underneath, a cloth on which was tied a metal symbol; and beneath that, a paper printed with Islamic texts. The Hindus would be very appreciative of such a practice. Their inclusivistic system allows for a high view of Jesus Christ. However, they can never agree to the exclusive claims of Christ—or of any other religious leader.

In the early church there was a widespread ancestor cult, as evidenced by many tomb inscriptions requesting the prayers of the dead for the living. This cult led to the modern phenomenon of saint worship. It is recorded that Monica, the mother of Saint Augustine, used to carry food and drink to the graves of the dead.[10]

Conclusion

The Old Testament speaks forcefully to the subject of syncretism. The people of Israel seemed so fickle in their obedience to Jehovah. Even while Moses was on Mount Sinai receiving the law, the children of Israel were in the process of "adding to" their God-given revelations. The idea of a golden calf seemed so attractive. It was something tangible to which people could attach their devotion. Repeatedly in the Old Testament the Jews were engaged in "running after other gods." As a result, the children of Israel frequently received rebuke and judgment from God.

10. Eugene Nida, *Message and Mission* (New York: Harper and Bros., 1960), p. 185.

Paul, in II Corinthians 4:2, states that he is "not walking in craftiness or adulterating the word of God." The dictionary defines "adulterating" as "adding an inferior substance." I well recall an instance of adulterating which took place in the town in which I resided. The farmers would rise up early in the mornings to milk their cows and would then walk long distances to town. Along the way, some of them would scoop up some pond water into their milk buckets. One day these men were squatting beside their pails at the milk market. They were busily haggling over prices with prospective buyers. One of the buyers suddenly pushed a small meter into a milk pail. He loudly proclaimed that the meter registered that a very high content of water had been added to the milk. With the shocked public firmly on his side, he threw the milk on the ground. He then went to every bucket of milk and carried out a similar check. With a great flair, he threw about half of all the milk out onto the soil. The dejected and chastised farmers quietly picked up their empty pails and headed for home. Perhaps they had learned their lesson concerning milk adulteration.

The Lord evaluates theological syncretism in a similar manner. No "inferior substance" can be added to the Word of God.

> I testify to everyone who hears the words of the prophecy of this book: if anyone adds to them, God shall add to him the plagues which are written in this book; and if anyone takes away from the words of the book of this prophecy, God shall take away his part from the tree of life and from the holy city, which are written in this book. (Rev. 22:18–19)

God will "spew out of His mouth" all efforts at syncretizing His Word with that which is inconsistent or incompatible with His own holy nature. The word *adulteration* is particularly relevant as anything added to Scripture would be of inferior quality.

In taking a stance against syncretism, however, we must not overreact to the point of refusing to engage in experimentation in the area of contextualization. We must avoid, for example, the type of mistakes which were made in Indonesia.

The Reformed Churches in the Netherlands, which have been largely responsible for the introduction of Christianity in Central and East Java, have been so motivated by fear of syncretism that a God-against-culture stance was hardly avoidable. The missionaries were so convinced of the purity of their (Calvinistic) Gospel, that they could see hardly anything of value in the Javanese tradition.[11]

Our discussion of syncretism closes with a few suggestions which should be kept in mind as we seek to spread the gospel in Muslim cultures:

1. We must be acquainted with the biblical teaching (particularly the Old Testament) on the subject of syncretism. New Testament passages on the uniqueness of Christ should be carefully observed. He is set forth as the one path to God. Any teaching which negates or waters down this standard should be firmly resisted.

2. Islam as a religion, as well as the unique Muslim culture which is found in a specific country, must be studied. Syncretism can be understood only when one takes an emic position.

3. An open approach is desired. Careful experimentation in contextualization need not lead to syncretism as long as one is aware of all dangers.

4. Contextualization needs constant monitoring and analysis. What are the people really thinking? What does the contextualized communication convey? What do specific forms trigger in the mind of the new convert? Is there progress in the grasp of biblical truth? Are the people becoming demonstrably more spiritual?

5. Cross-cultural communicators must beware of presenting a gospel which has been syncretized with Western culture. The accretions to Christianity that have built up over the centuries as a result of the West's being the hub of Christianity should be avoided as far as possible.

11. Hank Dewaard, "Transforming Supernaturalism in a Javanese Worldview" (paper presented to Charles H. Kraft, Fuller Theological Seminary, 1979), p. 5.

CHAPTER 3

Form and Meaning

Overview

Cultural forms are the high-profile practices or customs that are visible to the onlooker. Meanings lie behind the forms and are often hidden and misunderstood by the outsider. These meanings function at the deep level of one's world-view. The key to understanding the meanings, both for insiders and for outsiders, lies in interpreting the forms of a culture, since all meanings are expressed through forms. Cultural insiders have learned to automatically interpret their cultural forms correctly. Outsiders cannot be certain that they are getting the intended meanings through the forms of another culture (or subculture).

One interesting illustration of the interaction between form and meaning is an American wedding ceremony. One important meaning generally assumed by middle America is that such a ceremony legitimizes the right of the couple to live together and to have children. Other meanings may be formulated: in the minds of the couple, apprehension about an unknown future; for the parents of the bride, a great amount of debt; for the organist, an opportunity to display his musical talents; for the preacher, a significant addition to the weekly paycheck; for the guests, amazement that such a dull fellow could convince such a wonderful girl to marry him; and for the janitor, a great deal of extra work.[1] There was only one form. But there was a variety of meanings filtered through the minds of the various people who observed the wedding.

How does this relate to Christian expression? Charles Kraft's words are worth pondering:

> The principle here seems to be that Christianness lies primarily in the functions served and the meanings conveyed by the cultural forms employed, rather than in the forms themselves. . . . God seeks to use and to cooperate with human beings in the continued use of relative cultural forms to express absolute supracultural meanings. The forms of culture are important not for their own sake but for the sake of that which they convey.[2]

Our focus, then, should be primarily on meanings, rather than simply on forms. Cultural forms are described as relative; different forms may convey similar meanings in different societies. There are, apparently, no forms that convey exactly the same meanings to the peoples of every society. When God communicates to people of different cultures, therefore, He uses different cultural forms to convey the same absolute supracultural meanings. Kraft makes clear the significance of this fact for our day when he says that "Christians should function in today's contexts in ways equivalent to the ways that approved Old Testament and New Testament peoples functioned for God in their contexts."[3]

Many Bible translators have assumed that if they translated the form, the people would understand the meaning correctly. If in one language the word *lamb* is found, some translators have assumed that it is adequate to simply find a vernacular word that

1. Charles H. Kraft, *Christianity in Culture* (Maryknoll, NY: Orbis Books, 1979), p. 66.

2. Ibid., p. 99.

3. Charles H. Kraft, "Dynamic Equivalence Churches in Muslim Society," in *The Gospel and Islam: A 1978 Compendium*, ed. Don M. McCurry (Monrovia, CA: MARC, 1979), p. 115.

means "lamb" and to insert it in the appropriate place. The meaning will be clear. But this is unlikely to be the case since the same forms do not carry the same meanings in different languages. Actually, the more literally the form is translated, the greater the danger of losing the biblical meaning,[4] unless, of course, the form just happens to have a similar meaning for the receiving people. But what happens when the receiving people regard lambs (which were greatly appreciated by Hebrews) much as Westerners regard snakes?

Application

Muslims put great emphasis on external forms. Islam is built heavily on legalistic observances that are intended to prepare a person for eternity in heaven. In actuality, it is observed that often the deeper meanings of these forms are very inadequately understood by the Muslim.

> In practical life theology is not an important factor. The important thing is the performance of the rites and the adoption of such customs as differentiate the believer from others, for this means that the beliefs are accepted even though they are totally unknown.[5]

In 1947, a Muslim writer stated that

> all the movements that are stirring the Islamic world at present, amount to a real revolution. But it is a revolution in the forms and not in the principles. The Muslim countries desire to adopt modern forms, but at the same time, far from breaking with the Islamic system, they come back to it.[6]

4. Paul Hiebert, *Cultural Anthropology* (New York: J. B. Lippincott, 1976), p. 54.
5. J. Spencer Trimingham, *The Influence of Islam upon Africa* (London: Longmans, Green and Company, 1968), p. 53.
6. Zaki Ali, *Islam in the World* (Lahore: Muhammad Ashraf, 1947), pp. 180-81.

This was written in the days of modernization (Westernization) in countries like Turkey and Iran. It points to the distinction between modernized form and the underlying meaning, which is expected to remain unchanged. At present, the world is observing the interaction between those powerful principles and the forces of modernization. Religious leaders are using the principles as appeals to Muslims to move back into "authentic" form expressions of the Islamic faith. Thus, the *Shariah* (Muslim law) is being introduced in countries like Iran, Libya, and Pakistan. Women are being told to wear the veil. All eating establishments are being forcibly closed during daylight hours of the month of fasting. Amputation of a hand is being administered as the penalty for thievery. Forms are once again taking a prominent place in the expression of Islamic faith, even in countries which in the past twenty-five years have moved in the direction of modernization.

It is necessary for the cross-cultural evangelist to enter deeply into the Muslim understanding of form and meaning. Only then can he begin to grasp the mental processes involved when the Muslim encounters the faith and practice of the Christian.

The five pillars of Islam all involve participation. These forms are deeply imbedded in the very innermost being of every Muslim. Between the pillars of Islam and certain features of Christianity there is a basic similarity in form though not always in meaning. The *Shahada* (the Islamic confession that "there is no god but Allah, and Muhammad is His Prophet") has a biblical counterpart:

> And by common *confession* great is the mystery of godliness: He who was revealed in the flesh, was vindicated in the Spirit, beheld by angels, proclaimed among the nations, believed on in the world, taken up in glory. (I Tim. 3:16, italics added)

What *Shahada* could better replace the Islamic confession? They are both direct quotes from the holy books of their respective religions. *Prayer (salat)* is common to both religions. *Fasting* is an exhortation of Scripture as it is in the Islamic faith. *Almsgiving* is enjoined in the Bible as well as the Quran. The *pilgrimage* to Mecca bears a close semblance to the practice of thousands of Christians who take the "once in a lifetime" trip to the Holy Land "to walk where Jesus walked."

Of course, if we try to spread the gospel to Muslims by building on the similarities between Islamic practices and certain features of Christianity, these practices will all require a certain measure of reinterpretation. But it does seem that the closer we can relate to Muslim form, the more positive will be the response to our message, particularly in initial instances of evangelistic effort. As we have noted above, the more radical and strange Christianity looks, the more hesitant the Muslim will be to consider its deeper message.

It should be pointed out that the Muslim performs all these obligations as a means of obtaining merit. This, of course, is incompatible with the Christian message of grace. But what the Muslim needs is a change in focus (i.e., meaning) rather than a mere change in forms. An unconverted North American may be very faithful in church attendance, give to the poor, love his fellow man, and be moral and ethical in his business dealings. He, too, looks on these functions as building merit, leading to the assurance of eternal life. Such a man may then encounter the message of grace and experience the new birth. Does he now cease attending church, stop giving to the poor, begin to hate his friends, and commence unethical business dealings? No, such a thought is preposterous. He continues on in the same forms, but his purpose and perspective relating to these practices are totally changed. Gratitude and love to Christ have replaced merit-seeking. There is a new and deep meaning behind those external practices. The same basic dynamic can take place in the life of a Muslim as he infuses new meanings into forms which he retains— assuming these forms are in no way prohibited by command or principle in the Word of God.[7]

7. Bashir Abdol Massih, "The Incarnational Witness to the Muslim Heart," in *The Gospel and Islam: A 1978 Compendium*, ed. Don M. McCurry (Monrovia, CA: MARC, 1979), p. 89.

The following description of a Muslim wedding ceremony further illustrates the possibilities which contextualization of the Christian gospel might open up. How much more meaningful this ceremony appears than typical practices at Christian weddings in the West; for example, the showering of rice and the throwing of the bouquet to the bridesmaids.

> The Persian Muslim wedding is rich with meaningful symbols. The bride and groom sit side by side, facing a mirror, indicating that until that point they did not know each other directly. On a cloth in front of them is placed: 1) a Quran in the center, that it may be the center of their lives, 2) fresh greens, that their marriage may not grow stale, 3) goldfish, that their marriage might be full of life, 4) bread, that their table may never be bare, 5) an egg, that God may make them fruitful, 6) sugar lumps, to be broken over their heads that their lives together may be sweet and 7) a candle, that God may give them light on their new untrodden path. If the Bible were at the center with Christian content and message, could Christ become incarnate in this cultural form? I think he would be delighted.[8]

Experiments in contextualization continue to be made throughout the world. One of the most significant of these is the movement which calls itself Jews for Jesus, which is led by Moishe Rosen. This group is dedicated to offering American Jews the option of becoming followers of the Messiah without leaving their Jewish culture, without eating pork, and without cutting themselves off from their own Jewish identity. Several thousand Jews have accepted Jesus Christ as God through this movement. Rosen speaks about the aims of his mission:

> We don't think of ourselves as Jesus Freaks, although we've been called that. We're trying to be part of the Jewish community and be involved in Jewish organizations. We sincerely desire to support the Jewish community as much as they will let us. We want to be good Jews who follow Messiah

8. Ibid., p. 90.

Jesus. Some rabbis say we're apostates who have thrown away our rights as Jews. Our answer is that we have become completed Jews by accepting the Messiah as the final, once-and-for-all atonement for our sins. We observe the Jewish holidays and traditional family ceremonies and do all we can to preserve our Jewish identity.[9]

Recently, I attended a special program conducted by Jews for Jesus. Moishe Rosen gave a devotional after a group of singers had beautifully sung Jewish-type tunes, using appropriate musical instruments. This was an impressive presentation of a contextualized message directed toward a certain segment of non-Christian people. The unconverted Jew would feel an immediate identification with the various forms of communication. Only the core message would offend.

My proposal in this book is that we use this kind of dynamic as a contextualized approach to the evangelization of Muslims.

9. Quoted in James C. Hefley, *The New Jews* (Wheaton, IL: Tyndale House, 1971), p. 134.

CHAPTER 4

The Muslim
World-View

Definition of "World-View"

World-view is not synonymous with behavior. These two concepts have often been intermingled in people's minds. Behavior can be described as being on the outer rim, at the form level of culture. World-view is, on the other hand, at the hub, at the deep or meaning level of culture. The confusion arises from the fact that we as outsiders can discern world-view only by observing and analyzing behavioral patterns and then working back to the hub. There we find the core of the individual, his innermost being, his orientation to life on which his behavior is based.

Specific definitions of world-view are varied. Eugene Nida defines world-view as a "system of values."[1] Another short characterization of world-view is "the way a people characteristically looks out on the universe. [It] consists of general and comprehensive concepts and unstated assumptions about life."[2]

1. Eugene Nida, *Message and Mission* (New York: Harper and Bros., 1960), p. 50.
2. James P. Spradley and David W. McCurdy, *Anthropology: The Cultural Perspective* (New York: John Wiley and Sons, 1975), p. 465.

Robert Redfield sees world-view as a stage on which the "I" is the central character looking out on the rest of mankind.[3] James Sire postulates that "a worldview is a set of presuppositions (or assumptions) which we hold (consciously or subconsciously) about the basic makeup of our world."[4]

A longer and well-thought-out definition is given by Charles Kraft:

> Perceptions of reality are patterned by societies into concep-
> tualizations of what reality can or should be, what is to be
> regarded as actual, probable, possible and impossible. These
> conceptualizations form what is termed the worldview of the
> culture. The worldview, then, according to this model, is the
> central systematization of conceptions of reality to which the
> members of a society assent (largely unconsciously) and from
> which stems their value system. The worldview lies at the
> very heart of a culture, touching, interacting with and strong-
> ly influencing every other aspect of the culture.[5]

With these definitions in sight, the next section will focus on the specifics of a Muslim world-view. At best, this can provide only a general overview.

Analysis of the Muslim World-View

Having visited a number of different Muslim countries, and having talked to scores of missionaries who have worked in various Islamic nations, I am amazed at how broadly uniform the Muslim world-view is in the midst of such ethnic, linguistic, geographical, and cultural diversity. Though there are significant

3. Robert Redfield, *The Primitive World and Its Transformations* (Ithaca, NY: Cornell University Press, 1953), p. 86.

4. James Sire, *The Universe Next Door* (Downers Grove, IL: Inter-Varsity Press, 1976), p. 17.

5. Charles H. Kraft, "Intercultural Communication and Worldview Change" (Pasadena: School of World Mission, Fuller Theological Seminary, 1976), p. 1.

differences in detail, I believe the various ethnic groups have enough in common to permit us, without too much distortion, to speak of a single "Muslim world-view."

We must attempt to understand the Muslim's world-view from a broader perspective than merely his religious orientation. A total understanding of a people's way of life includes much more. And an effective presentation of the message of Jesus Christ must be based on an appeal to felt needs that pervade a Muslim's total life and thought.

Comparison with the Hebrew and Christian World-Views

Figure 1 attempts to compare the Muslim world-view with the world-views of the Old Testament Jew and the Western Christian. The chart shows that there is great similarity between the world-views of modern-day Muslims and of the Old Testament Hebrews, and that both contrast sharply with Western values— at least in the eleven areas under consideration. To recognize these similarities and differences is of utmost importance in any effective approach to evangelizing Muslims. The Old Testament, along with New Testament passages oriented to the Hebrews, is where evangelistic activity should commence. This concept will be developed further in Chapter 6.

1. Unity

Greg Haleblian, a Christian Syrian, writes of unity within Islam:

> One of the first principles most worthy of consideration is the Muslim's love for unity or oneness. This comes to the fore most notably when the contrast between the interior of the mosque on one hand, and the interior of the church on the other is sharpened. As one enters into the mosque, he finds himself submerged in an atmosphere of total unity: every element within its four walls is designed so as to avoid what is conspicuous and particular.... No individual part or pattern is emphasized over the other.... Muslims' love for

Figure 1
Comparison of World-Views

Concept	O. T. Hebrew and Muslim	Western Christian
1. Unity	Emphasis on unity in all of life	Emphasis on unity only if it has pragmatic value
2. Time	High respect for the past and tradition	*Orientation toward the future
3. Family	Solidarity	*Emphasis on individual
4. Peace	Harmony, integration Total way of life Internal and external characteristic	Contentment *A segment of life Internal characteristic
5. Honor	All-important consideration	High priority
6. Status	A matter associated with wealth, family name, age	*A result of accomplishment
7. Individualism	Subordination to emphasis on group	*High regard for independence
8. Secularism	A totally unacceptable trend	*A largely acceptable trend
9. Change	An undesirable phenomenon	*A highly desirable phenomenon
10. Equality	A theoretical ideal which is not practiced	A theoretical ideal which is not practiced
11. Efficiency	A matter of little or no concern	*An imperative

*In direct contrast to Hebrew-Muslim world-view

unity or oneness is by no means limited to religion. It is dominant in many areas of Arab culture and most notably in the
material products, such as houses and clothes. A Westerner
touring inner cities and villages in Syria, for example, will be
overwhelmed with the uniformity evident in the structure of
houses. Without zoning laws or government control, houses
are almost exact replicas of each other.[6]

Evidence of sameness can also be seen in Hebrew culture.
This is perhaps related, in both cases, to the emphasis on the unity
and oneness of God. On the other hand, the Western Christian is a
product of different cultural influences. The *Zeitgeist* of the West is,
"If unity is pragmatically worthwhile, keep it; if not, then discard
it." Variety, not uniformity, is highly regarded.

2. Time

Muslims have a high respect for historical perspectives. Lynn
Silvernale speaks of Muslim regard for the past:

> Bengalis are oriented toward the past...their past is their
> life. What they are now doesn't matter, they glory in what
> they were in the past.... The future enters very little into
> the thinking of the Bengalis.... To some extent Bengalis
> consider it presumptuous to talk about the future, probably
> due to the fatalism of their religion.[7]

The Jews gloried in what could be called "recital theology."
How they loved to recite the works of God in the great
deliverance from Egypt, the giving of the Ten Commandments,
and the crossing of the Jordan into Canaan. They were dedicated
to the perpetuation of tradition. The present is a definite consideration to the Jew and Muslim, but its impact is probably secondary to that of the past.

Haleblian says the Arabs are little interested in specific

6. Krikor (Greg) Haleblian, "World View and Evangelization: A Case
Study on Arab People" (Th.M. thesis, Fuller Theological Seminary, 1979), pp.
79-81.
    7. Lynn Silvernale, "Study of Bengali Culture" (private paper), p. 18.

designations of time. He contrasts the Arab and Westerner: "Where a Westerner will say, 'I will come and visit you tomorrow at seven o'clock in the evening,' an Arab would say, 'I will come to see you tomorrow evening.' The evening may mean anytime between five o'clock and ten or eleven at night."[8]

On the other hand, the Western Christian is strongly future-oriented. The past is seen as outdated and, in the main, irrelevant to the fast-breaking developments of the here and now. The present can be fascinating and enjoyable, but it must be measured in light of the criteria of the future. The challenge of life is the stretching out to grasp the future. Planning, strategy, goal-setting, and evaluations are all a kaleidoscope of activity that pushes the Westerner forward in the pursuit of a successful future.

The Western communicator of the gospel must come to grips with this clash of world-views. He must appreciate the time orientation that is deeply woven into the fabric of Muslim society.

3. Family

The interaction of the Muslim family is generally a beautiful thing to behold. Ties between family members run very deep. Haleblian describes these relationships:

> Generally speaking, the family lives either in one big house, or in several adjoining houses. Income and expenditure is shared by all members of the family, but controlled by "its head." Property is also held in common by the extended family. Over against the nuclear family structure characteristic of the West, the extended families enjoy a greater measure of security and solidarity. In events of economic hardship, physical illness or death, there are other members of the family to take over responsibilities. The extended family guides and assists the young married couples in child rearing, cooking, and other household chores.[9]

Muslims are criticized, often rightly so, for giving the

---

8. Haleblian, "World View," p. 42.
9. Ibid., p. 55.

woman a low status in life. But this view must be balanced by the positive aspects:

a. All Muslim women have the opportunity to be married.
b. Ideally, these marriages are arranged by concerned parents or other relatives.
c. Compared to the West, the divorce rate, in most Muslim cultures, is extremely low. There is security in marriage.
d. The family becomes a supportive unit that acts as a refuge from the harsh realities of life.

Having personally been a close observer of Muslim family life for many years, I want to express my opinion that the West has little to say to Muslims on the subject of family life. A so-called Christian nation like the United States with a national divorce rate approaching 40 percent can only shamefully repent of having strayed so far from biblical norms.

The Old Testament has close parallels to Muslim family structures. Arranged marriages, submission of the woman to the husband, the close-knit family, and the extended nature of relationships all bear strong resemblance to conditions in Islamic lands.

4. Peace

Islamic concepts of "peace" include: "to be well," "peace and health," "peace in this world as well as in the next."[10] The Muslim uses "Peace be upon you" as a greeting as well as a farewell. Like the Jew of Old Testament times the contemporary Muslim sees peace as harmony, integration, and a total way of life. It is both internalized and externalized. It embraces past, present, and future.

The Western Christian tends to internalize peace and put it more in a spiritual category. The Christian concept is not as broad or all-inclusive as the Muslim view of peace.

10. H. A. R. Gibb and J. H. Kramers, *Shorter Encyclopedia of Islam* (Ithaca, NY: Cornell University Press, 1965), p. 489.

5. *Honor*

The greatest tragedy in a Muslim's life is to see dishonor brought upon the family's name. Such shame will cause internal convulsions within the complete extended-family structure. The hurt, embarrassment, and perplexity of family dishonor will have a negative effect on the name and reputation of future generations. A crucial question in all marriage arrangements is, "Is he or she from a good family?" The Old Testament view of honor was similar.

The Western Christian also ascribes importance to being an honorable person. The New Testament continues the theme of the Old in this regard.

6. *Status*

In both Muslim and Hebrew society of old, status was more assigned than earned. This could arise from inherited wealth or property, an honored family name, or advanced age. I have often observed with amazement how a well-educated, middle-aged Muslim will go to his illiterate aged father for counsel. The father has a dual status arising from kinship as well as advanced age.

In the West, a Christian places emphasis on achieved status. A person can come from any background. The relevant criterion is what he has accomplished. One of my Christian acquaintances is a vice-president of Ford Motor Company. He was not born into that position. Family background is an irrelevant consideration. His status was earned by a tremendous volume of hard work.

7. *Individualism*

The Muslim does not value the autonomous approach to life. He derives strength and security from interrelatedness, not independence. Conformity has a much higher societal value than does nonconformity.

Haleblian summarizes the Middle Eastern perspective on this subject:

> The aspect of solidarity which characterizes the Arab society
> has important bearings on evangelism. It must be reiterated,

for example, that in such societies individual decisions are very curtailed. Before any relatively significant decision is made, the group mind has to be formed and consensus of opinion obtained. As opposed to Western societies where decisions are made purely on an individual basis, most of the decisions here are shared decisions.[11]

Silvernale writes of the individual in relation to the group to which he belongs. "To do something against an individual Bengali is to arouse the ire of the group, because the individual stands for the group and must be upheld."[12]

Note also the remarks of Michael Youssef:

As a Christian Arab, I know that Arabs do not like alienation. Their whole life is centered upon family, friends and peer groups. We, therefore, have put unnecessary barriers before them in emphasizing the individualistic approach in evangelism.[13]

This last point is of greatest importance. Up to the present, the most common form of evangelism employed by Westerners has been to win individuals to Christ. This has, in group-oriented cultures, led to extraction from society and, often, to total alienation. This approach should be repudiated. In Western culture, which sees individualism as a positive trait, this is an acceptable form of evangelism. In Muslim countries, however, it is abhorrent. New approaches must be probed which allow for groups to come simultaneously to Christ. The high value given to the interrelatedness of society must be retained. This is a good and positive sociological characteristic which must be appreciated and preserved.

8. Secularism

In Old Testament times there was always a tension between the true God and false gods (e.g., Baal). Both were religious forces.

11. Haleblian, "World View," p. 12.
12. Silvernale, "Bengali Culture," p. 4.
13. Michael A. Youssef, "Theology and Methodology for Muslim Evangelism in Egypt" (M.A. thesis, Fuller Theological Seminary, 1978), p. 80.

The supernatural was very real. Battles were waged; economic policies set; political treaties arranged—all with a deep cognizance of an external, super power. The devoted Jew recognized that force as being the God Jehovah of Israel.

To the Muslim, Allah is still very real—even in the midst of tremendous pressures to move toward a secularistic society. Current political events demonstrate a definite trend for Islamic nations to become even more orthodox in religious theory and practice. This is a reaction against the Western-introduced secularism of the colonial period. Islamic law is tied closely to nationalistic pride.

9. Change

In the West, change is looked on as synonymous with progress. Innovation is regarded as good for society. The "new look" carries with it built-in status. One of the most appreciated descriptive words of the West is "dynamic." From hemlines to car styles to breakfast cereals, change and variety are the "in thing."

The Muslim has been caught in an identity crisis in the twentieth century. Pressure from educated Muslim leadership influenced by Western norms has caused a great deal of tension at the grassroots level. On the other hand, the continuing attempts to shift back to the seventh-century Quranic value system have had the effect of restoring equilibrium to a vast segment of Muslim society. The rural Muslim masses can once more relax with the assurance that their revered traditional modes of life are secure.

10. Equality

The Jew recognized God as Creator of all men. This gave the human race a certain dignity. On the theoretical level the Jews believed in the equality of all. In practice, however, they were often quite discriminatory.

The Muslims proudly proclaim they are totally committed to the brotherhood and equality of all men. Often the example is given of the line of people at prayer time in the mosque. Literally, a beggar can be seen saying his prayers next to the richest man in the village. I have observed, however, that there is often great distance between people of various social and economic strata once the prayers are completed. Day laborers, ricksha pullers, and street cleaners are treated with disdain by the upper classes. Never would a person of status carry an article of great weight down a main street, nor would the same person stoop to clean a bathroom even in his own home.

11. Efficiency

The West highly regards efficient production. The assembly line is the realization of a high goal in Western society. Evaluation of the system focuses on the cars as they roll off the line and are loaded on railway cars for nationwide distribution. Quantity, profits, a well-known name—these are the aspirations of the car manufacturer. I once watched a penetrating one-hour special television program that concerned itself with the personal life of the assembly-line worker. The camera told a devastating story of boredom, frustration, family tension, and, ultimately, hatred of all that the worker's employer stood for! Yet, "efficiency" had been attained.

The Muslim has little concern for efficiency. He is person-oriented. His focus in life is much more on relationships with others. At present there are few assembly-line factories operating in Muslim countries.

Comparison of Muslim and Christian Concepts of Religious Terminology

Figure 2 addresses itself to the immediate reactions which various religious terms will elicit from the Western evangelical Christian and from the Muslim. The same word often triggers contradictory responses. The Christian must come to grips with these distinctives if he is to effectively communicate the message of new life in Christ.

1. God

David J. Hesselgrave sums up the contrast between the Christian and the Muslim understanding of God:

Figure 2
Concepts of Religious Terminology

Vocabulary	Muslim	Western Evangelical Christian
1. God	Distant Merciful Capricious Vengeful Almighty	Personal Loving Concerned Judgmental Holy
2. Christ	Prophet	God
3. Bible	Revelation from God Changed, corrupted	Revelation from God Authoritative
4. Trinity	God, Mary, Jesus	Father, Son, Holy Spirit
5. Faith	Object: God and Muhammad	Object: Jesus as God
6. Sin	Shame, embarrassment Rebellion against God	Guilt Rebellion against God (primarily) and man
7. Salvation	Requirement: faith and works Provider: God No assurance	Requirement: faith Provider: God in Christ Assurance
8. Sanctification	Emphasis on obe- dience and ritual	Emphasis on role of Holy Spirit
9. Love	Stress on family	Stress on community
10. Supernatural Powers	Belief in spirit world	Belief based on teach- ings of Bible

Muhammad's religion begins and ends with Allah. Allah is described as "One," "Single," and "Eternal." The Creator of all things and absolute sovereign, he has decreed both good and evil. He is mighty, forgiving, compassionate, all-knowing, wise and merciful, but he indifferently consigns men to heaven or hell. If these descriptions sound mutually contradictory, there is good reason because the Allah of the Koran is essentially unknowable. As for the Christian God, it is quite obvious that Muhammad thought that the Christian Trinity was composed of Father, Mary the virgin, and their child, Jesus. It is in light of this apparent misconception that we must understand the repeated insistence in the Koran on the unity of Allah.[14]

The Old Testament portrays God in terms of His majesty, power, and justice. But the New Testament conception of God centers around love, holiness, and personal involvement with mankind through Jesus. An important bridge in witnessing to Muslims is to explore the common ground of the Quranic and Old Testament views of God. For the Christian who accepts God as the God of both the Testaments, this is no problem. After a solid rapport is developed, it is natural to point out the incompleteness of the old covenant and the necessity of the new.

2. Christ

To the Christian, Christ is a precious name. Our hearts swell with gratitude as we consider the benefits we have received as a result of our faith in God through the intermediary work of Christ on the cross. Our minds are overwhelmed as we mentally reconstruct Christ's acts of love, self-sacrifice, endurance, compassion, and identification with sinful, rejecting mankind.

By the Muslim, however, the name *Christ* is greeted with ambivalence. On one hand, there is appreciation for the life and ministry of one of the greatest of all prophets. On the other hand, there are cynicism and disgust over the fact that around this man has

14. David J. Hesselgrave, *Communicating Christ Cross-Culturally* (Grand Rapids: Zondervan, 1978), p. 186.

risen a cult of deity worship that embraces close to one billion people. The Muslim respects Jesus, but in his heart despises Christianity. The person of Jesus has attracted him, but the system has repelled him.

3. Bible

Authority is a crucial issue to the Muslim. He is convinced the Quran is the final and fully inerrant revelation from God. Gabriel, the Muslim believes, dictated the words of the Quran to Muhammad, who faithfully recorded the communication in the Arabic language. Seldom has the authority of the Quran been questioned by Muslims anywhere in the world. Certainly the type of higher criticism so devastatingly leveled at the biblical record is unknown among Muslims.

"Changed" and "corrupted" are the two most common charges leveled against the Bible. The Quran speaks highly of the Law, Prophets, Psalms, and Gospels. But Muslim scholars charge that the manuscripts have been significantly changed and corrupted through transcription errors down through the centuries.

4. Trinity

To the Christian the issue is clear—either Christ is God, or Christianity is one huge hoax. The Father demonstrated His love to the human race through the gift of Jesus. A further manifestation of this love is the sending of the Holy Spirit to reside in the heart of each believer. The Trinity remains a mystery to millions of believers in Christ. Yet, it is a foundational doctrine to orthodox Christendom. Faith is regarded as the key to acceptance of this profound biblical teaching.

One plus one plus one can never equal one. The Muslim is amazed at the naiveté of Christians in seeing mathematical, philosophical, and doctrinal unity in three discernible gods with separate functions. Thus, the religion of Islam takes as its rallying cry, "God is One." This is a definite reaction against the Christian doctrine of the Trinity.

5. Faith

"There is no god but God, and Muhammad is His Prophet." The Muslim's faith is primarily in God, but increasingly devotion is being directed toward Muhammad.

The Christian finds his expression of love to God fulfilled in loyalty and commitment to Jesus Christ. Faith in Christ is the door to the relationship between sinful man and a holy God.

6. Sin

Guilt is a normal reaction of a Western Christian to sin. His conscience is smitten; this leads to remorse and often on to repentance. Sensitivity to and definition of sin depend on many factors. Conscience is conditioned by culture, moral codes, and parental teaching. Sin is regarded as a rebellion against God in the primary sense and against fellow man on a secondary level.

By contrast the Muslim focuses on the penalty for sin. He does not usually experience sin as guilt but rather as shame and embarrassment. Losing face is the crucial issue. Lynn Silvernale describes this reaction to sin in the life of a Muslim Bengali:

> Shame or embarrassment is a primary social control, that is, it causes a person to try to keep himself in a socially acceptable position.... The Bengali governs his behavior by asking himself, "What will people say?"[15]

Three-wheeled cycle rickshas are very common in one Muslim country. The drivers are notorious for their behavior on the road. Often the police will grab one of these drivers and punish him by making him grab his ears, stick out his tongue, and do scores of deep knee bends. The public laugh and ridicule as they pass by. The embarrassment of this simple, nonviolent mode of punishment burns deeply into the heart of the offender.

A consequence of the Muslim perspective is that it is difficult to communicate the biblical meaning of sin to a Muslim. His outlook is horizontal rather than vertical. Often, the key criterion

15. Silvernale, "Bengali Culture," p. 5.

of a definition of sin is whether or not a person is caught. The same phenomenon can, however, be observed in the lives of Old Testament characters. Repentance and tears come quickly to people with this perspective when they are apprehended in the act. But seldom does guilt lead such people to confess a sin of social consequence.

The ideal would seem to be a merger of the vertical and the horizontal—of guilt before God along with the shame and embarrassment one feels in relation to other human beings. These forces acting in concert can serve as an effective deterrent to sin.

7. Salvation

The Old Testament pattern of allegiance to God along with faith and doing good works as a means of obtaining salvation is parallel with Islamic belief. Acceptance of Muhammad as God's special prophet is an added essential ingredient. There is no assurance of eternal life until the Muslim reaches the day of judgment at which time it is commonly understood that all will be made to walk over the thin edge of a sword stretched across a deep abyss. Those who succeed will enjoy an eternity of sensual paradise. Those who fail will be consigned to torment in the raging fires of hell. Faith and good works during a person's life are believed to give assistance in passing this test. Muslims believe one's good and bad works will be weighed on a huge scale and influence whether he successfully crosses over the abyss into paradise. It is my observation that this teaching of future bliss or punishment has little practical bearing on the behavior of Muslims. They are more taken up with the here and now. The demands of life in the present obscure concern for future salvation.

Evangelical Christians rest in the finished work of Jesus Christ for their assurance of salvation. Works play a part in obedience and commitment. However, it is faith that seals the destiny of the believer.

8. Sanctification

The Christian desires to know God more intimately. A great variety of beliefs about sanctification has sprung up in the past seventy-five years. The common goal of them all, however, is a holier walk in Christ that is characterized by a love for God's Word, prayer, and witness. It is generally agreed that sanctification is gradual, but a large number of theologians stress crisis experiences with the Holy Spirit.

Muslims see sanctification in terms of obedience and pursual of religious ritual. Praying five times a day is central to the awareness of God in one's life. In general, there is little evidence of Muslims experiencing climactic, life-changing encounters with God. This personal dimension of God's directly interacting with man is lacking. The Sufi sect (which will be described in Chapter 6) is an exception.

9. Love

All religions teach love. Love is a universal concept beyond particular cultures and religions. Though the interpretation will vary from society to society, love is regarded as a positive quality among all of mankind.

Muslims tend to emphasize love within extended-family relationships. This is typical of kinship societies. Concern for those outside the family is, however, minimal. Friendships will be made, but they do not carry with them the same kind of commitment as do kinship relationships. This pattern is similar to that found in the Old Testament.

The love relationships of individualistic Western Christians tend to center around the nuclear family and/or friends. Often they will never meet distant relatives. Committed relationships tend to be formed with groups of people (whether relatives or not) who regularly interact and who share a similar outlook and interests.

10. Supernatural Powers

The Muslim world-view is saturated with consciousness of the spirit world. This phenomenon is not limited to any one country. The form will vary from group to group, but a basic animistic-type influence is nearly always clearly identifiable. Because this aspect of the Muslim world-view tends to be ignored (or regarded as aberrant) in most treatments, I quote rather extensively to support my contention.

Saint worship is widely practiced in many areas.

> Although the worship of the dead is forbidden in Islam, yet "Saint worship" is very common in Pakistan. A Muslim would claim, perhaps, that practices at tombs are not acts of worship, but are performed for the purpose of obtaining blessings. But at the shrines, people worship the saints more than God. The Muslims give great respect to their saints.[16]

Merle Inniger adds these observations:

> At Pakpaltan, in the Punjab, devotees flock to worship at the shrine of Baba Farid, a well-known 13th century saint, and to seek his intercession. Singers, instrumentalists, and drum beaters heighten the emotion of the scene, and dervishes dance themselves into "wajid" (ecstasy). Here is found the "Bahishti Darwaza" (Door to Paradise), and believers wait in long lines to pass through this door, for anyone who does so during the festival is promised a sure entrance to Heaven. Here one meets not only the poor and illiterate, but intellectuals, government officials, and wealthy landlords also. National leaders recognize the great influence of this festival which is usually inaugurated by some important official.[17]

Inniger also writes of the millions of Muslims who wear charms or amulets. These are designed to ward off evil spirits and bring good fortune. A verse from the Quran is written on a small piece of paper which is forced into the amulet.[18]

Bill Musk, who lives in the Middle East, has formulated a chart (Figure 3) which highlights the differences between "low"

16. Anwar M. Khan, "Strategy to Evangelize Muslim Jats in Pakistan" (Th.M. thesis, Fuller Theological Seminary, 1976), p. 47.

17. Merlin W. Inniger, "Getting to Know Their 'Heart Hunger' Is a Key to Reaching Muslims," *Evangelical Missions Quarterly*, January 1979, p. 38.

18. Ibid., p. 36.

Figure 3
The Differences Between "Low" and "High" Islam

Form	Meaning In "High" Islam	Meaning In "Low" Islam
1. Confession	Proves one is a true Muslim	Words are used to drive away evil
2. Prayer Ritual	Bodily purity for worshiping God	Demonic pollution removed by washing
3. Legal Alms	Responsibility to fellow-Muslim	Precaution against the evil eye
4. Fasting	Sign of commitment to Islam	Rituals for dealing with evil, sickness
5. Pilgrimage	Visit the epicenter for the faith	Rituals deal with evil, sickness, etc.

and "high" Islam.[19] Note that the practices of "low" Islam support the point under consideration.

Detmar Scheunemann of the Indonesian Bible Institute has also commented on these features of Islam:

> Working for many years in a Muslim country, I have come to the conclusion that the power of Islam does not lie in its dogma and practices, nor in the antithesis of the Trinity, against the Lordship of Christ and his redeeming death, but in the occult practices of its leaders, thus holding sway over their people.[20]

Throughout the Muslim world there is widespread belief in jinn or superhuman beings. In the rural areas of the Punjab in

19. Bill Musk, "Popular Islam: The Hunger of the Heart," in *The Gospel and Islam: A 1978 Compendium*, ed. Don M. McCurry (Monrovia, CA: MARC, 1979), p. 218.

20. Detmar Scheunemann, "Evangelism Among Occultists and Spiritists," in *Let the Earth Hear His Voice*, ed. J. D. Douglas (Minneapolis: World Wide Publications, 1975), p. 885.

Pakistan, young women will not dress themselves fashionably because of their fear of the jinn. When a small child will not stop crying, the mother will take a red chili, circle it around the head of the child seven times, and then throw it into the fire. The assumption is that a jinni wanted her child to play with his child; when the chili is thrown in the fire, the jinni runs away.[21]

In Ghana, Muslims have certain procedures that allow them to curse a wrongdoer:

> Muslims have different ways of cursing someone who cheats them or offends them. A Muslim has all sorts of things he can put on his body, that is, things he has made by way of a prayer (to be worn or used) on his body, or else prayers that can be done at home. Therefore, if this sort of thing happens, there are things he can say under his breath. Nothing may happen to the person at first, but before he reaches his home, he will bodily feel its touch.[22]

In central and east Java, nominal Islam is filled with expressions of magic and attempts to influence supernatural powers. In another Muslim country, if a person looks with greed on something belonging to another person, it is believed that some misfortune will come upon that object. This is the idea of the evil eye. To counteract the evil eye, people put spotted pots in gardens or outside their houses, a broom and basket on the roof of their house, a certain set of words or a design over their front door, or a spot of black on the side of a child's forehead.[23]

Hundreds of additional examples could be cited to show that these aspects of "popular Islam" must be recognized as deep-level, all-pervasive features of the Muslim world-view. Missionaries have traditionally dealt with Islam as a "high religion" based on the Quran and tradition. This approach is inadequate. Research must be aimed toward uncovering the real (as opposed to the ideal) system of beliefs that touches every segment of the

21. Khan, "Strategy to Evangelize," p. 51.

22. Patrick J. Ryan, *Imale: Yoruba Participation in the Muslim Tradition* (Missoula, MT: Scholars Press, 1978), p. 187.

23. Silvernale, "Bengali Culture," p. 32.

Muslim's life. At the same time, the influence of orthodox Islam on popular Islam should not be overlooked.

The Western Christian often naively believes that his understanding of the supernatural is biblically based. But how many Christians read horoscopes, cross fingers, wish their friends "good luck," are sensitive to certain numbers (there is no row thirteen on most American planes), won't walk under a ladder, and inwardly cringe when a black cat races across their path? Before criticizing the Muslim it would be well for the Christian to engage in some introspective analysis.

Basic Christian Truth

The Traditional View

It is vital that we have a firm grasp of the essentials of Christianity before we attempt to bring the gospel to the Muslim world. We must also be keenly aware of the points at which the Christian message clashes with Islam. Just what is the traditional view of basic Christian truth? As evangelicals, we are committed to understanding and propagating the Christian message as defined in the Bible. There is a great variety of evangelical statements that attempt to summarize the essentials of biblical Christianity; most of them approximate the following summary:

1. We believe that "all Scripture is given by inspiration of God," being historically trustworthy, including all the miracles recorded in the Old and New Testaments, and its teaching and authority final.
2. We believe in one God eternally existing in three Persons—Father, Son, and Holy Spirit.
3. We believe that Jesus Christ was conceived of the Holy Spirit, born of the Virgin Mary; that He is very God and very man and that all His teachings and utterances are true.
4. We believe in salvation by Divine sacrifice; that the Son of God gave "His life a ransom for many" and "bore our sins in

His own body on the tree" and that all who repent and believe in Him are justified on the grounds of His shed blood.

5. We believe that the body of our Lord was crucified, was raised from the dead according to the Scriptures, and that He ascended into Heaven and sitteth on the right hand of God as our High Priest and Advocate.

6. We believe that man was created in the image of God; that he has sinned and thereby incurred both physical and spiritual death and that all men are consequently born with a sinful nature: and we, therefore, believe in the necessity of regeneration by the Holy Spirit and on man's part repentance towards God and faith in our Lord Jesus Christ.

7. We believe in the personality and deity of the Holy Spirit who spake by the Scriptures of the Old and New Testaments, Who dwells in the believer, Who is the administrator in the Church and Who is also here to "reprove the world of sin, and of righteousness, and of judgment."

8. We believe that the supreme purpose of missionary work is to preach repentance and remission of sins through Christ's name among all the nations.

9. We believe that "this same Jesus which was received up from you into Heaven shall so come in like manner as ye beheld Him going into Heaven."

10. We believe in the resurrection of the just and the unjust; the eternal blessedness of the redeemed in Christ and the eternal punishment of those who have ignored or rejected the offer of salvation.

Many evangelical statements of faith, particularly of groups in the United States, include an additional reference to a premillennial and, often, a pretribulational view of eschatology. Other groups emphasize a particular view of sanctification.

Is it imperative for a Muslim to have a full understanding of these basics to become a believer? Must he pass a theological exam prior to entrance into the kingdom of God? What in this list must the convert accept immediately, and what may he learn more gradually after conversion? Are the presuppositions behind the titles of well-known tracts such as "Four Things God Wants You to Know" and "Four Spiritual Laws" correct?

In 1955, as a seventeen-year-old high-school senior, I first was presented with the message of God's redeeming love. As I left the meeting after receiving Christ, my heart was filled with an inexplicable joy, but my head was literally devoid of cognitive biblical truth. I knew nothing of the doctrine of the Holy Spirit, eschatology, inerrancy of Scripture, or a vast host of other teachings of the church. In fact, I wasn't aware that the Bible has an Old and a New Testament, much less that one of the key authors is Paul! What I did know was that I was a sinner, that Christ died for my sin, and that by simple faith I could receive assurance of forgiveness of sin and eternal life in heaven. Basic theology indeed! That wonderful step of faith in and allegiance to Jesus Christ immediately ignited a transforming process that continues even today.

The presentation of Christ, as I heard it, was adequate to sweep me into the kingdom. But what about the Muslim? Must we insist that what we present to a non-Christian Westerner as the basic gospel be presented in total to a Muslim who possesses an entirely different world-view?

A Redefinition

Great barbed-wire barriers of peripheral offense have often been erected by well-intentioned missionaries. The biblical message has become interwoven with economics, politics, and a very Western approach to religion.

Figure 4 focuses on external obstacles to successful communication of the gospel in a Muslim land. Before reaching the core message, the inquirer often counts the cost and turns away from salvation in Christ. But what cost is he counting? Is the offense the "offense of the cross" or is it the repugnance he experiences when presented with an offer of salvation that not only involves accepting a "foreign religion" but a "foreign culture" as well?

Figure 5 depicts the change in allegiance that most Muslims experience as they move from traditional Islamic belief to faith in Jesus Christ. Hebrews 11:6 affirms the existence of God and also

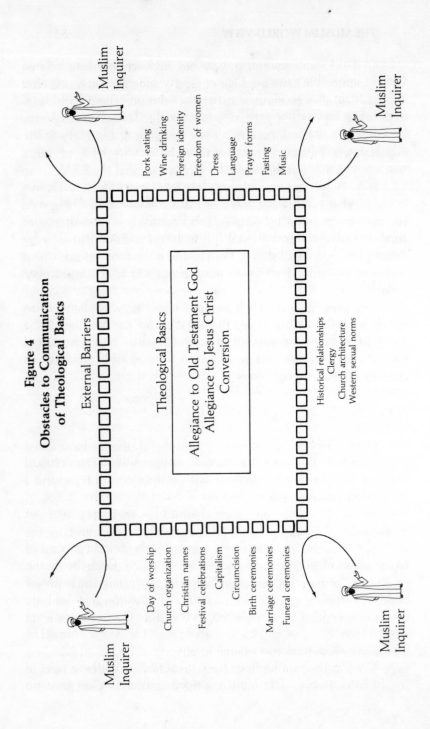

Figure 4
Obstacles to Communication of Theological Basics

External Barriers

Muslim Inquirer

Muslim Inquirer

Muslim Inquirer

Muslim Inquirer

Pork eating
Wine drinking
Foreign identity
Freedom of women
Dress
Language
Prayer forms
Fasting
Music

Theological Basics

Allegiance to Old Testament God
Allegiance to Jesus Christ
Conversion

Historical relationships
Clergy
Church architecture
Western sexual norms

Day of worship
Church organization
Christian names
Festival celebrations
Capitalism
Circumcision
Birth ceremonies
Marriage ceremonies
Funeral ceremonies

the fact that He interacts with man. All orthodox Muslims believe and act upon this premise. Deuteronomy 6:5 calls for a response of love from man to God. The average Muslim is convinced he is responding to God through adherence to the five pillars of Islam. He confesses, prays, gives, fasts, and, if at all possible, goes on the pilgrimage to Mecca. His cognitive understanding of Islam leads him on to specific religious behavior.

It is at this point that Christianity sets forth an exclusive teaching which Muslims have rejected. Romans 10:9 presents Christ as more than an exalted prophet. Christ was raised from the dead and, thus, provided a path for eternal salvation to all who believe on Him. The biblical teaching leads the inquirer on from a cognitive assent to a commitment of allegiance. This may occur at an identifiable moment or it may be obscured by a process of gradually coming to the truth of the gospel. My own conversion was sudden and dramatic. Many of my friends cannot specify the moment of their passage from darkness to light. The main point is they know they have been born again of the Spirit of God. I have observed that, for most Muslim converts, the day and hour of con-version cannot be specified.

How much cognitive understanding is necessary for a Muslim to become a Christian? In my own experience of salva-tion, this knowledge was a bare minimum. It is my opinion that a faith commitment can be made by a Muslim with little more than Romans 10:9. I am not at all dogmatic on this point. It is just that I am concerned lest we cram into a Muslim inquirer a lot of knowledge about the technical details of Christianity without stressing the dynamics of faith in and allegiance to Christ.

The point of conversion will commence a lifelong process of gaining the inspiring insights of the Word of God. Soon the believer, if he is well taught, will come to appreciate the truths of biblical authority, eschatology, and ecclesiology. He will be thrilled to see God's plan unfolded in the Bible. His response level will be high. His goal will be to grapple with the whole counsel of God, both cognitively and behaviorally.

My plea is for a limited, basic presentation of the gospel in the initial instance. The biblical record indicates Jesus gave no

Figure 5
Change in Allegiance

Action	"And without faith it is impossible to please Him, for he who comes to God must believe that He is, and that He is a rewarder of those who seek Him." Heb. 11:6	→ "And you shall love the Lord your God with all your heart and with all your soul and with all your might." Deut. 6:5	→ "If you confess with your mouth Jesus as Lord, and believe in your heart that God raised Him from the dead, you shall be saved." Rom. 10:9
Cognitive Understanding	God exists God interacts with His creation	One God ——→ (love response)	Jesus Christ as Lord → Resurrection Salvation by faith and confession

theological treatise to the lame and the blind. The focus of His call was for an active faith. Great numbers heeded that call and entered into the kingdom of God. Childlike faith in Christ was the only prerequisite.

Strategy for Implementing Change

Transformation of World-View

The Christian communicator should be a person of love and tenderness. He must fully empathize with the person of another culture to whom he is presenting Christ. Kraft has written on this subject with the concern befitting a Christian.

> One need not approve of the custom or attitude, but Christian concern dictates that one respect the point of view of the other culture. For those within that culture were taught the integrated lifeway of which that element is a part in the same way that we were taught our lifeway. And they accepted it as the correct way of life just as uncritically as we accepted our own culture. Cultural practices should be interpreted in their proper cultural contexts, however, not as a denial of scripturally revealed supracultural ethical standards, but as the first step toward advocating change in that direction.[24]

Following is a partial list of obstacles a Muslim may experience when a Western Christian urges him to accept Christ as his Savior:

1. There is a strong clash between world-views.
2. The Muslim has a deep-level nationalistic view of Islam.
3. The so-called Christian West is seen to be culturally and morally inferior to Islam.
4. Change is not desirable.

24. Charles H. Kraft, *Christianity in Culture* (Maryknoll, NY: Orbis Books, 1979), p. 361.

5. The Muslim has a great sense of personal pride.
6. Christianity doesn't seem to relate to felt needs.

Figure 6 pinpoints the need to work on the transformation of world-view rather than on external behavioral standards. This type of witness centers on the felt needs of the Muslim at the deep level of his world-view. As a person becomes convinced and commences to change his world-view, there will be a rippling or radiating set of influences that move out to affect behavior. In other words, in the transformational process, world-view, not behavior, should be the focus of our witness to the Muslim. This is not to minimize the importance of seeing changes in sub-Christian

Figure 6
The Centrifugal Rippling Effect of a
Change in World-View

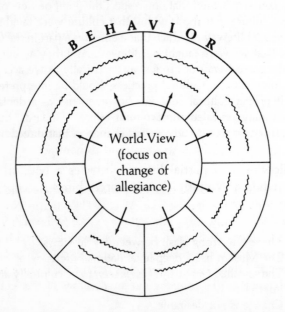

Note: This is the antithesis of enforcing peripheral behavioral changes, which cause inward-moving ripples that bombard the world-view, thus creating dissonance and disintegration.

behavioral patterns. This will come, but not through imposition. Rather, it comes through the individual's deep personal conviction. Needless to say, this type of commitment will be characterized by greater stability and permanence.

Everett Rogers and Floyd Shoemaker illustrate how at times, even in the West, innovation is often greeted with skepticism and slow acceptance. More than fourteen years were required for hybrid seed corn to reach complete adoption in Iowa. Public schools in the United States required fifty years to adopt the idea of the kindergarten, and, more recently, about five years to adopt modern math.[25] How much more patience should be shown toward cultures that regard change with much greater skepticism than does the United States!

The Muslim must see Jesus Christ as the initiator of a supracultural message for all mankind. Missionaries must present the word of reconciliation in such a way that it fits well into the value system of the society in which it is being proclaimed. The transforming of the world-views and allegiances of Muslims should be carried out as a process which involves minimal social dislocation.

Inside-Outside Advocates

Kraft succinctly differentiates between inside and outside advocates, comparing them to yeast and dynamite.

> I reflect back on God's encounter with Elijah. Here's the great big display. The earthquake. Was God in that?—No. The fire?—No. Big wind?—No. Where's God? Still, small voice. Yeast rather than dynamite. The competitive approach says, "Go and hammer them to pieces. Destroy in order to rebuild." I think God's approach is to take the culture as it is and appeal to the central conceptualizations of that culture,

25. Everett M. Rogers and L. Floyd Shoemaker, *Communication of Innovations*, 2nd ed. (New York: Free Press, 1971), p. 16.

their worldview, with the message that will transform them from the inside out.[26]

It is not easy to influence the inner core of individuals and society. But the attempt must be made if Christ is to become a viable option to the Muslim. To close this chapter, we present a few suggestions that may be helpful in attaining this desired end.

1. Muslim leaders must be contacted. It is very rare for civil and religious leaders to become Christian. They are vulnerable to the wishes of their followers. "Don't rock the boat" is their guiding philosophy. Yet, friendship will neutralize any overt opposition from this very important segment of society.

2. Second-level leadership should be an important focus of witness. Men who are opinion leaders but not in the spotlight are often open to consider other options. Also, they are highly respected members of the community.

3. Initially, the fringe of social rejects (within the target group) should not be a *focus* of witness. If the first converts come from this group, the image of Christianity will be very poor and will likely cause the larger group not to seriously consider the claims of Christ. Such people, however, should never be turned away or refused admission into the community of believers.

4. A group, either of friends or relatives, should be the initial target of witness. It is very difficult for an individual to stand alone against social opposition. It may be best to encourage secret belief until such a time as a number can together openly declare their faith in Christ.

5. In the initial witness, only basic and important changes should be introduced. Peripheral teaching and suggestions for change can come at a later period.

6. Adequate time should be given for assimilation to change. Frequently the missionary is guilty of introducing multiple changes at the same time. The convert is then overwhelmed and can become very confused.

26. Charles H. Kraft, "Dynamic Equivalence Churches," in *Conference on Media in Islamic Culture Report*, ed. C. Richard Shumaker (Marseilles: Evangelical Literature Overseas, 1974), p. 32.

7. The cross-cultural communicator will seek to become an "insider" as much as possible.

To the Muslim, his world-view is very precious. It is his whole way of life. Jesus Christ desires to become the very center and core of that world-view. To the Christian who is entrusted with the task of introducing and stimulating that change, the task is awesome, challenging, and sometimes frightening. But to those of us who have had the privilege of meeting transformed Muslims, the task is eminently worthwhile!

PART II

Application of Contextualization

CHAPTER 5

The Cross-Cultural Communicator

As mentioned in the Introduction, the purpose of this writing is to be extremely practical. We must focus on present realities rather than on dreamy ideals. And among those realities is the fact that, with only a few exceptions, it is the cross-cultural communicator from the West who is carrying the largest share of evangelistic ministry to the Muslim—however small that may be. In Muslim countries the national church often feels severely threatened by the majority community. Their caution leads them to shy away from evangelistic involvement with Muslims. In some ways, they feel they are aliens among their own people. There is a parallel between their situation and that of the Jewish exiles in Babylon who hung up their harps on the willow trees (Ps. 137:2). They felt discouraged at the difficulties in which they found themselves. It was hard to sing the praises of God when surrounded by the obstacles of an alien culture.

The missionary, however, does not face this emotional pressure. He retains an identity with the people back in his own homeland. His Western friends and supporters are a source of comfort and encouragement. He can then go forth confident that if things get too bad he has the option of a safe withdrawal. The national believer has no such possibility. Witness takes on a different perspective for the national believer. It is hoped that sensitive implementation of the principles enunciated in this book will lead to a growing evangelistic concern on the part of Muslim converts. Until that occurs, the Western missionary will continue to be in the vanguard of Muslim evangelization.

The missionary calling has unique features. The missionary must be reasonably well-educated, cross geographical boundaries, leave loved ones behind, often sacrifice financially, adjust to another language and culture, and work on a close-knit team. Many of these involve pressures little known by Christian workers in the West.

My conviction is that we as missionaries must open ourselves to criticism, both from friend and foe. We must be willing to reevaluate what has come to be regarded as sacrosanct methodology. "Change" must not be a dreaded word. Can the missionary to Islam be more effective? What is the Muslim's perception of the missionary? How can it be changed for the better?

I speak from a heart of love and concern—from within the camp. My observations will often be self-condemnatory. We are all learners. For that process a humble attitude will be regarded as the chief virtue.

The Incarnational Model

How would you evaluate the following instruction given to missionaries by their home board?

> Do not regard it as your task and do not bring any pressure to bear on the peoples, to change their manners, customs, and uses, unless they are evidently contrary to religion and sound morals. What could be more absurd than to transport France, Spain, Italy, or some other European country to China? Do not introduce all that to them, but only the faith, which does not despise or destroy the manners and customs of any people, always supposing that they are not evil, but rather wishes to see them preserved unharmed. It is the nature of men to

love and treasure above everything else their own country and that which belongs to it; in consequence there is no stronger cause for alienation and hate than an attack on local customs especially when these go back to a venerable antiquity. This is more especially the case, when an attempt is made to introduce the customs of another people in the place of those which have been abolished. Do not draw invidious contrasts between the customs of the peoples and those of Europe; do your utmost to adapt yourself to them.[1]

How many boards today encourage their missionaries to adopt such an appreciation of the target culture? Amazingly, these instructions were written in 1659 by the office of the pope in Rome and then sent to all Catholic missionaries in China! It would appear these missionaries desired to be "incarnated" into the mainstream of Chinese life. The cost was great. But they were not without a prior model.

No Scripture deals so succinctly and clearly with the incarnation of Christ as does Philippians 2:5–8:

Have this attitude in yourselves which was also in Christ Jesus, who, although He existed in the form of God, did not regard equality with God a thing to be grasped, but emptied Himself, taking the form of a bond-servant, and being made in the likeness of men. And being found in appearance as a man, He humbled Himself by becoming obedient to the point of death, even death on a cross.

What a gripping mystery! As God, our Lord was totally "other." In the expanse of heaven, He ruled with the earth as His footstool. There was no constraint on His actions—even from His erring created ones on planet earth.

Yet, this divine One possessed the great virtue of love. He could not remain oblivious to the acts of Satan among mankind. His concern spanned the light years of the universe. Involvement

1. Quoted in Stephen Neill, *Christian Missions* (Baltimore: Penguin Books, 1964), p. 179.

was not felt to be merely an option but rather an imperative. Love impelled the incarnation—"in the fullness of time."

Jesus chose the stable and the carpenter shop rather than the palace of Herod or even the center of power, the palace of Caesar. Christ identified with mankind in a full and unique sense. "God in Jesus became so much a part of a specific human context that many never even recognized that he had come from somewhere else."[2] Humility and love drove Him first to empty Himself, second, to become a man, and third, to go to the cross. The bond-slave image of the God-man Jesus is impressive. The cord that bound Him in slander, in hurt, in torture, and on the cross was simply *agape* love. Never has cross-cultural identification been so complete or so costly. The die of Jesus' model was cast in the furnace of concern and love.

For the missionary, *cross*-cultural ministry may indeed mean bearing the *cross* of the Lord Jesus. Incarnation into an alien environment may require forsaking comfortable housing, Western dress, familiar food, and personal privacy. The question naturally arises: To what limit must the dedicated missionary be willing to incarnate himself in the Muslim culture?

> God made Christ incarnate in Jew-like form to reach them, and Christ incarnate in Gentile-like form to reach them. Dare we follow the train of Jesus and Paul and say, "Christ incarnate in Muslim-like form to reach them"? Do we find a resistance in our hearts at this point? Surely this prejudice is not born of Christ's incarnational love. . . . How far are we willing to go to bring Christ incarnate in a Muslim context? . . . The incarnational witness is one in whom love has worked so deeply that he seeks in every way possible to become like the hearer so that he can manifest the gospel in thought, communication, and religio-cultural forms that relate meaningfully to the hearer.[3]

2. Charles H. Kraft, *Christianity in Culture* (Maryknoll, NY: Orbis Books, 1979), p. 175.
3. Bashir Abdol Massih, "The Incarnational Witness to the Muslim Heart," in *The Gospel and Islam: A 1978 Compendium*, ed. Don M. McCurry (Monrovia, CA: MARC, 1979), p. 87.

It is never easy for a person to incarnate himself in another culture. I can remember Muslim children throwing rocks on our tin roof throughout a long, hot summer evening. For them this was a few hours' entertainment. For my family it was a night of frayed nerves and serious questioning of how much we really loved these people. On other occasions, I have been insulted and even physically abused. I cannot say the command of Christ to love those who persecute you has always been easy to follow in my life. My frustrations have caused me to lose my temper more than once. Yet, what really is this temporal harassment in comparison to what our Lord endured for us?

Matteo Ricci, in 1579, pioneered mission work in inland China. Life was crude and taxing. The Chinese governor presented Ricci and his colleague the following list of edicts. They could either follow them without deviation—or immediately leave China.

> You must not be joined by other barbarians. You must continue to wear our dress; you must promise to conform to our habits; you must obey our magistrates; if you marry, you must choose a woman of our country. You will become, in all save your physical appearance, men of the Middle Kingdom, subject to the Son of Heaven. Are you willing to make these promises?[4]

The missionaries pondered deeply the significance of such an allegiance to a nonbelieving governor. Bowing three times to the floor, they repeated promises of submission and conformity. They then went forth rejoicing that they were privileged to engage in missionary work in a closed land of millions of lost souls. As one reads historical accounts of Ricci and others, he is struck with the immense deprivation and emotional testing they endured in order to incarnate Christ into the mainstream of Chinese life.

What mental processes were operative in Christ's keeping in touch with heaven? His prayers were full of passion and meaning

4. Vincent Cronin, *The Wise Man from the West* (New York: E. P. Dutton, 1955), p. 47.

as He talked to His Father. For in His humanity He experienced hurt, tears, perplexity, questioning, and temptation. Cannot the missionary take solace as he, too, goes through similar emotional responses to the incarnation process?

A price to pay, yes, but also a great reward and sense of satisfaction in accomplishing the assigned task. Paul, the missionary statesman, came to the end of his life and penned these beautiful words:

> For I am already being poured out as a drink offering, and the time of my departure has come. I have fought the good fight, I have finished the course, I have kept the faith. (II Tim. 4:6–7)

Dr. Saeed Khan Kurdistani was an outstanding Iranian Christian who died in 1942. In 1960, a man went to the area where Saeed had lived and ministered. An aged man of the community was asked by the visitor if he had known Saeed. The elderly man caught his breath and whispered: "Dr. Saeed was Christ Himself!"[5] Reverently, it can be said that this is the goal of the incarnation and the contextual process.

Finances

There is an overwhelming difference of opinion among missionaries on the subject of finances. Some feel it is imperative to "go native" and to denounce all who do not follow their example. Others feel equally strongly that they must live according to a Western standard for the sake of their family's mental and physical health. They defend their position by contending that the nationals will understand their needs. The important thing for the missionary, they say, is in the area of attitudes, not in lifestyle. Between these two extremes will be found every conceivable view. One can always be assured of a lively discussion among missionaries when this subject is raised!

5. Massih, "Incarnational Witness," p. 85.

Muslim countries are generally economically depressed. This reality sets the stage for the conflict of a great disparity between the living standard of the Western missionary and the Muslim. Chaeok Chun, a former Korean missionary in Pakistan who recently earned her doctorate from the School of World Mission of Fuller Theological Seminary, comments on this tension:

> I think it is significant that today's image of the Christian missionary endeavor from the Asian receptor's point of view is an image of comfort and privilege. Hence, Asians tended to reject the missionary and misunderstand his message.[6]

One national Christian observed the "luxurious" standard of missionary housing in a Muslim nation and questioned, "If the missionaries live on such a standard of affluence here, why do they speak so much of heaven? They have their heaven right here." Another national categorized as a "hell hole" a luxury hotel to which missionaries went on Saturdays to relax and swim.

Ralph Winter illustrates the problem:

> Let us envision for a moment the young United States mission candidate. He may have to scrounge around for the wherewithal to buy his family a car, a camera, and a washing machine (just the "bare necessities" of the U.S. life-style). Once on the field he will make expensive plane flights to the capital city for necessary medical help from real medical doctors. Even the most pitiable, poverty-stricken new missionary appears quite wealthy to the national Christian of most mission lands.[7]

The Irish monks of the seventh and eighth centuries were well known for their asceticism. Their entire outfit consisted of a

---

6. Chaeok Chun, "An Exploration of the Community Model for Muslim Missionary Outreach by Asian Women" (D.Miss. dissertation, Fuller Theological Seminary, 1977), pp. 142–43.

7. Ralph D. Winter, "The Highest Priority: Cross-Cultural Evangelism," in *Crucial Dimensions in World Evangelization*, ed. Arthur F. Glasser (Pasadena: William Carey Library, 1976), p. 324.

pilgrim's staff, a wallet, a leather water container, and some relics. When they received money from the wealthy, they quickly gave it away to the needy.[8] Is this a proper model for the contemporary missionary? In correspondence with me, Donald McGavran suggested that

> the missionary from affluent countries lives on a standard far higher than he needs to. What is called for—if we are to meet this problem head on—is an order of missionaries, celibate or married without children, who live . . . on rupees a hundred a month [i.e., ten dollars]. But any such move is at present "unthinkable" alas.

I would, at the risk of being controversial, like to pull some thoughts together on this very important issue.

1. It *does* matter what Muslims and converts think about the financial profile of the missionary community. Generally, they are appalled at the gap between their own living standard and that of the Western missionary. If we turn away from this concern in indifference, we are in danger of being insensitive to Paul's clear teaching on being a stumbling block to others.

2. Singles and couples without children can more easily make the adjustment to a simple lifestyle. This should be encouraged but not legislated.

3. Experimentation should be allowed. Take, for example, a missionary couple with a newborn infant living in a bamboo hut with a mud floor in a Muslim rural village. They should be supported. At the same time, they should not be made to feel embarrassment if at any time they feel withdrawal advisable.

4. Each family should be open before the Lord on the subject of finances. They should prayerfully evaluate their own physical and emotional needs. The goal is to live as closely as possible to the style of life of their target people without adverse results to anyone in the family. "Balance" is a key word.

5. Often the missionary can reside in stark simplicity in a

8. Sister Mary Just, *Digest of Catholic Mission History* (Maryknoll, NY: Maryknoll Publications, 1957), p. 22.

rural area and then take an occasional weekend trip to a nearby city for relaxation and necessary shopping. This accommodation to our cultural backgrounds is not, in my view, an act of hypocrisy. We must be realistic concerning our needs and various levels of capacity to endure deprivation within a foreign culture.

6. It is permissible to raise this issue with missionaries, but idle criticism, a judgmental attitude, and self-righteousness must be studiously avoided. Often, missionaries living in extreme poverty or those living in great affluence are the most opinionated and self-defensive. For the sake of unity in the body, it may be wise to avoid engaging these missionaries in heavy discussions on this subject.

Language

Christ in His incarnation had a distinct advantage over present-day missionaries. He learned His language as a child. The cross-cultural communicator must struggle with the acquisition of a new and frequently difficult language. It may be that the words are tonal, the verbs appear at the end of the sentence, and the writing reads from right to left. There can, however, be no really effective move toward contextualization until the missionary can communicate in the language of the people. Missions must make mastery of the language the first priority of every missionary as soon as (if not before) he arrives on the field.

Language acquisition is a continual process. Tom Brewster, coauthor with his wife, Betty Sue, of a valuable book entitled *Language Acquisition Made Practical*, has stated that "too often the new missionary completes language study and then his language skills settle on a plateau or even retrogress. The learner who knows how to learn can continue learning even after formal language study is over."[9] The alert mission will give incentives such as paying for language lessons so that their missionaries continue to pursue the goal of linguistic excellence.

9. E. Thomas and Elizabeth S. Brewster, "What It Takes to Learn a Language and Get Involved with People," *Evangelical Missions Quarterly*, April 1978, pp. 104–05.

William Smalley links respect for a people and culture with the process of learning their language:

> A missionary once remarked to me that the reason why his mission had an unusually splendid record for competence in the use of the language of their area of work was that they had a high degree of respect for the local culture. I think it would be possible to point to many cases where respect for local culture correlates with language competence. It would be possible certainly to point to many cases where strong disrespect for local culture correlates with abysmal language use. It may be coincidence, but the one country of the world where, in my experience, the people are most criticized by missionaries serving there is also the country which seems to have the lowest level of missionary language ability.[10]

Inadequate understanding of the language can lead to disastrous consequences. In my early days on the field I was having a particularly rough time with a landlord of one of the houses we had rented for the single ladies of our mission. This Muslim was forever making grandiose promises concerning essential house repairs, promises he never kept. My patience ran thin. In total exasperation one day I blurted out, "You are a very small person to make commitments and then not keep them." I uttered this statement in the vernacular—word for word. The Muslim houseowner flew into a rage. His eyes dilated and he screamed, "Who are you to call me such a thing? You too are a small person!" I was taken aback at the overwhelming force of his response. I explained the sequence of events to a friend. With a grave frown on his face, the Christian brother explained that I had used a very derogatory expression against the Muslim. Quickly, I returned to the houseowner and profusely apologized for what amounted to a vulgar cursing.

The missionary must be fully knowledgeable of the deeper meanings of the language he uses. Culture is very important in this process. "Son of a pig" is the ultimate term of disrespect to a Muslim. This is understandable when one considers how Muslim culture and Islamic religion view the pig.

It is the ultimate compliment to Muslims to learn their language well. This shows the missionary has a respect and esteem for that which is of primary importance and value to them. The opposite is communicated if the language is poorly learned.

Many missionaries conclude, often prematurely, that they have no linguistic aptitude. Just prior to going to the field, I took a course in phonetics—and it was a disaster. In desperation, I asked the teacher if she thought I could ever learn a foreign language. With a sober face, she said it would be very difficult, but she felt with a lot of hard work I would succeed.

During my first two-and-a-half years on the field, attempting to learn the language was extremely frustrating—and that is about all I did with my time. Most of the year my day commenced at 4:30 a.m. and often I studied well into the night. My wife, with the gift of a musical ear, spent a maximum three hours daily in study. The great encouragement to me was that our grades in the annual exams were almost identical. My application and determination had compensated for the lack of sharp linguistic skills. It is likely that almost anyone with the right attitude and the willingness to engage in a lot of hard work is capable of being, at minimum, an average communicator in a foreign language. The problem all too often lies in a lack of commitment and application.

Time

We have already alluded to this topic (pp. 67–68). A basic conflict between East and West is seen clearly in the sharp difference in orientation to time. The Easterner sees life in a casual event-oriented framework. The present is the most important consideration. A Westerner's life, on the other hand, is governed by the clock. He may be thoroughly enjoying an event, but if he glances at his watch and realizes the program is five minutes overtime, he suddenly begins to feel uncomfortable. This foundational clash can lead to serious interpersonal problems between missionary and national. In Ghana, for example:

> This difference of cultural background also underlies the dispute over the breakfast break. From the missionaries' time oriented background it was reasonable that the Africans should have their breakfast before leaving home, as they did, so that working hours could be spent in working. But the Africans customarily eat around 10 o'clock, and if they were to eat before leaving for work it would mean having their meal at about 6 a.m. The European sees the principle involved and the saving in time, but for the Ghanaian the event (in this case the meal) is more important.
>
> This difference in orientation explains many causes of friction. Missionaries often complain of "African time," implying the African is unpunctual, and it is a constant source of frustration why Africans are not punctual to church services, arriving anytime from the singing of the first hymn to the pronouncing of the benediction. But for many Africans the event, attending the service, is the most important thing, and the time of arrival is relatively trivial.[11]

Especially in rural areas the national is very relaxed concerning time. His schedule for farming is casual. This does not mean he is lazy. Frequently, the farmer is out plowing fields by sunrise. His midday break may extend to three hours, but he will be back at the plow until sunset.

The sun is often the only clock the farmer has. I recall one meeting with believers in which I suggested it was getting late and perhaps they would like to conclude in order to have time to walk back to their village by sunset. Immediately, as I spoke, all seven of the believers turned their heads in concern, looked out the door, made a determination of the placement of the sun in the sky, and agreed it was indeed time to be leaving. It was as coordinated and meaningful as the Westerner looking down at the face of his expensive wrist watch!

11. Donald Banks, "Causes of Friction Between Missionaries and Nationals," *Evangelical Missions Quarterly*, July 1976, p. 151.

What is often not realized is that the Easterner gets as frustrated with the Westerner's extreme concern about time as the Westerner gets upset over what looks to him like a lack of attention paid to time on the part of the Easterner. Charles Kraft tells of the time a young missionary sat chatting with the son of the local chief on the porch of the mission house. After some time had elapsed, the chief's son asked the missionary how long they had been sitting there. The missionary estimated about forty-five minutes had elapsed. The chief's son then said, "Do you know how long I would have been here if your predecessor were still here?" The missionary replied in the negative. "Five minutes," the chief's son replied. "Your predecessor would have come to the door when I called and asked me, 'What do you want?' I would have stated my business, gotten my answer, and been off again in about five minutes."[12]

This offense has been multiplied innumerable times. A national leader held in the highest esteem by all of his fellow countrymen told me he had once gone to a missionary's home. He rang the bell and soon the Westerner appeared. The missionary's first words were, "What can I do for you?" There was no invitation for the national to come inside the home. He replied, "There is nothing you can do for me," and turned and walked away in disgust. It was evident that even years later he still carried deeply the hurt of that moment.

Another national speaks to the issue:

> Moreover, in those days to see a missionary was a big problem in itself. One had to face a few obstacles to visit the missionary. First he had to face the missionary's dog; then the watchman. Moreover it was dependent upon the will of the missionary whether he had time to see anybody even if he had come from a far distant place.[13]

12. Charles H. Kraft, "God's Model for Cross-Cultural Communication—The Incarnation," *Evangelical Missions Quarterly*, Summer 1973, p. 212.
13. Anwar M. Khan, "Strategy to Evangelize Muslim Jats in Pakistan" (Th.M. thesis, Fuller Theological Seminary, 1976), p. 60.

The Westerner is taught that "time is precious." The Easterner is taught that "people are precious." The onus for change and adaptation is on the missionary.

Housing

The day of the mission compound is by no means over. These Western enclaves are found throughout the missionized world. They are often misunderstood and, in some cases, despised by the nationals. A Muslim convert questioned their existence by asking, "Am I wrong if I say that mission bungalows are often a partition wall between the hearts of the people and the missionaries?"[14] Paul Hiebert has researched the perception of these mission compounds in the minds of the onlooking community.

> In India the missionaries were called *dore*. The word is used for rich farmers and small-time kings. These petty rulers bought large pieces of land, put up compound walls, built bungalows, and had servants. They also erected separate bungalows for their second and third wives. When the missionaries came they bought large pieces of land, put up compound walls, built bungalows and had servants. They, too, erected separate bungalows, but for the missionary ladies stationed on the same compound.

> Missionary wives were called *dorasani*. The term is used not for the wife of a *dore* for she should be kept in isolation away from the public eye, but his mistress whom he often took with him in his cart or car.

> The problem here is one of cross-cultural misunderstanding. The missionary thought of himself as a "missionary," not realizing that there is no such thing in the traditional Indian society. In order to relate to him, the people had to find him a role within their own set of roles, and they did so. Unfor-

14. D. A. Chowdhury, "The Bengal Church and the Convert," *The Moslem World* 29 (1939): 347.

tunately, the missionaries were not aware of how the people perceived them.[15]

It is my view that the majority of all Western mission compounds that remain in Muslim lands should be dismantled. This would free the missionary to move into a community of Muslims and share his testimony among them incarnationally, rather than being shut off on a large plot of land that has very negative connotations in the minds of the people. It is preferable also for Christians to scatter out among the non-Christian townspeople rather than to live in a sealed-off community. Light must be diffused to be of any benefit.

Our first five-year term, living in a small town was a great learning and sharing experience. Adjacent to our bedroom window was the home of a Muslim lady who was separated from her husband. Her two young daughters lived with her. Quickly we became very intimate friends. The girls were always coming over to borrow a spice or an egg. We felt free to do the same. When the younger daughter had a raging fever, we brought her to our house and nursed her. From our bedroom window, we learned more about Muslim culture than scores of books could ever have taught us. Living in a mission compound would have denied us opportunity for personal involvement in the community.

The following critique by an outstanding Chinese Christian leader must not be taken lightly:

> In some places there is a bad image of Western missions. A Chinese church leader from Hong Kong once remarked to me that we could not expect many young people in Hong Kong to respond to missionaries while the image they had of missionaries was determined by Western missionaries in luxury housing in Kowlook Tong, driving around in Mercedes. While the old mission compounds are increasingly becoming museum places (though they may still be seen barbed wire

15. Paul Hiebert, "Social Structure and Church Growth," in *Crucial Dimensions in World Evangelization*, ed. Arthur F. Glasser (Pasadena: William Carey Library, 1976), p. 63.

and all in Korea and I gather sometimes in India also) it is still possible for missionaries to live in their hermetically sealed capsules, ivory towers from which they emerge periodically to distribute tracts and take prisoners. A fresh image of sacrifice, involvement and identification of Western missionaries may do more to encourage fellow believers in the Third World than anything else.[16]

I have found that many nationals, to some extent, resent it when missionaries preach on giving and sacrifice. It is true, the Westerner has given up his homeland and left many loved ones behind. But the overwhelming image in the mind of the national is a beautiful home and a car worth ten years or more of his salary.

The documents of Vatican II touch on the subject of the housing of Catholic missionaries:

> Priests and bishops alike are to avoid everything that might in any way antagonize the poor. More than the rest of Christ's disciples they are to put aside all appearance of vanity in their surroundings. They are to arrange their house in such a way that it never appears unapproachable to anyone and that nobody, even the humblest, is ever afraid to visit it.[17]

There needs to be some latitude, depending on whether one lives in a city, town, or village. Working with university students, for example, would demand facilities quite different from those needed in a rural village setting. The main concern is to relate to the group with whom one is working.

Food

Food is far more than just a substance to keep one's body cells replenished and healthy. There is a great deal to be learned

16. James Wong, *The Third World Missions* (Pasadena: William Carey Library, 1973), p. iv.
17. *Documents of Vatican II*, ed. Austin Flannery (Grand Rapids: Wm. B. Eerdmans, 1975), p. 896.

from a people and their food. For one thing, there is a close psychological relationship between the two. People feel their own choice of food is superior. The Westerner greatly appreciates ham, bacon, and pork roast. To the Muslim, this is totally repugnant. He cannot imagine a civilized person eating such despicable and unclean food.

When one expresses or even implies displeasure over another's food, he is communicating a powerful message of rejection. Many times I have conveyed my grateful appreciation for what, in my cultural grid, was an unsatisfying meal. But I refused to cause hurt and alienation by rejecting the values of my hostess. In her way of thinking, she was serving me the best food in the world.

For years, my family and I used to carry boiled water when going out on a village trip or when attending church feasts in the city. The result was, to some measure, a psychological barrier between national and missionary. In actual fact, there was little danger from the tube-well water that was usually served. When we ceased the practice, we, at least from our side, felt one more barrier give way.

Our initial reaction to curry was extremely negative. It was full of spices and red chilis. I didn't like the type of rice or the lentil soup that invariably came with each meal. We soon learned that there is a great difference between the ways in which these foods are prepared. One day we were invited to a very specially prepared meal. That was one of the best curries I have ever tasted. It launched me on a process of growing appreciation for a food which I now deem to be among the best in the world.

A Rhodesian who studied in America comments:

> One day a missionary lady who also had spent many years in Africa came to my wife and asked her to show her how to make an African meal. A church had asked her to make an African meal for their annual missionary conference. At first we laughed at her ignorance but became sad when we realized the significance of the whole thing. After only one year in America my village-raised wife, Winnie, was able to make

the most delicious apple pie and several other popular western dishes including mulligan stew, chicken kiev and beef wellington. The missionary lady had been in our country for over ten years but had not bothered to learn how to cook even one African dish.[18]

It boils down to a simple statement that rejection of a people's food is a rejection of themselves as persons. I have been asked scores of times by nationals what I eat and if I like curry and rice. An affirmative response always causes a look of appreciation to light up the face of the questioner.

Recently, a Muslim government official visited in our home. In the course of our conversation a mutual friend mentioned that my wife had compiled a cookbook of various Western and Eastern recipes. It has sold several thousand copies. The official became very enthusiastic and offered profuse congratulations to my wife on such a meaningful accomplishment. He had seen the book and was very pleased to meet the author. The compilation of the book conveyed a deep-level cultural acceptance that communicated powerfully to that Muslim.

Early in our career we came to see the value of hospitality centered around food. Over the years, my wife has served hundreds of meals to guests from several different cultures. Whenever possible, she researches ahead of time to see what dish will be appropriate and appreciated. This Martha-type ministry has been of real significance in the sharing of our home and testimony with others.

Dress

The dress styles of Muslim women are very conservative. They wear various types of apparel ranging from saris to an ankle-length dress with full-length baggy pants underneath. The women, in public, usually wear either a full or half-length veil, often black and shapeless. The face may or may not be covered. In

18. Pius Wakatama, *Independence for the Third World Church* (Downers Grove, IL: Inter-Varsity Press, 1976), pp. 92–93.

the most conservative societies this veil will cover all of the body from the top of the head to the foot. The woman is able to look out through a net which is sewed into the veil. The Quran directs that women wear the veil in order to protect themselves from the lustful stares of men. Girls start to wear the veil in many countries at the marriageable age of thirteen or fourteen.

Saudi Arabia is one of the strictest countries in regard to clothing. In the cities, "mosque policemen" go about denouncing foreign women who dare to appear in the streets or shops in Western-style dresses. Few foreign women wear such apparel for a second time in public!

The missionary woman often reacts against the Muslim style of dress. The sari is regarded as hot in tropical climates. Also, it seems impractical to wear while one does household chores. The veil causes an outrage of horror from anyone even remotely connected with the Western feminist movement! For almost all other foreigners it is simply undesirable. These strong opinions create problems in some countries. If a missionary wife wears a short skirt in a conservative area, she will be branded as immoral. Many Muslims already have a low view of the Westerner's morals due to exposure to films and novels which have been imported into their country.

The principle of contextualization should lead a missionary woman to weigh personal inconvenience against cultural offense. In several Muslim countries, the missionary woman has put on the veil while traveling out to remote, conservative villages. In one such instance the onlooking Muslims declared, "Look how the missionary loves and respects his wife. He is having her dress in our veil."

The Western woman may find herself surrounded by staring men whenever she goes out in public. This is hard on any self-respecting woman. It should be understood that a Muslim man seldom gets the opportunity to see a foreign woman. Basically, curiosity is at the root of his staring.

The missionary male should also dress like the group among whom he is working. This will vary according to status, occupation, and unique societal standards, and in general will create no undue hardship. Many missionaries grow beards because they are very common among Muslims.

Family

It is not particularly easy to raise a Western family in a Muslim country. There are many circumstances that create unusual tensions. One very positive point, mentioned in Chapter 4, is the high value which Muslims place on family life. I have been challenged over the years as I have observed the close interaction of the Muslim extended family. Parents often make great personal sacrifices in order to educate their children well. Meticulous care is taken in the selection of a marriage partner. Marriage, is, of course, following centuries-old tradition, arranged by the parents.

This pattern of family life with its many positive values creates a good climate for family-to-family interaction between Muslim and missionary. The child of a missionary is the center of attraction in any visit to a Muslim home.

There are, however, certain points of stress, certain problem areas which Western missionaries experience in relation to their families:

1. *Uniqueness.* A white face still creates a commotion in most Muslim countries. It is hard on Western children to be taunted and yelled at. I have seen fifty children lining the top of a wall that surrounded a missionary's home. The object of their curiosity and catcalls was an active five-year-old who was playing in the yard. This type of behavior can create a severe emotional strain on both child and parents. There are no easy answers. Making friends, consulting with the parents of rude children, and a lot of prayer can help.

2. *Loneliness.* Missionaries in remote stations should seek to make deep and meaningful friendships with nationals. Compatible children of the neighborhood should be invited to play with the missionaries' children. Adequate breaks must be provided so that families can enjoy Christian fellowship with people from their own country.

3. *Schooling.* There are a number of educational options available. Correspondence courses from accredited Western institutions make it possible for mothers to teach young children. Even though the mother is untrained as a teacher, she can still handle the early grades. Frequently, there is provision in the capital city for schooling of foreign children. If a boarding arrangement can be made, this is a helpful option. Many missionaries send their children to a distant country for education in schools particularly intended for missionary children. Surveys of such children indicate adjustments are amazingly successful.

It is my view that missions should allow maximum freedom to parents to work things out according to their own particular needs and preferences. A tight legalistic set of rules binding on all families with no room for the consideration of individual needs will likely lead to premature withdrawal from the field.

4. *Security.* I almost hesitate to bring up the subject of security in light of the high crime rate of the West. But Western females living in a Muslim society present a unique situation. There have been a number of cases of child molestation and attempted rape. Missionary wives and daughters must dress very modestly and take other sensible precautions for the sake of security. Mission leaders should also be aware of particular local circumstances.

The family is a great asset to an evangelistic ministry among Muslims. It is the norm of Muslim society. All Muslim girls are married, most of them by age sixteen. The male is usually married no later than thirty years of age. Muslims cannot really understand the single lady missionary. They have no category or role for her in society. This makes life, in a practical sense, very difficult for single ladies in a Muslim land. It is my opinion that they can best find fulfillment in institutional outreaches rather than seeking to engage in traditional evangelistic roles.

I have never witnessed directly to a Muslim lady. My wife has never shared Christ with a Muslim man. Our honoring the dictates of Muslim culture that one must communicate only with members of the same sex has been appreciated.

The family is a bastion of strength in times of deep hurt or discouragement. I have repeatedly stated that I could never have endured some of the stormy testings of life on the mission field without the presence of my unflappable, faithful wife. On many occasions she was the ballast that pulled me through times of adversity. A solid relationship of love and mutual commitment must be deeply cultivated in families desiring to effectively minister for Christ in a Muslim country.

Intellectual Life

Today many Christian colleges have become sensitive to the need for cross-cultural understanding in the field of communications, social psychology, anthropology of religions and many others. Many Christian scholars are also engaged in research in these areas. People with a grasp of the behavioral sciences, coupled with deep compassion, are the kind of missionaries needed in the Third World today. Mission organizations should require these vital subjects as prerequisites for all missionary candidates. Missionaries thus trained are able to witness more effectively to people of other cultures. They are also better able to assist them in thinking out their faith in reference to their cultural environments, thus formulating theologies which are expressed in indigenous thought forms and familiar terminology.[19]

The conditions under which missionary work is conducted have undergone a radical transformation since the end of the colonial era. New approaches and attitudes have been demanded. Pioneers like Donald McGavran have popularized the science of missiology. Hundreds of case studies and textbooks which can be utilized as resource material are now on the market. Important programs of missiological study are offered by such schools as Fuller Theological Seminary, Trinity Evangelical Divinity School, Columbia Bible College, Wheaton Graduate School, Dallas Theological Seminary, BIOLA College, and Moody Bible Institute. Extension study in missiology is offered through Fuller.

19. Ibid., p. 89.

Journals like *Missiology, Evangelical Missions Quarterly,* and the *Church Growth Bulletin* keep the evangelical missionary abreast of the latest concepts and applications. Any cursory look at mission fields to-day reveals the tremendous assistance these tools have been to the grassroots missionary. New groups have been reached with the gospel because of the sensitivity which these tools have helped evangelical missionaries to develop.

One relevant bit of advice to missionaries is that they should "keep an open mind, realizing that times change and one must make adjustments. Tactics of ten years ago will not work and even those of five years ago are outdated."[20] It is always sad to see missionaries get into ruts and become inflexible. The orientation and allegiance of some (both older and younger) to traditional methodology make it seem to them that a careful move into new areas of experimentation is almost a denial of truth. Younger missionaries arriving on the field with a more venturesome approach become frustrated. Their ideas and zeal are often lost in a patronizing "Keep it under your hat for a few years. Experience will mellow you and mature your input." There must develop a fresh and nonthreatening relationship between the senior and junior missionary. One adds experience while the other (if he has received up-to-date training) brings the latest in theory and enthusiasm. United, they are almost unbeatable. Divided, they are a catastrophe, not only to the team of missionaries, but also to the perceptive onlooking national Muslim and Christian communities.

Our commitment to Jesus Christ means that we want to be the best servants possible for His glory. It means stretching, not only in spirit, but also in intellect. A consecrated use of academic opportunities leads to greater effectiveness, not to pride or snobbery. We must beware of vegetating on the mission field. Both our hearts and our minds must stay alive and alert. Colossians 1:9 captures this thought with an exhortation for Christians to be filled with "spiritual wisdom." A helpful book on the subject is

20. Joseph A. McCoy, *Advice from the Field* (Baltimore: Helicon Press, 1962), p. 144.

Kenneth Pike's *With Heart and Mind, A Personal Synthesis of Scholarship and Devotion* (Grand Rapids: Wm. B. Eerdmans, 1962).

Attitudes

Forever fresh in my mind is a statement of Harold Cook, who was for many years professor of missions at Moody Bible Institute. One morning in 1959, he walked into class and began to lecture to one hundred students, all of whom looked forward to service on the mission field. As I sat taking notes near the front of the lecture hall, the following words were burned indelibly into my heart:

> Students, the single most important area of your life and ministry will be in the realm of attitudes. It is here you will either succeed or fail as a missionary. Attitudes touch every nerve end of life. Your relationship to Christ, fellow missionary, national believer, and non-Christian will be deeply affected by proper or improper attitudes.

There is no hyperbole in that statement. In every crisis I have tried to consciously analyze how my attitude was affecting my mental processes.

There are a number of ingredients in a positive attitude toward the Muslim people. One is empathy.

> Empathy gives the ability to correctly interpret the attitudes and intentions of other people by being able to see the world through their eyes. A person with this ability is able to perceive situations from the others' standpoint and thus understand and anticipate their behavior. No genuine communication is possible without this ability and the degree to which empathetic capacity is developed correlates closely with the quality of the social interaction which can be achieved. Through empathetic responses, which enable one person to take the role of another, there arises the "feeling of oneness" which is basic in the process of identification.[21]

21. William F. Muldrow, "Identification and the Role of the Missionary," *Practical Anthropology* 18 (1971): 216.

Let me illustrate empathy. Each morning at sunrise a Hindu neighbor in our village would rise, wash, and go out and stand near his cow. He would then look up at the sun, fold his hands, and go through a ceremony that involved worship of both the sun and the cow. I watched our Hindu friend perform this ritual scores of times. One day the cow became ill and died suddenly. Grief struck the Hindu household. This was indeed a tragic loss to them. I personally disagreed with worshiping a cow, but I somehow had entered into the world-view of the Hindu. He hurt and I hurt. Quickly I learned a few appropriate phrases (as we were new in the country) and went along to the Hindu's shop. I stuttered out a few incorrectly pronounced words about being sorry that his cow had died. My Hindu friend was deeply touched. Though we were worlds apart in culture and religion, yet he knew I cared. I had for a brief moment stepped into his life.

Charles Taber exhorts missionaries to

> abandon triumphalism and develop sincere respect, appreciation, and sensitivity for Muslim persons, for their faith, and for their way of life. Mission characterized by any other attitude *ipso facto* mutilates and misrepresents the gospel.[22]

Our ethnocentrism shows through when we begin judging another culture. It seems natural to criticize all we see as inadequate or substandard. The negative comes through with great force and clarity. Such an attitude is quickly perceived by the Muslims.

We must wean ourselves from judgments on culture that are narrow and bigoted. Harold Lindsell comments on Pharisaism:

> No attitude is more distressing than that of the Pharisee who measures conduct and life by his own standard and who never makes a sincere effort to get to the bottom of the standards and conduct of other men. Christ consistently pronounced judgment upon Pharisaism and exposed its sham and hypocrisy. This does not presuppose that everything in

22. Charles R. Taber, "Contextualization: Indigenization and/or Transformation," in *The Gospel and Islam: A 1978 Compendium*, ed. Don M. McCurry (Monrovia, CA: MARC, 1979), p. 150.

any culture is perfect, but there is a difference in attitude or approach which is all important.[23]

There is a line from James Russell Lowell's "Vision of Sir Launfal" which contains a great deal of truth: "The gift without the giver is bare." Missionaries are giving people. Their job demands that role. They may be engaged in relief work, teaching, medicine, or some other ministry that necessitates the act of sharing. But the act of giving is inadequate in itself. What is the force behind the action? Is there love? Is there a deep concern for the other person? Has giving become a professional obligation? These are heavy questions.

I was once required, on behalf of another person, to go and request a gift of money from an elderly man. In fear and trembling, I, a mere ten-year-old, put forth my request. When the elderly man responded with a curse, I cringed in fear. At last, he took the money out of his wallet, threw it on the floor, and stomped out of the room. With hurt and anger in my heart, I leaned down, picked up the few dollars, and quickly retreated. I had received the money, but at the moment I had an intense dislike for the giver.

No, the missionary doesn't act in such an overtly non-Christian manner. But I do wonder if at times the gift is given without the giver. If so, no national fails to notice, whether he acknowledges the fact to our face or not.

I believe that the attitudinal qualifications of today's missionary must be summed up in the word "servant." They must take the principles of mission from the Great Missionary Himself. He was a humble and lowly servant who took time to listen, to share and even to receive from those He came to minister to. He helped people without demeaning them, but preserved their dignity and human pride.

Unless present-day Western missionaries are willing to examine their attitude toward other races and cultures and . . .

23. Harold Lindsell, *Missionary Principles and Practice* (Westwood, NJ: Fleming H. Revell, 1955), p. 281.

to humble themselves enough to listen, the future of the missionary in the Third World may be questionable.[24]

It is my experience that the one quality most associated with true godliness in the mind of a Muslim is humility. A "proud missionary" like a "proud *imam*" is a contradiction of terms. This observation can only drive us to our knees.

Length of Ministry

It is time now to consider briefly the ministerial focus of the missionary. In looking at New Testament missions, we see that Paul's involvement was exceedingly temporary. Paul came, stayed a few weeks or months or at most a few years, and left to go into new areas of challenge. The churches he planted did not remain in his control. Even if heretical influences came into the churches, Paul could only exhort the Christians to walk in truth. He had no funds to cut off. The believers were totally free. Certainly the contemporary picture of missions is different from that in Paul's day.[25]

Lesslie Newbigin writes of Paul's totally entrusting leadership into local hands. He pungently comments that Paul didn't do what modern missionaries have done: "He does not build a bungalow."[26] In several places, Paul could have rightfully contended that there was enough work to warrant his settling down. But he resisted the temptation and kept on the move.[27] Yet, as Roland Allen points out, Paul didn't neglect the churches. He continued to visit and correspond with them. But the basic leadership responsibility was all put in local hands.[28]

24. Wakatama, *Independence*, p. 94.

25. Donald A. McGavran, *How Churches Grow* (London: World Dominion Press, 1959), p. 114.

26. Lesslie Newbigin, *The Open Secret* (London: S.P.C.K., 1978), p. 144.

27. George W. Peters, "Issues Confronting Evangelical Missions," in *Evangelical Missions Tomorrow*, ed. Wade T. Coggins and E. L. Frizen, Jr. (Pasadena: William Carey Library, 1977), p. 162.

28. Roland Allen, *Missionary Methods: St. Paul's or Ours?* (Grand Rapids: Wm. B. Eerdmans, 1962), p. 151.

Today, we observe that the Western church has a very difficult time completely turning over control to the younger church. At times, missionaries may be withdrawn as denominational budgets flounder. Yet, even in these cases, funds often continue to go directly to the church, thus perpetuating dependence. And, worst of all, the missionaries are not redeployed to virgin areas for new church planting. Rather, they are brought home because it is assumed that now the emerging church will take care of its own evangelistic responsibility.

In other situations, missionaries have been content to work in one mission station among a small cluster of churches for a full missionary career of thirty-five years. In many ways, the ministry is fulfilling. One experiences joy in seeing children born, later becoming Christians, getting married, and settling in to good professions. There are continuity and routine in such a life. National Christians, too, feel good about having a foreign missionary around to assist them in their times of need. Recently, it appeared that a Muslim government would imminently expel all missionaries. One distraught Christian leader was asked to list in order of their priority the reasons he would miss the missionary presence. His answers were illuminating:

1. Funds would cease coming to the church.
2. There would be fewer employment opportunities for Christians.
3. The missionary would no longer be able to help the nationals represent themselves to the government.
4. The last point was that the missionaries would not be around to give Bible teaching!

Following Paul's example, the missionary should move on as soon as possible after worshiping groups have been established. Converts should not be allowed to depend on the missionary rather than on the Lord.

Having travailed, given birth, and cared for young churches, the missionaries (whether Tamilian or Naga or American or Australian) should turn over authority to indigenous leaders.... Travail must not go on too long. It must be followed by weaning and pushing out of the nest. Then the missionary goes on and repeats the process.[29]

Many missionaries with a burden for Muslim evangelism are locked into ministries of nurture in traditional and well-established churches. They should consider requesting release in order to go out to pioneer new areas.

Donald McGavran, at the ripe age of eighty years, wrote an excellent paper entitled, "The Entrepreneur in Modern Missions." His comments are crisp and relevant:

> Surrender of initiative in evangelism to National Denominations—done with the best of motives on both sides, of course—has led and is leading to major failure in achieving the fundamental purpose of both Church and Mission. The disease afflicts many denominations. Camouflaged as it is under the guise of "exercising the respect due to sovereign nations" and "treating our Latfricasian [Latin American-African-Asian] brothers with scrupulous fairness," surrender of evangelistic initiative quietly sabotages the basic ends of Christian Mission. Consequently, this entrepreneur has recently bent his energies to developing strategies and implementing tactics to enable both Missions and Churches to devote themselves to the supreme and controlling purpose of the Christian Mission to the world. It is clear that the honor and respect due to Latfricasian Churches ought to be preserved. This will best be done by evangelizing out beyond them, if possible with their blessing, but without burdening them with administrating such efforts.[30]

The missionary must keep before him constantly the imperative of pressing out to new frontiers. He will need to resist the tendency to become a permanent fixture of the established church.

29. Donald A. McGavran, *Ethnic Realities and the Church* (Pasadena: William Carey Library, 1979), p. 130.

30. Donald A. McGavran, "The Entrepreneur in Modern Missions" (Pasadena: Fuller Theological Seminary, 1978), p. 5.

CHAPTER 6

Theological Bridges to Salvation

Value of Bridges

The construction of a bridge is a matter of great complexity. Engineers must first survey the terrain with meticulous care in order to choose the best possible site. They have to plumb the depths of the river, measure the swiftness of the current, and check out high and low water levels before they begin to build. Correct materials must be gathered which will bear the pressure of rushing waters. Costs must be estimated and correct budgets drawn up. Without proper handling of these factors, bridge-building can be an exercise in futility—or worse yet, a total disaster. In one Third World country, great effort and funds were expended in the construction of a much-needed bridge. Every newspaper in the nation carried photos and a write-up of the dedication ceremony. Particularly significant was the fact that this was one of the first bridges to be designed and supervised by engineers who were citizens of that country. Within a few months, the bridge developed severe cracks and was declared unsafe for traffic. It stood for years in silent mockery of those who feel there are easy shortcuts to effective bridge-building.

127

There is a raging current flowing between the banks of Islam and Christianity. In certain places, the river is narrow and the banks are close to each other, while in other areas the gap appears totally unbridgeable. One could postulate that inadequate attention and energy have been devoted to building bridges of *salam*, understanding and communication between the two largest religions on planet Earth. There is One, however, who set the example.

> Why did God send Christ to bridge the gulf between heaven and earth, between divinity and humanity? The people of this world did not ask for it, and when Christ came He was not accepted even by those who should have been prepared for His coming. God's love constrained Him to do so, and the same love constrains Christians to do likewise. God Himself built the bridge to humanity. . . . Just as Christ Himself became the bridge between God and man and the channel through which the divine blessings flow, in like manner we have to become bridges to our fellow men—here to the Muslims—and channels through which the life-giving waters flow. That alone should be our objective and that alone justifies our going to these foreign lands as missionaries.[1]

Among people of the West there has been an appalling ignorance concerning the Islamic religion. An American who attended a school run by the Arabian-American Oil Company in New York reported on one particular session:

> The questions "What is Islam?" and "Who was the Prophet Mohammed?" brought forth some interesting answers. One of our members thought that Islam was a "game of chance similar to bridge." Another said that it was "a mysterious sect founded in the South by the Ku Klux Klan." One gentleman believed it to be "an organization of American Masons who dress in strange costumes." The Prophet Mohammed was

---

1. Erich W. Bethman, *Bridge to Islam* (London: George Allen and Unwin, 1953), pp. 201–02.

thought to be the man who "wrote the *Arabian Nights*." Another said he was "an American Negro minister who was in competition with Father Divine in New York City." One of the more reasonable answers came from one of our men who said, "Mohammed had something to do with a mountain. He either went to the mountain or it came to him."[2]

These responses would be rather humorous if it weren't for the fact that the respondents were all college graduates who were preparing for employment in one of the Middle Eastern Muslim countries. One can't help but wonder if Christian laymen in Western churches are any better informed—even in these days of intense focus on the Middle East. If a sensitivity is not developed on the part of the church worldwide, then it is doubtful if effective bridge-building can be accomplished between Islam and Christianity.

Often, a simplistic approach has been utilized by which Islam is totally attributed to satanic inception. Nothing in the religion or culture of Muslims is praised. Methodology of evangelism is limited to an imposition of a Western religion in Western garb. Results of such a technique are predictable.

Fuad Accad is a Muslim convert who has been successful in winning his former coreligionists to Christ. He speaks of the necessity of relating to Muslims:

> I pray that in the spirit of our Lord who gave Himself as Servant of the whole world, we will start to build the broken bridges over the gulf which has separated us from our brothers' love and friendship all these hundreds of years.[3]

This chapter is devoted to an exploration of a few key bridges which can assist in facilitating understanding between Islam and Christianity.

2. "The Elephant in the Dark," in *Christianity, Islam, and the Sufis*, ed. Leonard Lewin (New York: E. P. Dutton, 1976), pp. 4–5.
3. Fuad Accad, "The Qur'an: A Bridge to Christian Faith," *Missiology* 4.3 (1976): 339.

Scriptural Authority

It is necessary to appreciate the Muslim view of the Quran. This holy book is held in extraordinary esteem even if it is not comprehended by the illiterate masses. Surah (Chapter) 56:78 says, "Let none touch it but the purified." Often the orthodox resent the Quran's being possessed by a person of another faith. I well recall being severely reprimanded by a Muslim for placing my feet too near his Quran while on a journey in an extremely crowded launch. The average Muslim wraps his Quran in an expensive cloth and places it in a position of honor. It is very difficult for the Muslim to understand the casual manner in which a Christian may place his Bible on the floor or mark it up with pen or pencil. This amounts to desecration of that which is sacred.

The Sufis (see pp. 147–51) speak of "seeking to be drowned" in the verses of the Quran. This holy book is regarded as the uncreated Word of God. Many Sufis spend their whole lifetime in reciting the Quran. Though non-Arabic-speaking Muslims will derive little benefit from reading the Arabic Quran, yet they feel their minds are penetrated and cleansed by the consciousness that they are partaking of the Divine Word.[4]

Many Muslims wear a miniature copy of the Quran enclosed in a bag which is suspended from the neck. Others wear around their neck or arms amulets in which verses and chapters of the Quran are placed. Most Muslims feel these practices assist in protecting them from evil and sickness.[5]

Recently, Urdu New Testaments were sent to every phone subscriber in Pakistan. Hundreds of these Scriptures were refused and had to be returned to the post office. Tons of these New Testaments accumulated and were sold for "waste paper." Soon, Bible portions were appearing all through the marketplace as wrappers for small quantities of merchandise. The Muslim could only shake his head in disbelief that such a desecration of Scripture could take place.

4. Martin Lings, *What Is Sufism?* (Berkeley: University of California Press, 1975), p. 25.

5. L. Bevan Jones, *The People of the Mosque* (Calcutta: YMCA Publishing House, 1939), p. 61.

The Quran frequently places a high value on the Bible and the "People of the Book":

Dispute not with the People of the Book save in the fairer manner, and say, "We believe in what has been sent down to us, and what has been sent down to you; our God and your God is One and to Him we have surrendered." (Surah 29:45)

The Bible is variously termed "the Word of God, the Book of God, a guide and a mercy, a light and direction to men, the testimony of God along with guidance and light."[6]

Muhammad himself spoke of the Bible as being trustworthy. In one instance, he referred to the *Taurat* (the Law) to settle certain controversies regarding food which had arisen between him and the Jews. Surah 3:94 records, "Bring ye then the *Taurat* and read it, if ye be men of truth."

A clearly defined statement on the Bible by Muhammad is found in Surah 5:72, "O People of the Book, ye have no ground to stand on, until ye observe the *Taurat* and the *Injil* [Gospels] and that which hath been sent down to you from your Lord." Surah 4:49–50 also reflects Muhammad's high view of biblical authority:

And in the footsteps of the Prophets caused we Jesus, the son of Mary, to follow, confirming the *Taurat* which was before him. And we gave him the *Injil* with its guidance and light, confirmatory of its preceding *Taurat*: a guidance and warning to those who fear God; and that the people of the *Injil* may judge according to what God hath sent down therein. And whoso will not judge by what God hath sent down—such are the perverse.

It would be good if the discussion could end at this point. That, unfortunately, is not the case. Contemporary Muslims are taught to believe that the Bible presently in circulation is not

6. W. Goldsack, *Christ in Islam* (London: The Christian Literature Society, 1905), p. 6.

trustworthy. They often use the emotive word *corrupted* to describe textual alterations they believe were made in the transmission process.

It is true that Muhammad in his discussions with Jews often accused them of unfaithful exegesis of their Scriptures. Surah 7:161–62 says, "The ungodly ones among them [Jews] changed that word into another than that which had been told them." Surah 2:72 states, "Some are there among them [Jews] who torture the Scriptures with their tongues, that ye may suppose it to be from the Scripture, yet it is not from the Scripture." And Surah 3:64 adds, "Woe to those Jews who with their own hands write the Book and then say, 'This is from God.'"

An evaluation of the historical context of Muhammad's time may shed some light on this controversy. At Mecca, Muhammad developed a sincere respect for the Jews and for their Book. He mixed freely with them in the hope that he could win them over to his message. Muhammad took a real interest in the Jewish prediction of a Messiah. He claimed to be that anointed one. The Jews vehemently denied any and all claims made by Muhammad. In retaliation, Muhammad accused the Jews of improper scriptural interpretation. So, the character of this dispute was largely personal. As history clouded the issue even further, it was soon believed by Muslims that Muhammad had been prophesied in the original scriptural writings, but that these references were later omitted.[7]

Almost all Muslims believe the Bible has been abrogated by the Quran. There is, however, not a single word in the Quran to support this opinion. The word *nasakha* (in the sense of "to abrogate") occurs only twice in the Quran (Surah 2:100; 22:51), and in neither of these instances is it used with reference to any part of the Old or New Testament.[8]

Translations of the Quran into vernacular languages abound. But all Muslims agree that only the Arabic version is the true and authoritative Quran. God directly revealed His Word to Muham-

7. Jones, *People of the Mosque*, pp. 272–76.
8. C. G. Pfander, *The Mizanu'l Haqq ("Balance of Truth")* (London: The Religious Tract Society, 1910), pp. 56–57.

mad in Arabic and it was duly recorded in that heavenly language. It would be well for communicators of the gospel to consider a Bible with face-to-face translations in Arabic and the vernacular. Even though Muslims may not have a full comprehension of the Arabic, there will be an appreciation of the presence of what is considered to be the special language of Allah.

In sharing Christ with a Muslim, careful use should be made of Quranic passages that point to a high view of Scripture. Care for the Bible should parallel the manner in which a Muslim handles his Quran. The Bible can be placed in wooden stands such as Muslims use for their Qurans. First-class, attractive printing on a good quality of paper should be utilized for scriptural productions. Pictures should be omitted as they are offensive to the Muslims. In Lombaro, Muslim converts place the Greek and Hebrew Testaments in the front of the church as a sign of reverence for the original languages of the Bible.

The current controversy over the possibility of scientific and historical errors in the Bible is a confirmation to the Muslim that the Bible is not universally accepted as authoritative. Muslims, worldwide, fully accept the inerrancy of the Quran. They cannot conceive of errors in God's special revelation. I would agree strongly with William Miller, one of the great living authorities on Islam, who says, "If a Christian has any doubts regarding the authenticity and authority of the Bible, he would do well to resolve these doubts before talking with a Muslim about his faith. If he does not trust the truth of the Bible, he will have no ground to stand on."[9]

A. Nakhosteen has stated, "There is no more speedy way for the advancement of the Kingdom of God in a Moslem land than to spread forth the knowledge of the Bible."[10] J. Christy Wilson, Sr., reinforces this view by observing that "in a great number of instances, those who have become Christian attribute their first real knowledge of Christ and their conversion to reading the Bible

9. William McElwee Miller, *A Christian's Response to Islam* (Nutley, NJ: Presbyterian and Reformed, 1977), p. 71.

10. A. Nakhosteen, "The Bible in Moslem Hands," *The Moslem World* 35 (1945): 302.

or hearing it read. Bible distribution is an old method in the world of Islam, but it should be continued and increased in every possible way."[11]

Of course, the Bible is at places most profound. One could legitimately question whether Muslims can comprehend such deep mysteries of God. Wilson addresses the issue:

> No earnest inquirer should be discouraged because the Bible contains mysteries beyond the comprehension of the greatest intellect. For humble Christians in every age and every land, as they follow Christ step by step, have been led by the Holy Spirit to ever increasing knowledge of the deep things of God. As one of our great evangelists in Iran has said, though the stream of Christian truth is deep enough in places to drown an elephant, there are also still waters where little children may wade.[12]

Old Testament Prophets

In the Islamic religion, prophets are men especially appointed by God to be His messengers. Theoretically, all prophets are to have the same status. In practice this is not true. Certain prophets are accorded special status by all Muslims.

It is reputed that there are 124,000 prophets. Of these, 313 are called apostles, nine are called "possessors of constancy," eight are *rasuls* (those having a separate people for whom they are responsible), six are lawgivers, and six have special qualities. Only 28 of the 124,000 are mentioned in the Quran.

Most Muslims probably know the names of only Adam, Noah, Abraham, Ishmael, Moses, Jesus, and Muhammad. One popular extra-Quranic source of information on the prophets is

11. J. Christy Wilson, Sr., "Moslem Converts," *The Moslem World* 34 (1944): 177.

12. J. Christy Wilson, Sr., "The Bible and Moslems," *The Moslem World* 27 (1937): 248.

the Persian book of legends called *Qisas-ul-Ambia* (i.e., "the stories of the prophets"). This widely translated book is not reliable.[13]

Muslims believe all prophets are human and never regarded as divine. They are simply recipients of a revelation from God. The Lord never speaks directly to a human. Usually an angel is sent to convey His message. At times the prophet may just experience a sense of inspiration which motivates him to write the Word of God. Muhammad is accepted as the last and greatest of the prophets; in him all the messages of former prophets were consummated. His greatest miracle was the writing of the Quran. Gabriel transmitted the words of this holy book to the heart of Muhammad. At times Muhammad could see and hear Gabriel while on other occasions he was in a semidazed trance.[14]

The "prophet of the day" is an Islamic concept. Obedience is expected to the prophet whose teachings are valid and binding for a particular historical period. God sends a message for a specific time through a specially anointed prophet. It is important to note that common Muslim belief dictates that any new revelation supersedes all previous revelations. It is said that if it were possible for an earlier prophet to rise from the grave and come back to the world, even he would have to adhere to the current law. Muhammad is reported to have stated that "if the illustrious Apostle Moses were alive today, he, too, would be following the Divine law brought by me."[15]

It is not within the scope of this book to go into detail concerning the life, message, and position of the Prophet Muhammad. Hundreds of books have been written on the subject. A few comments, however, are in order.

Can Christians not legitimately praise the positive accomplishments of Muhammad? In his day in Arabia, social and economic conditions were extremely poor, causing great hardship

13. Jens Christensen, *The Practical Approach to Muslims* (Marseilles: North Africa Mission, 1977), pp. 602–03.

14. "Islam," *Encyclopaedia Britannica, Macropaedia,* 1974 ed., vol. 9, p. 914.

15. Mohammad Manzoor Nomani, *Islamic Faith and Practice* (Lucknow: Academy of Islamic Research Publications, 1962), p. 36.

for the masses. Women were being exploited. Animistic-type worship was common. Muhammad protested these injustices and insisted on monotheism. Few would doubt the sincerity of Muhammad. He was personally convinced he was a vessel of communication from God in heaven to sinful mankind.

One definite problem is, however, a trend toward the even greater exaltation of Muhammad. Constance Padwick speaks of "a type of prayer or meditation based on the high doctrine of Muhammad's personality and position, glorifying him by placing all other prophets far beneath him, and in a state of dependence on him."[16] In one Muslim country I have seen religious television programs in which numerous songs and poems were rendered in what amounted to almost a worship of Muhammad.

We should avoid the prior "Christian" strategy of openly denouncing Muhammad as a tool of Satan. Sensitivity demands a love for all Muslims—and this love should also embrace the memory of Muhammad. The exaltation of divine Jesus incorporated in a positive Christian witness will automatically put the memory of Muhammad back in its proper historical position.

In summary, it can be said that the common ground of the Quran and the Old Testament in regard to the prophets should be thoroughly explored. This may well eventuate in the Muslim's giving serious consideration to the message that leads on from prophecy to prophetic fulfillment.

Jesus in the Quran

Can Quranic teaching concerning Jesus Christ be a valid bridge to a vital experience of salvation and assurance of eternal life? Don McCurry comments on his change of position in this regard:

My second area of re-thinking concerns my use of the Quran. It is widely known that many Muslims have come to Christ

16. Constance E. Padwick, "The Language of Muslim Devotion," *The Muslim World* 47 (1957): 17.

by first being pointed to him by the Quran. True, they later encountered him in the New Testament and from then on the Quran no longer remained a reference book for them. But the point is, I should not feel shy about using the Quran as a beginning point for introducing the subject of Jesus. And Paul has given us endorsement of this approach by his use of Greek literature in his Mars Hill sermon.[17]

Geoffrey Parrinder states that "Jesus is always spoken of in the Quran with reverence, there is no breath of criticism, for he is the Christ of God."[18] Michael Youssef, too, recommends using the Quran in witnessing to Muslims:

Rather than tell the Muslim to ignore his Quran, one ought to sit down with him and try to read the Quran together to see what it says about Jesus and how Mohammed perceived Jesus. Many, I think, would be shocked to learn that Mohammed thought very highly indeed of Jesus . . . . Mohammed affirmed, for example, his virgin birth. He called him the Spirit of God, the work of God. He believed that Jesus raised people from the dead and was a miracle worker. The Quran called Jesus pure and sinless.[19]

A number of references to the birth of Jesus are found in the Quran. Consider how closely Surah 3:45–47 parallels the biblical account:

The angels spoke to Mary, saying: "Oh Mary! Allah giveth thee glad tidings of a word from Him, whose name is the Messiah, Jesus son of Mary, illustrious in the world and the Hereafter and one of those brought near [unto Allah]. He will speak unto mankind in his cradle and in his manhood, and he is of the righteous." She said: "My Lord! How can I have a

17. Don M. McCurry, "Cross-Cultural Models for Muslim Evangelism," *Missiology* 4.3 (1976): 280.

18. Geoffrey Parrinder, *Jesus in the Quran* (London: Faber and Faber, 1965), p. 16.

19. Michael A. Youssef, "Theology and Methodology for Muslim Evangelism in Egypt" (M.A. thesis, Fuller Theological Seminary, 1978), p. 102.

child when no mortal hath touched me?" He said: "So [it will be]. Allah createth what He will. If He decreeth a thing, He saith unto it only: Be! and it is."

A more detailed passage concerning the birth of Jesus is found in Surah 19:16–36. Here it is recorded that God sent His spirit, commonly regarded as Gabriel, to announce to Mary that she would become the mother of Jesus. Mary protests that this is impossible as she has known no man. Gabriel then assures her that nothing is impossible with God.

During Mary's pregnancy, God puts a stream beneath her feet to provide drinking water. She is also nourished by dates which fall from a nearby palm tree. After Jesus is born, Mary takes Him to her people whereupon she is accused of immorality. Jesus speaks in her defense. He then informs the people of His prophethood.[20]

Later in life, Jesus is said to have had the power to perform miracles. He brought a clay bird to life, cured the blind and the leprous, and raised the dead.[21] These acts authenticated the mission of Jesus. But they are always stated to be "by the permission of God." There is no recognition of the fact that Christ possessed personal divine authority.[22]

Concerning the death of Jesus, the statements of the Quran are contradictory. Surah 3:55; 5:17; and 19:33 all mention the death of Jesus, but Surah 4:157 obscures the picture:

And for their saying we have killed the Messiah, Jesus, Son of Mary, the messenger of God: they killed him not nor did they crucify him but they thought they did.

Muslim scholars claim that it was not Christ who was crucified, but someone who closely resembled Him. It is thought Muhammad chose this interpretation because it was inconceivable

20. Ibid., p. 14.
21. James Robson, "Muhammadan Teaching About Jesus," *The Moslem World* 29 (1939): 39.
22. Aubrey Whitehouse, *The Qur'an Says* . . . . (Birmingham: The Fellowship of Faith for the Muslims, n.d.), p. 8.

to him that a prophet of God could suffer such an ignominious death as crucifixion.[23]

However Jesus died, He is now reputed to be in heaven and to have access to the throne of God. He is expected to return to this world shortly before the day of judgment.

> A number of remarkable happenings will occur in connection with this event. This is a firm belief among Muslims, although there is only one verse in the Quran with rather obscure wording that has a reference to the second coming of Jesus. "Verily, he (Isa) is only a servant whom we favoured and made an example to the children of Israel; and if we pleased, we could have given you angels as offspring. And verily, he (Isa) is the knowledge of the last hour"; that means, by his coming the nearness of the "Hour" will be known. Others read it, "He is a sign of the last hour."[24]

Around this verse tradition has built a whole eschatological structure. It is mentioned in the *Hadith* (traditions) that Isa (Jesus) will descend on a mountain path in the Holy Land, probably near Afiq. In His hand will be a spear with which He will kill the Antichrist. He will then enter the mosque, where He will fall into line and pray behind the *imam*, according to the rites of Islam. Following this, Isa will kill all swine, break a cross, destroy all synagogues and churches, and then kill all Christians who have not accepted Him.

Isa will reign for forty years and then die and be buried in Medina between Muhammad and Abu Bakr. Upon completion of Isa's mission, the sound of the trumpet will be heard and the great day of judgment will be ushered in.[25] It is noteworthy that all Muslims believe that Isa will return to this earth. This unique demonstration of power and authority is reserved only for Jesus.

The most exciting title given to Jesus in the Quran is "God's Word." Surah 4:171 states, "The Messiah, Jesus son of Mary, was

---

23. H. A. R. Gibb and J. H. Kramers, *Shorter Encyclopedia of Islam* (Ithaca, NY: Cornell University Press, 1965), p. 173.

24. Bethman, *Bridge to Islam*, p. 60.

25. Ibid., p. 61.

only a messenger of Allah, and *His Word* which He cast into Mary, and a spirit from Him. So believe in Allah and His messengers." W. Goldsack notes that "the Arabic shows that it means 'the Word of God,' not merely a word of God."[26]

It is instructive to compare this title for Jesus with those assigned by the Quran to other prophets:

> Adam—The chosen of God
> Noah—The prophet of God
> Abraham—The friend of God
> Moses—The speaker of God
> Muhammad—The messenger of God[27]

For Muslims, the eternal words of God appear in the form of the Quran. For Christians, the eternal Word of God came to earth in the form of the God-man, even our Lord and Savior Jesus Christ:

> In the beginning was the Word, and the Word was with God, and the Word was God. He was in the beginning with God. All things came into being through Him; and apart from Him nothing came into being that has come into being. In Him was life; and the life was the light of men. . . . And the Word became flesh, and dwelt among us, and we beheld His glory, glory as of the only begotten from the Father, full of grace and truth. (John 1:1–4, 14)

Does the Muslim designation of Jesus as the Word of God help us bridge the gap which exists between the Muslim and Christian understanding of Jesus' person and His relation to God? Certainly this title is more helpful than others such as "Son of God" or "Lamb of God." This designation can be a launching pad to show the Muslim that Jesus is God's eternal Word of redemption, rather than just another prophet.[28]

26. Goldsack, *Christ in Islam*, p. 15.
27. Youssef, "Theology and Methodology," p. 5.
28. Ernest Hahn, *Jesus in Islam: A Christian View* (Hyderabad: Henry Martyn Institute of Islamic Studies, 1978), p. 36.

The Quran refers to Jesus in other ways which may help bridge the gap—Spirit, Prophet, Apostle, Preeminent One, Example, Sinless One, and Miracle Worker.[29] Other designations include: Sign, a Mercy, a Witness, Messenger, and Servant.[30] Muslims are not supposed to mention the name of Jesus without repeating the formula, "Peace be on Him."[31]

Another notable fact is that the ninety-nine names of Allah as listed in the Quran (with one or two exceptions) are also found as attributes of Jehovah in the Old Testament Scriptures.[32] With that in mind consider the following two statements:

> I have never met a Muslim convert who regards the God he previously sought to worship as a wholly false God; instead, he is filled with wonder and gratitude that he has now been brought to know that God as He really is, in Jesus Christ our Lord.[33]

> I have yet to meet a single such individual who has the feeling that he came to meet a new God when he became a Christian. The experience in every instance has been the same—that God, who was far off, has suddenly come close in Christ.[34]

Are the God of Christianity and that of Islam one and the same? There is a stand-off among evangelicals on this subject. There are highly-regarded scholars on both sides of the controversy. I see no need for an ultradogmatic stand. Love and sensitive understanding should transcend the issue. Polarization and attacks

29. Robert Christy Douglas, "Strategic Components in Proposed Experimental Approach to Evangelism of Muslims" (project presented to the School of World Mission, Fuller Theological Seminary, 1977), p. 41.

30. Youssef, "Theology and Methodology," p. 1.

31. J. W. Sweetman, "A Muslim's View of Christianity," *The Moslem World* 34 (1944): 280.

32. Samuel Zwemer, "Islam's Allah and the Christian God," *The Moslem World* 36 (1946): 308.

33. John D. C. Anderson, "The Missionary Approach to Islam," *Missiology* 4.3 (1976): 295.

34. James Paul Dretke, "Opening a New Door to Dialogue Between Christians and Muslims in Ghana" (D.Miss. dissertation, Fuller Theological Seminary, 1974), p. 46.

should be studiously avoided. If a Muslim convert perceives the God of Islam and Christianity as one, then who are we to deny such a possibility? The essential element is that the new believer come to a full-orbed faith in and acceptance of God as revealed in the Old and New Testaments.

A much larger controversy which has polarized Christians and Muslims for over thirteen hundred years relates to the doctrine of the Trinity. Surah 4:171 sums up the problem:

> O people of the Scripture! Do not exaggerate in your religion nor utter aught concerning Allah save the truth. The Messiah, Jesus son of Mary, was only a messenger of Allah, and His Word which He cast into Mary, and a spirit from Him. So believe in Allah and His messengers, and say not "Three"—cease! [It is] better for you!—Allah is only one God. Far is it removed from His transcendent Majesty that He should have a son.

Some years ago, in South India, an educated Muslim said to an evangelist, "Whenever you Christians speak of Jesus as the 'Son of God' it makes our blood boil."[35] In actual fact, there is little similarity in the thought processes of Christians and Muslims when they hear this term. The language of the Quran has in view not a Trinity, but a triad—something after the manner of the Hindu Brahma, Vishnu, and Shiva; or the Egyptian Isis, Osiris, and Horus.[36] The Muslim is fiercely monotheistic and any suggestion of polytheism is immediately inflammatory.

Muslims generally believe the dynamic of the Trinity consists of God the Father's having sexual intercourse with Mary the mother of Jesus, who was the second member of the Trinity. This union resulted in the birth of Jesus as the third person of the Godhead. Emphasis is placed on the physical. The Holy Spirit is omitted from this list of the three members of the Trinity.

The Trinity is not presented in creedal form in Scripture. The doctrine was not officially formulated until the fourth century. Nevertheless, the New Testament does contain the basic truth

35. Jones, *People of the Mosque*, p. 277.
36. Ibid., p. 281.

which later contributed to the formalizing of this doctrine. Most Christians would agree with W. Montgomery Watt, the famous British scholar of Islam, who stated, "The doctrine of the Trinity is extremely difficult and is not well understood by ordinary Christians."[37] There is an element of mystery in God's becoming man, an element of mystery that surpasses intellect and carries us into the realm of naked faith.

Without apology, every Christian can affirm monotheistic belief. Recall Jesus' response when one of the scribes asked Him, "What commandment is the foremost of all?" (Mark 12:28). Jesus quoted Deuteronomy 6:4–5: "Hear, O Israel; the Lord our God is one Lord; and you shall love the Lord your God with all your heart." If Jesus could so clearly endorse monotheism, we can and should do likewise.

Aristotle pointed out that the word *one* is used in more than one sense. It can be used to indicate oneness of quantity or oneness of essence. For instance, a molecule of water may be "one" numerically without being one or single in its essence, as its formula H_2O indicates.

No Christian believes that the word *begotten* when referring to Jesus is to be taken in a human or literal sense. The Bible deals with spiritual subjects, but uses human terminology to describe spiritual relationships. The words *Father, Son,* and *begotten* must be viewed as figurative and metaphysical. Arabs utilize such figures of speech as *ibn al'sabil,* which literally means, "the son of the road." All Arabs know that a road has no son and that the real meaning is "traveler."

Muslims have good reason to be confused on the subject of the Trinity. It is likely that in Muhammad's time Mary was venerated by some Christians as a member of the Godhead. Consider the present position of the Roman Catholic Church in their exaltation of Mary.

Edwin Calverley proposes certain terminological changes in order to communicate the Trinity more effectively to Muslims:

37. W. Montgomery Watt, "Thoughts on Muslim-Christian Dialogue," *Hamdard Islamicus* 1.1 (1978): 22.

Changes in terminology may be suggested in presenting the Trinity to the Muslim mind. Our conventional theological vocabulary uses the word Person for each of the Divine Beings. This is a word that has corporeal, physical, concrete, human connotations. Would not the abstract term "personality" preserve better the immaterial ideas associated with God? Also, the word "generate" does not necessarily have the exclusively sexual associations of the word "begot." A statement of Christian theology about God for Muslim thinkers could say: "God is the one and only Divine, eternal and infinite Spirit with Unity of Essence in a Trinity of Personalities as Father, Son and Holy Spirit, perfect in wisdom, power, holiness, justice, goodness, truth, and love."[38]

The bridge of the person of Christ is central to the task of Muslim evangelism. Utilization of this bridge will demand careful and sensitive exegesis of relevant Scriptures. Quranic truth can be utilized in the process of sharing the gospel, but in the end, the Muslim must come to an acceptance of the stumbling block that has hindered conversion over the centuries, that is, the "absolute truth" that Jesus Christ is God incarnate.

Qurbani Id (Id Al-Adha, or Sacrifice Festival)

And the camels have we appointed you for the sacrifice to God: much good have ye in them. Make mention, therefore, of the name of God over them when ye slay them, as they stand in a row; and when they are fallen over on their sides, eat of them, and feed him who is content and asketh not, and him who asketh. Thus have we subjected them to you to the intent ye should be thankful. By no means can their flesh reach unto God, neither their blood; but piety on your part reached Him. Thus hath He subjected them to you, that ye might magnify God for His guidance: moreover, announce glad tidings to those who do good deeds. (Surah 22:35–38)

38. Edwin E. Calverley, "Christian Theology and the Qur'an," *The Muslim World* 47 (1957): 289.

According to tradition, Aisha (Muhammad's favorite wife) reported that Muhammad had once said:

> Man has not done anything on the Idul-Adha more pleasing to God than spilling blood; for verily the animal sacrificed will come, on the day of resurrection, with its horns, its hair, and its hoofs, and will make the scales of his good actions heavy. Verily its blood reacheth the acceptance of God before it falleth upon the ground; therefore be joyful in it.[39]

The great feast of sacrifice falls on the tenth day of the last month of the Muslim year. It is celebrated in remembrance of Abraham's willingness to sacrifice his own son Ishmael (not Isaac, as Jews and Christians believe). In all Muslim homes a male goat, a lamb, a cow, or a camel should be slain. Poor families purchase shares of an animal—or they may just sacrifice a chicken. The animal must be without blemish and young.

At the time of the sacrifice, the animal's mouth is turned towards Mecca and the following words repeated, "In the name of God, accept this sacrifice as thou didst accept the offering of thy friend Abraham." In some countries the eyes of the animals are dried and kept. They are then used as charms against the power of the evil eye.[40]

An important time of worship precedes the actual killing of the animals. Cn an auspicious occasion like *Id*, the Muslim population (often only men) gathers either in a mosque or in an open field in an act of public worship of Allah. At the close of the service, the Muslims salute and embrace each other. This is a special occasion for wearing new clothes.

A controversial point is whether Muslims look on this sacrifice as an integral part of receiving cleansing from their sin, or regard it as just a commemorative act initiated by the Jews and adopted later by Muhammad. It is my opinion that, in popular

39. Jones, *People of the Mosque*, p. 125.
40. Anwar M. Khan, "Strategy to Evangelize Muslim Jats in Pakistan" (Th.M. thesis, Fuller Theological Seminary, 1976), p. 45.

Islam, the average Muslim links the sacrifice to a sin offering, much as the Jew did in Old Testament times. I have had confirmation of this from several Muslim countries.

The feast of sacrifice is a potential bridge between Christianity and Islam. Numbers 29:7-11 describes the Jewish sin offering. This ceremony can be compared with the Muslim *Id*. Psalm 51 can then be presented as a transitional passage from "burnt offerings" to the offering of "a broken and a contrite heart." Hebrews 9 and 10 expound the path to a full and complete sacrifice for sins:

> And every priest stands daily ministering and offering time after time the same sacrifices, which can never take away sins; but He [Jesus], having offered one sacrifice for sins for all time, sat down at the right hand of God. . . . For by one offering He has perfected for all time those who are sanctified. (Heb. 10:11-12, 14)

A carefully written booklet could put together Quranic references, *Hadith* sayings, Old Testament law, and New Testament grace. The underlying theme would be God's great provision for a sin offering, for every person and for all time. Special care would have to be given to the fact that the Islamic practice was instituted in a post–New Testament framework. Emphasis would be laid on identifying the *Qurbani Id* with pre-Christian Jewish sacrificial ceremonies. The cross and empty tomb of Jesus, the Savior of all mankind, would be presented as symbols of the ultimate sacrifice.

If converts emphasize the element of remembrance, might they not be allowed to continue to observe *Qurbani Id* much as traditional Christians celebrate the Lord's Supper? If Muslim converts have a clear understanding that the purpose of the ceremony is not to receive forgiveness of sins, but rather (1) to focus attention on the complete and sufficient sacrifice of Christ, and (2) to provide a continuing identification with Muslim people, would it not be acceptable to observe *Qurbani Id*? Might this not be a unique time of witness rather than one more link in the chain of alienation that often widens the gulf between Muslims and Christians?

An anonymous convert leader proposed a different kind of *Qurbani Id* celebration:

> Our Christian festivals [Christmas and Easter] could be called "Christian Qurbani Ids." *Qurbani* means sacrifice and *Id* is defined as a festival. Thus, we would have a "festival of sacrifice." The Bible speaks of the sacrifice of praise, therefore, the *Id* would be a time for an offering of praise. On the Christian *Id* days, new clothes would be purchased for the family, a great feast would be served and special portions of food would be allotted for the poor. The focus of the day would be a special open air church service where the Good News of the Gospel would be openly proclaimed.

It is clear from all these suggestions that experimentation with the festival of sacrifice should be carried out with a view to narrowing the distance between Islam and Christianity.

Sufism

The question of the origins of Sufism has long been debated. The *Encyclopaedia Britannica* states that Sufism "appeared in pious circles as a reaction against the worldliness of the early Umayyad period (A.D. 661-749)."[41] These early mystical Muslims were constantly meditating on the Quranic teaching concerning the day of final judgment. They were distinguished by their close adherence to Quranic injunctions, by their many acts of piety, and by their all-night prayer meetings. Sufis engaged in repetitive recitation of the Quran which led them to feel a closeness with God. Like other ascetics of the time, Sufis chose to wear a frock

41. "Islamic Mysticism," *Encyclopaedia Britannica, Macropaedia,* 1974 ed., vol. 9, p. 943.

made of coarse wool as a mark of penitence and renunciation of the world. The term *Sufi* means "a person clad in wool."

Sufism emphasizes a program of spiritual ascent. This involves a number of stations in progressive order that the Sufi must reach under the guidance of his master. Whether a station is attained is believed to be determined by the level of effort and desire manifested by the individual. Yet at the same time, attainment of these spiritual "stations" is regarded not as a result of human action, but as a divine gift.

Before proceeding, it will be helpful to present a brief summary of Sufi doctrine:

1. God exists. He is in all things and all things are in Him.
2. All visible and invisible beings are an emanation from Him, and are not really distinct from Him.
3. Religions are matters of indifference: they however serve as leading to realities. Some for this purpose are more advantageous than others, among which is Islam, of which Sufism is the true philosophy.
4. There does not really exist any difference between good and evil, for all is reduced to Unity, and God is the real Author of the acts of mankind.
5. It is God who fixes the will of man: man therefore is not free in his actions.
6. The soul existed before the body and is confined within the latter as in a cage. Death, therefore, should be the object of the wishes of the Sufi, for it is then that he returns to the bosom of Divinity.
7. Without the Grace of God no one can attain to spiritual union but this can be obtained by fervently asking for it.
8. The principal occupation of the Sufi while in the body is meditation on the unity of God, the remembrance of God's names and the progressive advancement in the journey of life so as to attain unification with God.[42]

With regard to speculations about God, Sufis can be divided into two main groups. The larger of these is composed of pan-

42. Thomas Patrick Hughes, *A Dictionary of Islam* (London: W. H. Allen and Company, 1895), p. 609.

theists, to whom everything is God and all is of one essence. Those forming the second group explain away the pantheistic expressions of Islamic mystic writers, interpreting them in the sense that the existence of the universe and all that it contains is so far transcended by the reality of God that these things count for nothing.[43]

In his spiritual journey the Sufi passes through three distinct conceptions of the Absolute Being. At first, the simple creed, "There is no god but Allah," implies three things: there is no agent but Allah; there is no object of worship save Allah; and there is no existence save Allah. In the second phase the creed takes the form, "There is no god but Thou." In the final stage the creed becomes, "There is no god but I." This is the final goal of the Sufi's journey along the Path.[44]

The aim of the Sufis is to present to the world a universal "idea" filled with spiritualism, love, and liberty. They seek to free man from institutional shackles, hypocrisy, and rigid rules. A new world is to be opened up with emphasis on honesty and purity of heart.[45]

The *pir* is the religious leader of the Sufi community. He has a large following of people who regard him with great respect and devotion. I have observed huge gatherings of Muslims spending whole nights in worship of Allah under the direct guidance of a *pir*. Those who attach themselves to a particular *pir* are called *murid*.

The form which Sufi worship takes is vividly described by Bevan Jones.

> Since one of the principles of Sufism is to fix the mind on some object of thought, it is a common practice to repeat the name Allah over and over again. In particular, a disciple learns to repeat the "kalima" with special stress on the words, "illa'-llah," which he repeats with great vigour and much jerking of the head and body. This practice is known as "dhikr"

43. Jones, *People of the Mosque*, p. 155.
44. Ibid., p. 156.
45. Nasrollah S. Fatemi, *Sufism* (New York: A. S. Barnes, 1976), pp. 46–47.

or remembrance. Men assemble together for the performance of "dhikr" and frequently go to such lengths as to fall un-
conscious; women on the other hand often appear to go
through the recital alone, though they also continue until the
head becomes dizzy.[46]

Sufism shifts the emphasis from the external rituals of
religion to the mind and heart. God is thought of not as a distant
ruler, but as a close friend. Sufis hold that God may be reached
only through love. Good deeds, without a pure heart, are
useless.[47]

> Sufism is that form of life in which, under the negation of
> the world and I, the complete union of the soul with God is
> longed for and striven after as the summum bonum. Leave
> yourself outside, it advises, and then go in.[48]

Sufism has come into conflict with mainstream Islam in areas
like "saint worship, visiting of tombs, musical performances,
miracle mongering, degeneration into jugglery and the adaptation
of pre-Islamic and un-Islamic customs."[49] The pantheistic tendencies of Sufism are abhorrent to orthodox Islam. Yet, there remains
an interesting truce between Sufism and other forms of Islam like
Sunni and Shia.

Can Sufism have a positive effect on bridge-building between Muslims and Christians? Consider the following
statements:

> Sufism provides another area of theological permutation
> which lends itself to creative missionary approaches.[50]

46. Jones, *People of the Mosque*, p. 304.
47. Freeland Abbott, *Islam and Pakistan* (Ithaca, NY: Cornell University Press,
1968), p. 27.
48. Fatemi, *Sufism*, p. 35.
49. "Islamic Mysticism," p. 948.
50. Bill Musk, "Roles: God, Communicator, Muslim" (special project for
Dean Gilliland, Fuller Theological Seminary, 1978), p. 77.

Islam has a high regard for Christ, who plays a particularly significant role in certain phases of Sufism.[51]

Certain beliefs and practices of Sufism can be helpful in communicating the gospel. I would cite the following possibilities:

1. The Sufi view of God. Allah is above all and totally in control of His creation.
2. The Sufi stress on a personal relationship with God.
3. The deemphasis of the value of ritual and form.
4. The necessity of a hunger for God.
5. An awareness of the working of God's grace in the lives of men and women.
6. A similar goal of being with God one day.
7. A belief in intermediaries between God and man. This is a natural bridge to an effective presentation of Jesus as mediator for estranged mankind.

On the other hand, care must be taken lest, in using Sufism as a bridge, the Christian seem to condone pantheism. We, however, must meet Muslims where they are. An informed understanding of Sufism can potentially be very helpful in sharing the Christ who once said, "Blessed are those who hunger and thirst for righteousness, for they shall be satisfied" (Matt. 5:6).

Supernatural Experiences

How did Islam so easily expand in many countries of animistic Africa? There are multiple answers to this question. Certainly, conquest was a chief method of expansion. But it should be noted that Islam was able to identify very closely with the felt needs of Africans. Muslims have always believed in Satan, jinn, the evil eye, angels, and the power of amulets for protection. Thus, Islam came in with a similar, yet distinct, message. God was

51. Seyyed Hossein Nasr, *Ideals and Realities of Islam* (London: George Allen and Unwin, 1966), p. 34.

presented as an all-powerful force who could subdue evil spirits. Healing was carried out by Muslim practitioners. Other specific needs were met.

In like manner, Christianity must involve itself with Islam in areas where there are felt needs and unfulfilled desires.

> At some point God puts His finger on needs in the Muslim's life: fear of evil spirits, of death, of loneliness, some sickness or family disaster. The communicator identifies and empathizes with the Muslim in this exposure of need, but holds forth a message of hope in the person of Jesus. Jesus can exorcise, can deliver from death, from fear and loneliness, can heal or move miraculously in men's lives.[52]

Charles Kraft reinforces this observation:

> It is not illegitimate in our day to encounter evil spirits in the name of Christ, to expect God to speak in dreams and visions, to communicate, educate, lead, ritualize, and otherwise structure Christianity in ways reminiscent of the Old Testament and Gospels. For the Bible shows such means to be adequate as expressions of Divine-human interrelationships.[53]

An amazing number of Muslims have come to Christ as they experienced dreams of a supernatural dimension. William Miller writes of one Muslim who in a dream saw a huge palace with a cross on its roof. A voice told him the palace belonged to Jesus Christ and only He could open the gate. Sometime later, the Muslim was reading *Pilgrim's Progress* and was startled to see on one of the pages a picture that was identical to his dream. This experience led to his conversion.[54]

Bilquis Sheikh is a devout Pakistani Muslim convert. She

---

52. Musk, "Roles," pp. 54–55.

53. Charles H. Kraft, "Dynamic Equivalence Churches in Muslim Society," in *The Gospel and Islam: A 1978 Compendium,* ed. Don M. McCurry (Monrovia, CA: MARC, 1979), p. 116.

54. William McElwee Miller, *Ten Muslims Meet Christ* (Grand Rapids: Wm. B. Eerdmans, 1969), p. 79.

writes autobiographically in her book, *I Dared to Call Him Father*, of the dream in which she first encountered Christ:

> I found myself having supper with a man I knew to be Jesus. He had come to visit me in my home and stayed two days. He sat across the table from me and in peace and joy we ate dinner together. Suddenly, the dream changed. Now I was on a mountain top with another man. He was clothed in a robe and shod with sandals. How was it that I mysteriously knew his name too? John the Baptist. What a strange name. I found myself telling this John the Baptist about my recent visit with Jesus. "The Lord came and was my guest for two days," I said. "But now He is gone. Where is He? I must find Him! Perhaps you, John the Baptist, will lead me to Him."[55]

Shortly thereafter, Bilquis Sheikh was in the home of TEAM missionaries David and Sinova Mitchell. It was there that she heard further of both John the Baptist and the Lord Jesus. It is my privilege to know Bilquis Sheikh as a beautiful Christian. She has suffered much for her faith. Her pilgrimage commenced with a vivid dream experienced in her lovely home in the majestic rolling hills of northern Pakistan.

Max Kershaw of International Students, Inc., has written of his contacts with Muslims in America:

> Two nights ago, a Muslim friend who was visiting in my home asked me what I thought about dreams. I told him that the Bible contained many stories of dreams and their significance. He's been dreaming a lot of late and he's thinking about them. I have known several Muslim converts where dreams have been used as stepping stones to Christ.[56]

Other supernatural occurrences have communicated powerfully to Muslims. In one country, a healing campaign was conducted with the goal of presenting Christ to Muslims. The

55. Bilquis Sheikh, *I Dared to Call Him Father* (Waco, TX: Chosen Books, 1978), p. 35.
56. R. Max Kershaw, in a personal letter to the author, 8 January 1979.

meeting was held in an open field with just a makeshift platform. There was no emotional content to the program. At the conclusion, each Muslim in the crowd was told to place his hand over the place he was in pain. The evangelist then prayed for the audience. Remarkable testimonies of healing followed. Especially significant was one six-year-old girl, blind from birth, who received her sight. By the fourth night, over ten thousand people had gathered for the simple service. Just before the meeting began, police moved in and arrested the team, which included foreigners and nationals. The expatriates were deported. The national interpreter was kept in jail for several weeks and then released. Never in the history of that country have so many Muslims gathered in one place to hear the gospel preached. This method of communication allows for a holistic approach to ministry with minimal financial involvement. Future efforts of this nature, however, should probably be conducted on a much smaller scale.

Consider the supernatural dynamics of this anonymous story of three recent converts who were about to be killed because of their faith in Christ:

> The sun had reached its zenith hours ago and the afternoon was sultry and foreboding. The mob had conveniently arranged for men to come with bamboo poles, used to crack the skulls of wild animals or thieves. The three prayed, yet the first blow never came. Suddenly, a crazy man, who was known to be a spirit worshipper, burst into the ring of beaters. He was always a little weird, carrying chains and uttering incantations. At this moment he went from man to man staring at each and muttering in a monotone, "These men are righteous men; do not harm them; these men are righteous men; do not harm them." The village Muslim is an unorthodox breed, and the incantations of this man had a lot of weight. The religious leaders reconvened and decided that it was better not to beat them, but to have them all pray and show respect to Allah. The believers were delighted and prayed concluding each prayer in Jesus' name. After the trial was over, the crowd of Muslims dispersed. The crazy man was not to be found. One of the converts offered his explanation, "The crazy man was an angel."

It is reasonable for the Muslim to want to meet God in a demonstrable manner. It is human nature to desire that one's needs be met. Jesus and the early church made it their business to meet the needs of those around them, and the result was often conversion. It is our responsibility as Christians to seek an anointing that we may be powerful instruments in the hand of God. Muslims must come to realize that our God is alive—and that He confirms His existence with tangible proofs.

CHAPTER 7

The Muslim-
Convert Church

Mosque and Church Structure

John Stott comments on the possible development of "Jesus mosques":

The very word Christian is associated in a Muslim's mind with all that he abominates most—the memory of those brutal Crusades, the materialism and moral decadence of the West, and our (to him) incredible espousal of Zionist imperialism. It is inconceivable to him that he should ever betray his Islamic inheritance. To become a Christian would be treason as well as apostasy and would deserve the death penalty. So the question is whether a whole new way of presenting the Gospel can be developed. Can we show that "however much new converts feel they need to renounce for the sake of Christ, they are still the same people with the same heritage and the same family" (Willowbank Report), and that "conversion does not unmake, it remakes" (Kenneth Cragg)? Is it possible to conceive of converts becoming followers of Jesus without so forsaking their Islamic culture that they are regarded as traitors? *Can we even contemplate Jesus*

mosques instead of churches and Jesus Muslims instead of Christians?
(italics added)[1]

Is it not possible to see a church evolve that is maximally contextual to the Islamic way of life and worship? We will explore
some of the options that seem to call for further experimentation.

Mosque Patterns

The mosque is both a religious and a social center. People
may be seen lounging in the mosques, talking over a broad range
of secular as well as religious topics. Mosques are never closed.
Travelers and guests are welcome to put down a bedroll and sleep
in the mosque. The religious significance of the mosque is evident
in the following injunction of Muhammad, as recorded in the
Hadith (traditions):

> The prayers of a man in his own house are equal to the
> reward of one prayer, but prayers in a Masjid near his home
> are equal to twenty-five prayers, and in a central mosque,
> they are equal to five hundred prayers.[2]

The only requirement of the law of Islam regarding the
building of a mosque is that it should face Mecca. The *Hadith* further recommend that all buildings should be as simple as possible.
Adornments should be avoided. The mosques are unfurnished except for mats or carpets and a pulpit from which the Friday sermon is delivered. The chief decorations of the mosques are the
writings on the walls, in mosaic, of Arabic verses from the Holy
Quran.[3]

In 1976, I had an extended interview with an orthodox
Muslim layman who had made the pilgrimage to Mecca three

1. John R. W. Stott, "Christians and Muslims," *Christianity Today* 23.5
(1 December 1978): 35.
2. Thomas Patrick Hughes, *A Dictionary of Islam* (London: W. H. Allen and
Company, 1895), p. 330.
3. Maulana Muhammad Ali, *The Religion of Islam* (Lahore: The Ahmadiyya
Anjuman Ishaat Islam, 1936), pp. 288–89.

times. He was a willing and gracious informant who dealt with each question with clarity and precision. The following description of the administration of the mosque is a composite of my notes written up after our meeting.

Each mosque is basically governed by a local committee of those who worship there. The committee appoints a secretary. Often this secretary is a man of influence who may well have donated a large sum of money for the construction of the mosque. No one person, however, is allowed to give all the money for building a mosque as this may lead to pride, which is a terrible sin. Subscriptions are taken from the local community to meet necessary expenses.

The committee gives oversight to the needs of the mosque. They meet informally and irregularly on the basis of some specific need. In most mosques there is no political infighting or divisive tendencies. Only where there is an abundance of money would there be a temptation for someone to seek the position of secretary.

Each mosque is autonomous. The committee runs its own affairs without outside interference. There is no "union of mosques." There is no *"imams'* fellowship." There is no "Pope *Moulana.*" This system definitely cuts down on jealousy, power struggles, and the pursuit of self-promotion. Each person is free to worship in any mosque he chooses. Ritual is so prescribed that there is little to choose between different mosques. The Friday lecture does, however, open itself to a comparison of the abilities of the various *imams* in the area of expositional skills.

The committee can discipline an *imam.* The actual judgment must be presided over by a Muslim priest. My informant mentioned lying and cinema attendance as serious sins for any Muslim religious leader.

In light of the attitude which the Muslim has toward the mosque, imagine the shock experienced when he enters a church in his home district and finds people "defiling the house of God" by wearing shoes. He then encounters chairs, musical instruments, and pictures on the wall. Prayer time is conducted with people casually sitting in their chairs. The Muslim is told that there is no hospitality arrangement and the church will be locked thirty minutes after the Sunday morning service concludes. Before the Muslim confronts theological barriers, he has experienced not the offense of the cross, but rather the cultural offense of what is basically, to him at least, a repugnant foreign import. Is there not a better way?

The Homogeneous Church

In Islamic lands, the body of believers is often composed largely of non-Muslim converts. This, combined with a Western church flavor imported by missionaries, has caused the church to be perceived as totally alien by the onlooking Muslim community. It can be safely assumed that the church of non-Muslim converts in a Muslim country will be resistant at this stage to any overtures toward change that will break sacrosanct tradition and move it toward a more culturally acceptable (to the Muslim) identity. Therefore, serious consideration should be given to the establishment of a homogeneous church, that is, a church made up of recent converts to Christianity from Islam. This church would not be in competition with the established body of believers, but rather would be a parallel structure.

The early church had distinctions between Jewish and Greek-speaking segments (Acts 6). There were Christian movements among the Samaritans, the priests, and the Pharisees (Acts 15:5). It is reasonable to suppose that these homogeneous groups heard the gospel in their own social units and then believed. It is also reasonable to suppose that those who came to Christ then wanted to communicate the Good News to those who had been in their same social grouping. In this way, the gospel grew among existing social units.[4]

Today, in a similar homogeneous church, there would not be a bar to others from disparate backgrounds joining the church. The doors would be open to all. But the flavor of the church

4. Montgomery W. Smith, "Homogeneity and American Church Growth" (D.Miss. dissertation, Fuller Theological Seminary, 1976), p. 168.

would be distinctive and would thus naturally attract mostly converts from Islam. They would feel at home in such a church. This would be a great step toward overcoming the problem the Muslim inquirer faces when he enters a church composed largely of non-Muslim converts: he finds "his faith doubted, his presence mistrusted, and his interest questioned."[5] Instead of receiving such a reaction from traditional Christians, the inquirer would find in the homogeneous church a reservoir of understanding and acceptance from people who, like him, have been on a pilgrimage of faith from Islam to Christianity.

Frank Khair-Ullah is an evangelical Christian leader in the Pakistani church who comes from an Islamic background. In his writings he has illustrated this tension between the church and Muslim converts:

> Recently, we were having an informal meeting of those who are interested in Muslim evangelism. Two Pakistanis were also present. The question under consideration was how to help the new converts become a part of the Church. A suggestion was made that as a transitional step, there should be a fellowship of other Muslim converts and sympathizers. Fear was expressed spontaneously by one Pakistani, that such a step might give to the new convert an undue sense of superiority and that one should be careful about this.

> This is a typical and symptomatic attitude of the church leaders. A certain unwillingness to share the good news with our "unconsciously regarded enemy" neighbor. Most Christians have an in-built hatred for the Muslim, which we, by God's grace, need to overcome.[6]

Church Administration

It is often observed that human nature enjoys political-type activities within a sociological group. Christians are no different.

5. Kenneth Cragg, *The Call of the Minaret* (New York: Oxford University Press, 1956), p. 351.

6. Frank Khair-Ullah, "The Role of Local Churches in God's Redemptive Plan for the Muslim World," in *The Gospel and Islam: A 1978 Compendium*, ed. Don M. McCurry (Monrovia, CA: MARC, 1979), p. 567.

In many countries the quest for power and leadership has led to deep divisions, thus negating any positive influence for Christ. Parties and groupings have been perpetuated down through the generations. The export of Western denominational structures to the church in Muslim countries has introduced problems which should have been avoided. A hierarchy of elected offices, often accompanied by status and comparative wealth, has set the stage for egocentric, power-hungry individuals who are determined to win election—at any cost.

The mosque structure seems to parallel fairly closely that of the Plymouth Brethren. Would not the convert church function best with maximum autonomy for each congregation? Elected leadership would be minimal, thus disallowing scope for internal politicking. The churches would informally fellowship with each other, but would shun administrative structures and a leadership hierarchy.

A small committee of dedicated laymen could be given the oversight of church affairs. Their meetings would take place only when a situation required their decision. The complete emphasis of the church structure would be on conducting the work of God. Spiritual realities would be stressed. Potential for the self-aggrandizement of any individual would be minimized.

Day of Worship

Christians have universally accepted Sunday as the day of worship for many centuries. Scripture gives some indications of a precedent for Sunday worship, but there is no specific command or exhortation. Conversely, the Bible issues warnings against legalism:

> Therefore let no one act as your judge in regard to food or drink or in respect to a festival or a new moon or a Sabbath day—things which are a mere shadow of what is to come; but the substance belongs to Christ. (Col. 2:16–17)

Sunday worship is a definite problem to Muslims. Muhammad appointed Friday as the special day of community prayer:

> O ye who have believed, when proclamation is made for the
> Prayer on the day of the assembly [Friday], endeavor to come
> to the remembrance of Allah and leave off bargaining; that is
> better for you, if ye have knowledge. (Surah 62:9)

A great deal of Muslim tradition has built up around Friday as a day of religious significance. Friday is said to be the best day on which the sun rises, the day on which Adam was taken into paradise, and the day of the coming resurrection. There is also a certain hour on Friday (known only to God) during which a Muslim obtains all the good he asks of God.[7]

As Friday worship is of such importance to Muslims, cannot the convert church agree to hold special services on Friday at 1 p.m., when the rest of the populace is at prayer? Iran is one country where Christians do worship on Friday. Merle Inniger reports that the business holiday in Pakistan has recently been changed from Sunday to Friday. Christians, however, are allowed a few hours off from work on Sunday morning to attend the church of their choice.[8] In a Muslim country it may be quite feasible to have services on both Fridays and Sundays.

Designation for Believers

The word *Christian* has long been a serious offense to the Muslim. One experienced missionary to Islam has stated that even baptisms are not as dangerous as the word *Christian*. Charles Kraft suggests alternatives:

> For to be labeled a member of a Christian Church is often tantamount to being called a Communist. For many, these labels connote "traitor," one who has sold out to his enemy. "Are you a Christian?" The national answers, "No," thus he is untrue to his Lord. It is a dilemma most of us from non-Muslim lands can barely imagine, much less understand. Surely there are more acceptable terms, like People of God, People of Faith, Descendants of Abraham. Terms that do no discredit

7. Hughes, *Dictionary of Islam*, p. 130.
8. Merlin W. Inniger, in a personal letter to the author, 11 January 1979.

to our Lord, whose earliest followers were known as Followers of the Way, and only later, in Antioch, were dubbed "Christians."[9]

As mentioned earlier, in Lombaro, the term "followers of Isa" has been used in place of "Christian." This whole question needs further research.

Clergy

The structures of Islamic leadership should be closely examined. How does the Muslim leader of the mosque interact with his congregation? What qualifications are required of a Muslim teacher? Is there a standard salary scale? What are the social taboos for a Muslim priest? Answers to these questions will provide a foundation for a Christian leadership which will, in turn, be more easily understood and appreciated by the surrounding Muslim community.

It is important to have an overview of the offices of Muslim priesthood. Richard Nyrop has defined the more important of these:

Although no formal ecclesiastical organization exists in Islam, and in theory the existence of special access to God conflicts with Muslim teachings, in fact a learned quasi-priestly class known as the *ulema* (those possessed of religious knowledge) has grown up to interpret and administer religious law. At the lower levels are *imams* of individual mosques; *maulvis*, who have completed ten years of basic religious training; *mullas* and *munshis*, who have completed fewer years; and *maulanas*, who have received some advanced training in Muslim law and theology. A fakir is a religious mendicant,

9. Charles H. Kraft, "Dynamic Equivalence Churches," in *Conference on Media in Islamic Culture Report*, ed. C. Richard Shumaker (Marseilles: Evangelical Literature Overseas, 1974), p. 75.

believed possessed of *barakat* (special spiritual powers), and a *pir* is a Muslim spiritual guide.[10]

A Dictionary of Islam stipulates that an *imam* must know the Quran thoroughly.[11] The actual word *imam* is found twelve times in the Quran and carries the meaning of "model, pattern, leader." Surah 25:74 uses the word *imam* in the following context: "Make us a *model* to the pious"; and Surah 36:11 says: "Everything we have set down in a clear *model*."[12] It is obvious that the *imam* is to live an exemplary life of holiness, righteousness, love, and involvement in helping others.

Technically, *imam* is not a profession; the *imam* is an *imam* only so long as he is actually engaged in leading the prayer.[13] But in actual practice, the *imam* is usually assigned to one mosque and engages in part-time or full-time ministry among the persons who attend.

In the cities, an *imam* may be a person of higher learning. In rural areas this is seldom true. He has studied long enough to learn by rote the prayers that he recites. It is possible he may know the Arabic script well enough to read Quranic verses, but with limited comprehension of what he is reading.

The superstitious elements of Islam are seen in the rural areas:

> The villagers call upon the *Mullah* for socioreligious functions and may also consult him to determine whether a particular kind of behavior is permissible, although in important matters of this sort they may travel some distance to consult someone of higher reputation. More commonly they come to him for amulets and charms consisting of Quranic phrases written on bits of paper that are believed to cure sickness,

10. Richard F. Nyrop, *Area Handbook for Bangladesh* (Washington: U.S. Government Printing Office, 1975), p. 113.

11. Hughes, *Dictionary of Islam*, p. 204.

12. Ibid., p. 203.

13. H. A. R. Gibb and J. H. Kramers, *Shorter Encyclopedia of Islam* (Ithaca, NY: Cornell University Press, 1965), p. 165.

snakebite, and sexual impotence; to ward off evil jinns; to ensure the birth of sons; and to bring good luck in projected undertakings. Many villagers have implicit faith in such cures for disease and appear to benefit from them. Some *Mullahs* derive a significant portion of their income from such sales.[14]

In olden days it was demanded that an *imam* work some sort of miracle in order to prove his divine credentials. This idea was rigorously opposed by the *imams* themselves who frequently utilized Surah 17:110 as their proof text, "I am a man like yourselves."[15]

What really is the societal perception of the Muslim religious leader in rural areas? The following is rather typical:

> The term *Mullah* may be used to refer to a *maulvi* or to a local *Imam* of some natural wisdom and dignity, but usually it is a rather derogatory term that connotes a semiliterate, backward, often bigoted village *Imam*. As the recognized religious leader of the community the *Mullah* may be very influential and possess considerable authority in some villages; in other villages he may be regarded with friendliness and indulgence but little respect.[16]

In the village, the *imam's* identity centers around religion. In cities, Muslim priests at times become involved in politics. It, however, is the secularist rather than the orthodox Muslim who usually ends up in the fray of political life.

It is an uneven picture. Generally, it depends on the individual, much like the Christian minister of the West. I have met some outstanding men of high intelligence and character among Muslim priests. A group possessing the opposite traits has also been encountered.

The Muslim teacher is to be a man of otherworldly character. His life is to be marked by holiness and prayer. There are a number of taboos he must observe:

14. Nyrop, *Area Handbook*, p. 117.
15. Gibb and Kramers, *Shorter Encyclopedia*, p. 166.
16. Nyrop, *Area Handbook*, p. 117.

1. Cinema attendance
2. Strong drink
3. Eating of pork
4. Gambling
5. Smoking (usually)
6. Contact with women outside of his family
7. Television
8. Reading romantic novels
9. Wealth
10. Dancing

As is consistently the case in Islam, there is a tremendous emphasis on the externals. Ritual, abstinence, and outward displays of piety are highly valued. This is not to deemphasize other Islamic teaching such as humility and love. But, on the practical, empirical level, there seems to be an overwhelming emphasis on surface piety.

The Muslim priest is not a wealthy person. He serves a local mosque out of devotion rather than hope of financial remuneration. It is true, an *imam* of a large city mosque would be much better off financially than his counterpart in the village. Yet, I have never heard of a Muslim priest anywhere in the world drawing a salary comparable to the $40,000 annual income of some pastors of large American churches. This type of inflated salary is entirely incompatible with the Muslim understanding of a holy man who lives simply and is not taken up with a desire for worldly and material success.

This does not mean that a man is not worthy of his hire. The *imam* has financial needs just like others in society. The situation in one particular Muslim country affords a sketch of how the system is usually worked out:

Despite their considerable prestige, members of the *ulema* generally do not enjoy a high material standard of living. A prayer leader's income is not secure; he may be paid out of voluntary contributions, funds from trust property, or a conventional share of village produce at harvest time. He looks after the mosque, collects its revenues, leads the prayers, and delivers the weekly sermons. He also acts as a consultant on points of Muslim law and is usually called upon to participate in religious functions, marriages and funerals in exchange for gifts or cash. When a mosque is used as a school, the *imam* is the teacher, the studies being confined to the learning of the Quran.[17]

In Ghana, the *imam* adds to his salary by performing other religious duties. It has been said that "he feels no scruples in quite simply asking for a stipend before he renders a specific religious service."[18] In a typical Muslim village, it is common to see subscriptions being taken up to help pay for the *imam's* salary. A box is placed in the rear of the mosque for receiving contributions. The mosque committee oversees fund disbursements and sets the salary of the *imam*.

It appears to me that the emerging convert-church could accept most of the roles of the *imam* as a guideline for their spiritual leader:

1. The pastor would be a man of the Word of God. This is his specialty. Memorization of Scripture would play an important role in his preparation. He would be competent to teach the Word.

2. The leader would feel a particular pastoral responsibility to his people. His congregation would feel free to call on him in times of spiritual need. Particularly, it would be helpful for him to have a real prayer ministry for the sick and oppressed.

3. Holiness, love, and righteousness would need to be an integral part of the leader's life. There must be community consensus that he is a man who walks with God. It is not right for him to be bound up with legalistic negatives as regards behavior. On the other hand, there is a higher law of love which is operational. A "man of God" is a person who does abstain from what society perceives to be questionable behavior (I Tim. 3:2). Therefore, it would behoove the pastor, in deference to others who do not

17. Ibid.
18. Patrick J. Ryan, *Imale: Yoruba Participation in the Muslim Tradition* (Missoula, MT: Scholars Press, 1978), p. 160.

understand Christian liberty and grace, to quietly refrain from certain acts which could be misinterpreted and, in turn, reflect on his personal integrity as well as the testimony of his church.

4. Financially, the pastor should manifest a lifestyle similar to that of the local *imam*. He should be entirely dependent on offerings of his congregation for his livelihood. In the interest of having a truly contextualized ministry, no foreign money should be accepted.

There is a great deal of sacrifice involved in being a minister of the gospel in a Muslim country. The pastor will be at times seriously misunderstood and maligned. His life may even be in danger in certain situations. Yet, his calling is among the highest in the world. It is his privilege to serve Jesus Christ. For this honor, he is willing to become the servant of all. His day of reward will surely come!

Laity

The emphasis in Islam is on the laity. The layman has full authority to lead in prayer and to teach the Quran. Salaried religious leaders are more auxiliary than central.

In Christian circles the word *ministry* has come to refer to the professional clergy, but in the New Testament *diakonia* (ministry) is not the function of one class. It is a role to which all believers are called. In I Corinthians 12:4–30, Paul speaks of the different gifts bestowed by the Holy Spirit as "varieties of *diakonia*" (v. 5) and he includes all believers in his picture of the body.[19]

The New Testament does not focus on one leader in the local church. The churches met in homes and were guided by groups of elders. Acts 20:17–38 speaks of Paul's interaction with the *elders* from Ephesus. There is no focus of attention on one leader in this passage. It has been suggested that there were few full-time clergy in the first and second centuries.

D. James Kennedy sees the main responsibility of the pastor

19. Neil Braun, *Laity Mobilized* (Grand Rapids: Wm. B. Eerdmans, 1971), p. 105.

as that of preparing laymen to go forth to do the work of the ministry:

> In the fourth chapter of Ephesians we read that Christ has given to the Church "some, apostles; and some, prophets; and some, evangelists; and some, pastors and teachers; for the perfecting of the saints, for the work of the ministry, for the edifying of the body of Christ." This is the way it reads in the King James translation. This, however, is not a very accurate rendering of the Greek text. Instead of the preposition "for" being repeated three times, the Greek word would better be rendered: "for," "unto," "unto." A more literal translation, then, would be that Christ has given pastors and teachers to the Church "for the equipping of the saints unto the work of the ministry, unto the upbuilding of the body of Christ."[20]

Neil Braun, after careful scriptural and historical research, concludes that "it is abundantly clear that the pattern of each church having its own paid pastor is required neither by the New Testament nor by the history of the Christian Church."[21] Luther's conception of the church in his earlier writings was rather revolutionary. In his manifesto, "To the Christian Nobility," he boldly proclaimed that "all Christians are truly priests and there is no distinction amongst them except as to office. . . . Everybody who is baptized may maintain that he has been consecrated as a priest, bishop or pope."[22] Roland Allen, a great missiologist of the turn of the century, urged that no church be placed in a situation where, because of a shortage of professional leadership, it is unable to observe the rites Christ commanded. His solution was to ordain unpaid, voluntary lay leaders.[23] In a lecture delivered at Fuller Theological Seminary, Donald McGavran reinforced Allen's call for a

20. D. James Kennedy, *Evangelism Explosion* (Wheaton, IL: Tyndale House, 1970), p. 6.

21. Braun, *Laity Mobilized*, p. 39.

22. Hendrik Kraemer, *A Theology of the Laity* (Philadelphia: Westminster Press, 1958), p. 61.

23. *The Ministry of the Spirit: Selected Writings of Roland Allen*, ed. David Paton (Grand Rapids: Wm. B. Eerdmans, 1962), pp. 170-73.

lay ministry made up of dedicated volunteers. These men would have equal authority with the professional clergy in officiating at all church functions, including the dispensing of the sacraments. These laymen could conduct marriages and funerals. They would be ordained by the church. Accountability would be to the church body. A special theological course by extension or through night classes could be arranged to train these leaders.

A number of illustrations of this emphasis on lay leadership are emerging. In a recent letter to the author, Fred Plastow, a veteran missionary with the Gospel Missionary Union, writes of the emphasis on shared leadership in the Moroccan church. The believers work toward a consensus of opinion which guides their actions.

Lesslie Newbigin writes of an experiment with church planting in India. When converts were baptized in a new area, the temptation to send in a salaried worker in the usual fashion was resisted. Rather, the sovereign act of the Holy Spirit in using a humble layman was respected; and he was, at least for the time being, recognized as the one through whom the Spirit would lead the new converts. From time to time, he was assisted by trained leaders. An era of unusual growth followed in this particular area. In twelve years, the number of congregations increased from thirteen to fifty-five.[24]

Among the Bataks in Indonesia, a similar story is told. Local leaders serve as part-time pastors and part-time schoolteachers. These pastors in turn send out deacons who are each responsible for twenty-five families. They visit the sick, teach the catechism, and encourage evangelism. In one area, out of a Christian community of twenty thousand, nearly two thousand men and women volunteered for evangelistic work, calling themselves "Witnesses for Christ."[25]

Stephen Neill sums up the syndrome that frequently occurs in the transition from emphasis on laity to a paid, professional

24. Braun, *Laity Mobilized*, p. 203.
25. Harold R. Cook, *Historic Patterns of Church Growth* (Chicago: Moody Press, 1971), pp. 96–97.

clergy. He writes from the perspective of one who could legitimately be called a "missionary statesman."

> Almost every new Christian group starts with the idea that it will not become an institution; it will return to the simplicity of the primitive days and will refuse to be weighed down by the worldly considerations that come with wealth and property. Some such groups have been more successful than others in avoiding the steps by which a society is turned into an institution; but the beginnings of the process are observable in almost all of them. At the start there is no ordained ministry. But ere long one or two begin to stand out as specially gifted, and responsibility comes more and more to fall into their hands. As numbers grow, the work of the ministry becomes more exacting, and can hardly be carried out in the spare time of those who are already earning their daily bread in the world. A demand for a better-educated ministry begins to make itself felt and men must be trained. Most groups find it necessary to own some kind of place of meeting—and at once are launched on all the problems involved in the possession of property.[26]

Thus, a system is introduced that is very difficult to reverse. The church has moved a long way from the situation Chrysostom described in his comments on the lives of the rural bishops of Antioch in the fourth century: "These men you may see sometime yoking the oxen and driving the plough, and again ascending the pulpit and cultivating the souls under their care; now uprooting the thorns from the earth with a hook, and now purging out the sins of the soul by the Word."[27]

The central function of the laity must be to proclaim the gospel. Often the church is accused of poor ethics as it seeks to "persuade" people to accept the gospel. Should the church respond to society and its dictates or be answerable to the risen

26. Stephen Neill, *Christian Faith and Other Faiths* (London: Oxford University Press, 1977), pp. 211–12.
27. Braun, *Laity Mobilized*, p. 38.

Lord? Montgomery Smith believes that "the church must remove the blanket of bias against persuasion placed over it by society and get on with the work of God."[28] Donald McGavran makes a related comment concerning the mission of the church:

> Mission in the New Testament was never proclamation for proclamation's sake, never simply living as Christians, indifferent to whether men obeyed or not. According to the record, the passion that was God's for the salvation of mankind of which the Cross is the supreme expression, was not shown in detached witness, or a kindly living out of the Gospel, hoping that sinful men would notice the Christian's life and seek its Source. It was never simply discharging a duty to witness. It focused not on what Christians should do, but on saving men. It was witness and proclamation, that men might believe.[29]

Vedanayakam Azariah was the first Indian to become a Protestant bishop. His heartbeat was evangelism. On one occasion he stated that "too much of the energies of ministers and churches is being spent in taking permanent care of hereditary Christians. The church exists not to save itself, but to save others."[30] Another time Bishop Azariah told of going around to the churches and having baptized members place their hands on their own heads and repeat after him, "I am a baptized Christian. Woe unto me if I preach not the Gospel."[31]

C. Peter Wagner has documented that the phenomenal growth of the Pentecostal Church in Latin America is due mainly to the effectiveness of a lay witness to the community of non-Christians. Believers are motivated to go forth onto the streets,

28. Smith, "Homogeneity," p. 200.
29. Donald A. McGavran, *How Churches Grow* (London: World Dominion Press, 1959), p. 63.
30. Vedanayakam Azariah, "The Place of the Church in Evangelism," *Evangelism*, vol. 3, Tambaram series, p. 42.
31. Vedanayakam Azariah, "The Church and Its Mission," *Addresses and Other Records*, vol. 7, Tambaram series, p. 42.

among their friends, and into the factory with the message of a transforming gospel. As a result, believers are multiplying and churches are being planted at an incredible rate.

A laity highly motivated and enthusiastic about their faith in Jesus Christ will be the key to effective outreach among Muslims. Resources should be directed toward the establishment of such a lay movement.

Theological Training

What are the needs of the layman and pastor in the area of theological training? It should be kept in mind that the focus of this book is on the rural Christian community in a country where the majority are Muslim. The training needs of an urban pastor or the leadership of a highly developed ecclesiastical structure are not germane to this particular consideration.

In rural areas, the most common occupation is that of farmer. The emerging Muslim-convert church may well be filled with nonliterate or semiliterate people. This presents its own set of unique problems. Church members will likely be a part of a huge majority in developing nations who are consigned to a marginal existence. It is not possible for these believers to spend significant amounts of time away from their farms and families. Theological education must be tailored to meet their needs.

These concerns were felt keenly by a group of missionaries in Latin America. Their excellent Presbyterian seminary had been serving the denomination for twenty-five years. But in 1962 it was discovered that only ten pastors who were graduates of that outstanding seminary were actively serving the church. The outlook for the future was bleak. Only five students were enrolled that year. This was totally inadequate in view of the fact that the Presbyterian Church had two hundred growing churches for which it was responsible.

This very real problem led the missionary trio of Ralph Winter, James Emery, and Ross Kinsler to work through to a practical solution which has been duplicated throughout the world. Theological Education by Extension (TEE) is the product of those intense first years of experimentation. It is my judgment that this approach has a definite potential for assisting in the dissemination of biblical knowledge to converts spread throughout the Muslim world. This will become apparent once we have analyzed a few of the shortcomings of the traditional seminary approach and some of the features of TEE which are applicable to the training of Muslim converts.

Shortcomings of the Traditional Seminary Approach

Extraction

> Traditional seminary programs extract men from their natural environment in the world and insulate them from real life situations. The "ghetto mentality" produced by this artificial learning situation reinforces the concept of the church as a place to which the world is to come rather than as a staging base from which it penetrates the world. Inflexible attitudes are developed in training with little possibility of adjustment to the changing forms of ministry and church planting demanded.[32]

This problem is exactly what we are seeking to avoid. The new believer must remain part and parcel of society. His roots must be deep in the soil of his own culture. How many good men have been lost to their own people through the dislocation suffered from attending a seminary at a great distance from home? This phenomenon of extraction doesn't refer exclusively to study outside one's country. A villager may have never gone to the capital city of his own nation. Such a move would break him into a complete new world which is culturally a significant distance from his own people.

32. Ralph R. Covell, "The Extension Seminary and Church Growth," in *Crucial Dimensions in World Evangelization*, ed. Arthur F. Glasser (Pasadena: William Carey Library, 1976), p. 455.

Expense

Training by extraction is very expensive. Heavy subsidy must be granted by the foreign parent-denomination. This leads to the student's developing a spirit of dependence on the establishment. He expects to be supported by the denomination after graduation. The whole procedure leads to professionalism. It is then necessary to perpetuate the full-time leader, so the supply line of funds clearly leads back to a Western mission. Such a syndrome is in clear violation of the goal of self-supporting churches.

Elitism

"The graduate from such a program has the status of a semi-professional. He has gone away to school and now qualifies to move into the elite leadership of the church."[33] It is hard on the seminary-trained leader to return to his people as humble as he left them. And the other believers regard this somewhat sophisticated intellectual (in relative cultural terms) as a person to be more revered and feared than as one of themselves. It is often felt that he has lost his roots. The logical sequence is for the seminary-trained man to seek a pastorate in the city.

Irrelevant Courses

The seminary is structured to meet the training needs of the full-time Christian worker. Course content is often technical and even dull. It can seem very remote from the grassroots level of life. There is little stimulation to go forth in active evangelism and church planting.

How many men can the church afford to train in this traditional manner? Leadership training tied into the seminary system is extremely limited. It simply does not lead to aggressive church growth.

What about the layman? Generally there is no place for him to receive a structured course of study. The most instruction he receives is from a thirty-minute sermon on Sunday morning. Often the sermon illustrations he hears are centered on men like

33. Ibid.

Dwight L. Moody and Billy Graham, whose names are as foreign to his ears as Kumbie Luambai is to ours! He hears few parables or stories centered on village life to which he can easily relate. No wonder Christianity takes on such a foreign flavor.

TEE Features Applicable to Training Muslim Converts

Geographical Extension

Many gifted church leaders cannot leave their homes—nor should they. TEE proposes to go to them in the form of extension seminars. Classes would meet locally, conducted by a trained teacher. These sessions would take place weekly or as often as practical. All cultural and employment patterns remain intact. The teacher travels out to various villages; the students need not leave their responsibilities and go to the city. There is an adequate amount of home study to keep the leader or layman busy between classes.

Flexibility in Time

During the harvest time, all classes may have to be set aside. The monsoon rains may provide the perfect opportunity to double up on sessions. Afternoons may be the best time for classes. Lack of electricity in rural areas often means that night sessions are impossible. The time schedule for each individual situation is set up only after coming to group consensus.

Theological Education Adapted to the Culture

Molds of thinking in each sub-culture are different, and proper theological education will be tailor-made for each one. Institutions that are not extended will often require that a student from one culture take his training within another one.... Leaders of rural churches in South Viet Nam, for example, were discussing the problems that sending their ministerial candidates to study in the city raised. They said, "When our men return to the country they are not the same. They want their salary in cash, not in rice and chickens; they won't walk through the rice paddies because they will get their trousers wet; they are not even able to sit and talk with us because they have brought their city schedules back with them and no longer have any time."[34]

Forcing students to adapt to another culture must be avoided if the church is to have any effect on society.

Academic Programs Developed for the Target Audience

Why is there such a concern for academic degrees in relation to training simple village people in the Scriptures? There is no need for a rural pastor to possess a master of divinity degree. He does, on the other hand, need an in-depth, relevant knowledge of the Word of God. It is probably better for ministerial academic standards to be determined by the academic levels of the people in the pews rather than by an elite denominational board sitting in some remote city.

There should be two programs of study, one for the full-time pastor and one for the layman. These two programs will generally cover the spectrum of need. Courses must be written with the target audience in mind. They should be made as simple as needed. Certificates should be presented upon finishing each course as well as an attractive diploma given for the successful completion of the entire program.

The illiterate is a special problem. However, the capacity of a person to memorize must not be overlooked. Memorization can be linked into chanting, singing, and repetition. One of the greatest demonstrations of memory occurred when Aleksandr Solzhenitsyn was in a Siberian prison for six long years:

Solzhenitsyn learned that a prisoner's memory cleansed of superfluous knowledge was surprisingly capacious. He would write snatches of 12-20 lines at a time, polish them, learn them by heart and burn them. Every fiftieth and hundredth line Solzhenitsyn memorized with special care, to help him

34. C. Peter Wagner, "Changing Patterns of Ministerial Training," in *Crucial Dimensions in World Evangelization*, ed. Arthur F. Glasser (Pasadena: William Carey Library, 1976), pp. 407–08.

keep count. Once a month he recited everything he had written. If the fiftieth or hundredth lines came out wrong he
would painstakingly go over and over the lines until he had
them right.[35]

By the time Solzhenitsyn left prison he had over twelve thousand
lines committed to memory. Perhaps this standard is unrealistic
for anyone short of a genius. But I have been amazed to see the
facility for memorizing in students from developing countries.
Their minds are trained in this art from their first year of schooling. As an adjunct to literacy courses, this ability should be utilized in teaching converts about the Scriptures.

Reduction in Cost

Usually the seminary is one of the last institutions for which
the church can assume full financial responsibility. The George
Allan Theological Seminary in Bolivia found that the urban-
residence program of Bible teaching cost $90 annually per student-
subject. Contrast this to their program of extension study which
cost only $15 per student-subject.[36] This factor is of extreme im-
portance in the development of a contextualized Christianity in
the rural area.

Local Church–Seminary Interaction

The divorce of the seminary from the local church is to be
lamented. TEE offers a necessary and welcome corrective to that
situation:

> Placing theological training back in the local church has been
> a welcome by-product of some extension seminaries. In
> many cases classes are actually held on church premises.
> Seminary professors visit the churches and interact with
> church members as well as with students, keeping themselves

---

35. Philip Yancey, "Lessons from the Camps: Isolating the Human Spirit,"
Christianity Today 23.15 (4 May 1979): 25.
36. Wagner, "Changing Patterns," p. 409.

in direct touch with their thinking and attitudes. This makes them ever so much more effective as teachers.[37]

Very few Bible colleges offer "missions" as a subject. Almost no missionary training schools exist in Asia.[38] This needs to be corrected. Even in the early stages of TEE, the imperative and challenge of missions must be brought to the fore.

TEE's philosophy has been summed up well by C. Peter Wagner:

> The extension philosophy involves starting with the *person* rather than the *institution.* If a given person should be receiving ministerial training, the institution should see that he gets it, according to this new mentality. No possible alteration of the structure of the institution should be discounted which will enable more of God's chosen men to take theological studies. As the seminary or Bible school conforms to the student to be trained rather than vice-versa, it is to that degree "humanizing theological education."[39]

Thus, we see the potential of TEE for the Muslim-convert church. I do not minimize the hard work and long hours involved in setting up such a program. It is always difficult to find adequate staff. Costs, even though minimal, pose a problem. The development of a suitable curriculum is a huge obstacle. Each church and mission must determine priorities. If TEE is a top-level need, then other items, legitimate though they may be, must take second place.

In the fall of 1973, the North Africa Mission launched a TEE program for their Muslim-convert church. This is one emerging example of using this form of Bible education in a small church in a predominantly Muslim society. Initial results have been encouraging.

37. Ibid., p. 410.
38. James Wong, Peter Larson, and Edward Pentecost, "Missions from the Third World," in *Crucial Dimensions in World Evangelization*, ed. Arthur F. Glasser (Pasadena: William Carey Library, 1976), p. 388.
39. Wagner, "Changing Patterns," pp. 404–05.

CHAPTER 8

Problematic Christian Practices

Social Action

Problems in the Present Approach

All too frequently the following account is typical of a convert's pilgrimage.

> Halim Ali is a young man of nineteen, dissatisfied with life on the farm. He lives in a small bamboo hut with an extended family of parents, five brothers and sisters, two grandparents, one uncle, two widowed aunts. Halim's assigned task is to stand on a wooden plow behind a sickly ox and work the family plot through the long, hot summer days.
>
> One evening a tall, white-faced man briefly stops by Halim's home and leaves a packet of Christian tracts. The local teacher is brought in to read this literature to the illiterate Ali family. Interest is sparked in Halim's impressionable young mind, so he walks five miles to the town where the mission compound is located. There he is overawed by the sight of a large clinic, industrial training center, experimental farm, elementary school, and two beautiful homes (by relative standards) in which the missionaries reside.

Halim shares his desire to become a Christian with local believers. Food and shelter are provided while he undertakes a thorough catechism, which leads him to accept Christ as his Saviour. Soon thereafter he returns to his home and family where he proudly announces to all that he has become a Christian. Reaction is immediate and severe. Halim is regarded as a traitor to family, friends, country, and religion. The options are recant—or flee.

Soon thereafter Halim reappears at the doorstep of the missionary with his tale of persecution and rejection. Within six months he is baptized and given a new name. One year later Halim marries a Christian girl and completes his mission-sponsored teacher's training course. Consider perspectives:

The *missionary* rejoices that a brand has been plucked from the flaming fire; the *home church* in the U.S.A. enthusiastically adopts the support of this courageous young man who has "forsaken all" for his faith; the *villagers* symbolically bury an old pair of Halim's sandals in retribution against a despicable outcaste who dared to reject all societal norms and accepted a foreigner's religion where adherents eat filthy pig meat and worship three gods. Alienation is total.[1]

Not only do scenarios of this type impede church growth, they are terribly offensive to the Muslim. A former prime minister of Indonesia was a guest speaker at a "World of Islam Conference" in 1976. In the course of his speech he admitted the economic needs of developing Muslim nations. He decried the fact that many witnessing Christians are going to Islamic countries under the guise of being "doctors, engineers, nurses, and ordinary people." He stated that it was their aim to build friendship which would lead to the conversion of local Muslims. He spoke of this activity as "very dangerous" and went on to say that it is easier to counter Communists than missionaries because "the Communists have made all kinds of promises, but we cannot see anything they promise come to fruit; however, the missionaries pay cash and everybody sees results and thinks they are wonderful."

    1. Phil Parshall, "Evangelizing Muslims: Are There Ways?" *Christianity To-day* 23.7 (5 January 1979): 28–29.

In one Muslim country a seminar took place in which Muslim speakers complained about several foreign volunteer organizations which took advantage of poverty to induce people to change their religion.[2] Regardless of the truth or falsity of such a charge, the main consideration is how orthodox Muslims *perceive* Christian social activities.

A broad range of missionary and other Christian agencies have replied to these accusations, focusing their attention upon the Christian obligation to those who are entrapped in a system of poverty from which there appears to be no way of escape. All dehumanizing influences are antithetical to the liberating Good News of the gospel of Jesus Christ. The Christian must involve himself in structures that allow a ray of hope to pierce the deep gloom of hurt and despair that often engulfs the Muslim peasant.

The tension between evangelism and social concern has been well articulated in a statement in an article by Robert Pickett and Rufino Macagba:

> Nothing has been more misunderstood by Muslims than the biblical concept of the gospel meaning God's concern for the whole man. How many times we have had to face the charges that we "use" any physical, medical, and educational inducements to try to "make" Christians out of unfortunate Muslims. . . . No matter what Muslims, Christians or anyone may say, we believe that God's good news in Jesus Christ is meant to be for the whole man—his physical, psychological and spiritual needs. We do believe that the old polarization between the evangelistic concerns versus the social concerns hurts people.[3]

Johannes Verkuyl, in his introduction to missiology, emphasizes that "God calls His messianic people to wage war against sickness and every form of psychic disorder with every weapon in

2. "The Mosque Should Be Used as the Centre of Community Service," *Dainik Bangla*, 1 August 1977, p. 1.

3. Robert C. Pickett and Rufino L. Macagba, Jr., "Food and Health as Partners of Muslim Evangelism," in *The Gospel and Islam: A 1978 Compendium*, ed. Don M. McCurry (Monrovia, CA: MARC, 1979), p. 553.

its arsenal. Hence, the call to mission includes an appeal to engage in social and medical work."[4] Waldron Scott, general secretary of the World Evangelical Fellowship, tells of recently returning from Rhodesia

> where missionaries [who] admirably identify with the local people in terms of housing, food, dress, etc., are nevertheless trying to relate the gospel to almost everything except the one thing 94 percent of the people of Rhodesia want more desperately than anything else: the power to determine their own destinies.[5]

Peter Dyck, writing from a Mennonite perspective, reinforces the view that spiritual manipulation through social assistance is unacceptable:

> People want to be accepted as they are, to be confirmed in their beings. Each in his own idiom is crying for identity, longing for fulfillment and true selfhood. Jesus fully recognized and satisfied this basic need. Nor did he ever take advantage of their helplessness. Service that recognizes the worth and dignity of a person will never stoop to exploit another, least of all for the sake of winning him to Christ. It is simply another case of ends not justifying means.[6]

It would be convenient to end this discussion at this point. Christian responsibility involves praxis; that is, biblical truth must lead to action. The believer must be involved in alleviating hurt and poverty—wherever they may be found. However, pragmatic realities render such a view oversimplistic. Other considerations come into play.

Missions, in early days, went out from colonizing countries to Muslim lands where economic development was not advanced.

---

4. Johannes Verkuyl, *Contemporary Missiology: An Introduction*, trans. Dale Cooper (Grand Rapids: Wm. B. Eerdmans, 1978), p. 202.

5. Waldron Scott, in a personal letter to the author, 26 December 1978.

6. Peter Dyck, "A Theology of Service," *Mennonite Quarterly Review* 44.3 (July 1970): 272.

Simple compassion called for the sharing of the good things of life. In these situations missionaries had problems that did not confront Paul in the first century. Paul went to cultures more technologically advanced than his own. He felt under no obligation to offer educational or medical services to the citizens of Ephesus or Corinth.

Missionaries today still flow largely from wealthy communities to poor communities. This tension creates innumerable problems in the communication of the gospel. Many mission societies still hire national workers to evangelize the unreached. These men know their culture, are expert in the local language, can survive on a minimal salary, and are extremely mobile. But the credibility gap that exists between their life and message is often severe. The non-Christian tends to regard such "agents" merely as paid employees of the foreigner. They have no more status than a medicine salesman. Preaching is looked upon as a profession, not a passion for which no sacrifice is too great. It is all too easy for the Muslim to sneer at and ridicule such paid evangelists.

The problem extends to the local church. There is little motivation to give when there is subtle assurance that the mission will supply all needs. Why, then, should a convert receiving a salary of forty dollars per month sacrificially give to the church?

A New Model

A basic presupposition underlying the model presented here is the existence of, at minimum, one small cluster of Muslim converts organized into an informal church. It is necessary for these families to be living in fairly close proximity to one another. This "ideal" (the Muslim-convert church) can be realized only by tenaciously refusing to capitulate to the old method of "conversion and extraction." If a Muslim becomes a believer, he should be urged to witness quietly and carefully to his friends and family. If necessary, he may have to share his faith more by deed than by word. There is no option to flee if the situation becomes difficult.

A mighty volume of prayer must be raised for this one to multiply to at least ten.

Donald McGavran wrote perceptively on this subject to all missionaries ministering in one Muslim country.

> The cruel dilemma will not really be solved till thousands in groups have been baptized. When that happens, then the sheer numbers involved and the fact that they see the missionary so seldom, guarantee—a) that they will continue on in their ancestral ways and be reasonably well fed while doing it; and b) that the spiritual meaning of becoming Christian will have a chance to shine through. When converts come one by one against the family, it is very difficult for the spiritual blessings of Christian faith to shine forth above the material blessings which compassionate Christians (nationals and Westerners) naturally give.[7]

In dealing with the realities of Muslim evangelism, I would encourage Christian workers to put our new model into operation long before thousands have come to Christ. This plan can be practically implemented with even a small group.

Another requirement of our new model is that there be a Christian social agency within the country. In most areas of great need, there is at least one such organization. If not, then a group of Christians could initiate an invitation to a concerned evangelical agency to fill the gap.

What follows represents the new approach. The missionary agency sends out personnel who are trained and funded to engage in evangelism. They have expertise in missiological methodology, are enthusiastic to give themselves wholly to the task, and refrain from all forms of institutional involvement. A parallel, though independent, Christian social service agency is also established. The staff of this group is trained for ministries in areas such as medicine, education (including the teaching of handicrafts and industrial arts), running orphanages, and child care. These dedicated

7. Donald A. McGavran, in a personal letter to the author, 4 October 1977.

believers have the complete focus of their attention riveted on alleviating physical need. Usually the Muslim government is happy to have such agencies in their country (especially if the field workers are nationals). Their work is performed in Christ's name, but does not have an overtly evangelistic flavor about it.

Together, these two groups combine to effect a ministry to the total man. Each group does its work in the name of the Lord, and each is staffed by evangelical Christians. However, they hold to their specialties. The missionary refrains from involving himself in dispensing aid. The social worker emphasizes his commitment to the needs of the body. Informally, the missionary can offer counsel to the social workers, but he does not directly work with them.

How does this work out practically? Let us suppose that in a specific village there is a small group of converts surrounded by a sea of Muslims. The normal pattern for any individual convert in need of help has been to go directly to the foreign missionary. In the new situation, the convert knows that his only assistance will come from native Christian neighbors. It would be carefully explained to all concerned that by this method Christianity will gain high credibility among the surrounding community. The Muslims must see Christian love in action—from people who have the same color of skin and speak the same language. Foreign help in this situation of individual need would speak to Muslims of a vested interest. The societal pattern for generations has dictated that help come from family or neighbors. It is up to the Christians to continue this precedent.

But what would happen in case the need for help is so great that the native Christian community cannot fill it? For example, what if a natural disaster, such as a cyclone, caused widespread damage among both the Christian and Muslim population of a village? Normally, the missionary would mobilize relief efforts and move into the area with assistance, giving first to the Christians, but also to the Muslim community. Again, the fact that the financial assistance is of foreign origin becomes prominent.

In the new approach under consideration, the missionary would go immediately to the Christian social agency and request their help for the afflicted village. The agency would then respond with their expertise and resources. The assistance would be given equally to Muslims and Christians, all in Christ's name, but without the stigma of evangelistic emphasis. The foreign character of the assistance would be minimized as the field workers of the agency would all be nationals. The Christians would be told of the missionary's concern and how he had immediately contacted the agency in behalf of them and their Muslim neighbors. It is hoped that such a procedure would not be necessary very often.

The service agency also might supervise and fund other types of assistance for the people. This assistance would be open to all and Christians would receive no special preference.

In a village setting, a recent Muslim convert came to the home of a young Western missionary and requested warm clothes for his children. The cool night air and the shabbiness of the believer's own clothes confirmed the need. Immediately, the missionary realized he was being pushed into a no-win situation. If he consented, he knew all the Muslims in the village would say the convert became a believer only for financial gain. This would mean the end of a witness that was only in its initial stages. If the missionary refused, he would do so at the risk of totally alienating the convert.

After a quick prayer for guidance, the missionary explained the reasons he could not give the clothes. He then went on to promise to fast and pray for thirty-six hours that the Lord would provide for the needs of the children. He would express his empathy with the situation by means of self-deprivation. The convert went to his home and returned four days later. His face was beaming as he told the missionary that God had provided the clothes. This new believer in Christ had learned an unforgettable lesson of vertical rather than horizontal dependence. He went on to win many of his Muslim neighbors to Christ and is today the acknowledged leader of a small, but dynamic, assembly of convert believers.

It is recognized that the proposals in this section need a great deal more experimentation before they can be put into full operation. However, any type of innovative effort needs a first step.

There are many arguments, many of them legitimate, that can be mustered in opposition to any plan that disturbs the status quo. One is the Scripture which exhorts Christians to do good to the household of faith (Gal. 6:10). My response is: in the long run, what really is good for them? Will foreign money actually contribute to the spiritual maturity of the converts? The future has often been sacrificed by an immediate action that we interpreted to be right.

Another problem relates to Muslim countries where the only way a Christian can enter is through a social-service type of ministry. The door is closed to evangelistic missionaries. In that case, it is necessary to take maximum advantage of any possible opportunity of entry and witness, even if that means a restricted type of "presence evangelism." There must be flexibility as well as a lack of dogmatism in these vital areas.

In many Muslim lands, the missionary has an open door to work in a virgin territory without past precedents hanging as a millstone about his neck. A courageous and innovative approach in the area of contextualized finances could very well mean the difference between building on a foundation of rock or a foundation of sand.

Baptism

Problems with Traditional Forms

What does the Christian rite of baptism as practiced within an Islamic country convey to the onlooking Muslims? The ceremony is seemingly harmless. A group of Christians gather together at a pond or river with a young Muslim who has recently professed faith in Christ as Lord and Savior. After a few songs are reverently sung, the national pastor either sprinkles a bit of water over the head of the convert or totally immerses him. There is no coercion or force. Nothing antistate or anticulture has been verbally communicated. Yet, the impact of this simple initiation rite is very weighty.

Implications of this ceremony reverberate throughout nearby villages and towns. Abdul Muhammad has openly declared himself a traitor to Islamic social structures, political and legal systems, economic patterns; and, worst of all, the religion of his fathers has been profaned and desecrated. He has now become a worshiper of three gods, a follower of a corrupted religious book, an eater of pork, a drinker of wine, and a member of an alien society of warmongers and adulterers. This Muslim societal perception of Christian baptism is not isolated or localized. In talking to missionaries who minister throughout the Islamic world, I find this caricature of baptism is nearly universal.

There is, unfortunately, just enough semblance of truth in these accusations to render them almost impregnable. Individual baptisms of Muslim converts have almost always led to exclusion from one's own native society and inclusion in a foreign-influenced Christian community. Identification with an alien way of life further provokes the Muslim onlooker because he has come to regard Christian culture as degraded. Locally available Western novels and sexy films have served to foster this belief.

In October, 1978, the North American Conference on Muslim Evangelization took place in Colorado Springs, Colorado. Over 150 delegates from a score of different countries were present. Anthropologists, experts on Islam, mission executives, missionaries, and professors of missions were in attendance. I took advantage of this opportunity to have eleven persons fill in a questionnaire for me on the subject of contextualized baptism (see Appendix, p. 257). These eleven people had worked at some time in Pakistan, Turkey, Lebanon, Egypt, Cyprus, Israel, Jordan, India, Afghanistan, Morocco, Algeria, France, Saudi Arabia, and Bangladesh. Their combined time working among Muslims totaled 158 years.

There was unanimous agreement that baptism is one of the largest problems confronted in evangelism among Muslims. In each country the true biblical meaning of baptism was not properly understood. Problems noted with regard to traditional baptism forms were that they lead to alienation and are viewed as indicative of a change in identity or even treason. In addition, the different modes of baptism create confusion in the minds of Muslims.

With one exception, secret baptism with only a few Christians present was regarded as acceptable. The Ethiopian eunuch was cited as a New Testament example. One person felt the family and friends of the convert should be present. Baptism in a distant place was generally agreed to be suitable if necessary.

Self-baptism was more controversial. Five were adamantly opposed, while three agreed with serious reservations. One person felt self-baptism fails to depict the "body celebration." Several said it is not biblical and also fails to present a testimony to new life in Christ. Two found the practice acceptable, with one pointing out it was a practice in the Old Testament when proselytes were accepted into the Jewish community.

The overwhelming response to the suggestion that under extreme circumstances baptism might be forgone was negative. A few pointed out that delay is acceptable, but that omission of this command of Christ is unacceptable. Only one person disagreed.

Various comments on the possibility of some type of baptismal substitution or variation included:

It must show the death and resurrection of Jesus.
Stick to what the evangelical church does.
I am barely open to it.
Yes, substitute something that doesn't cause discrimination.
I hesitate to change what is clear in Scripture and was practiced by Jesus and the apostles.
Baptism has universally included water and should be given weight.

Overall, these observations are probably quite representative of missionary thinking. There is a recognition of the problem, but there is a hesitancy to move away from what is regarded as biblically normative.

Possible Variations

Delayed Baptism

Kenneth Cragg, in his *Call of the Minaret,* proposes a delay in the baptism of converts until such time as a larger number from one area can be baptized together. He agrees that "the theological truth about the final place and necessity of baptism must be recognized and upheld."[8] Cragg argues for an intermediate status for converts between conversion and baptism in which the believer could be known as a "lover of Jesus."

> It may be argued that this will be jeopardizing the disciple's own chances of growing in what he has found and of finding it further. In answer, it is said that any such pioneer status, not yet baptized, should have the fullest fellowship and spiritual support of the Church. It will demand qualities no less tenacious than those which characterize the finally baptized. It is offered as something to which the Church must encourage new seekers and in which it must stand with them, as a creative venture. The Church must be ready to think out and sustain in prayer and fellowship all the implications of the new status. What is believed is that "Lovers of Jesus," or a fellowship under some other designation, may go further in preparing Christ's way among Muslims than would the same people promptly and singly baptized into a fellowship still largely alien, not of Muslim background, and set (by one initial transaction) out of reach of the Muslim mind.[9]

There can be little argument against the wisdom of delayed baptism in certain situations. The key question relates to the length of delay. So, in balance, it can be said there is general agreement on this variation from the New Testament norm wherein the convert is almost always seen to be baptized immediately upon profession of faith in Christ.

8. Kenneth Cragg, *The Call of the Minaret* (New York: Oxford University Press, 1956), p. 350.
9. Ibid., p. 349.

Secret Baptism

In Scripture, we have records of secret believers (e.g., John 3:2; 19:39). These are persons who have put their faith in Jesus, but have, for social or political reasons, hesitated to publicly declare themselves as Christians. Perhaps this is analogous to the Muslim who goes off quietly to a distant city to be baptized. This convert will still face a problem when Muslim friends and neighbors ask, "Are you a baptized Christian?"

Many missionaries protest that a secret ceremony violates the command to witness. To this, two replies may be given. First, there will be a witness presented by the convert to the believers in attendance at the baptism in the distant city. Second, the Bible doesn't directly link profession and witness to baptism. This can be given prior to or following the ceremony.

Of course, no one would declare anything esoteric as the Christian ideal. Believers are people of the light. Secret baptism should be reserved for difficult situations.

Self-baptism

Few arguments can be advanced from Scripture to support self-baptism. One line of reasoning has developed from the fact that the purification rites of the Old Testament were self-administered in many instances.[10] Some scholars have questioned how three thousand persons could be baptized in one day if they did not baptize themselves. That must remain as an argument from silence. From historical writings (though not from Scripture) we know that the proselyte converts to Judaism went into the water and submerged themselves.

Recently a Muslim convert was convinced from his Bible study that water baptism is a command of Jesus Christ. He detected a hesitation on the part of the missionaries to arrange for his baptism. One day, after completing his bath in the river, he quietly said, "I now baptize myself in response to the command of Jesus Christ." He then submerged his body under the water.

10. *A Dictionary of the Bible*, ed. James Hastings (New York: Charles Scribner's Sons, 1951), vol. 1, p. 238.

Within a few weeks, this believer went on to baptize two other converts from the area. The missionaries have accepted this believer's baptism as legitimate.

A similar situation occurred when Bilquis Sheikh decided it was God's will to baptize herself:

> I walked into the bathroom and stepped into the deep tub. As I sat down, water rose almost to my shoulder. I placed my hand on my own head and said loudly, "Bilquis, I baptize you in the name of the Father and of the Son and of the Holy Ghost." I pressed my head down into the water so that my whole body was totally immersed. I arose from the water rejoicing, calling out, and praising God. "Oh Father, thank you. I'm so fortunate."[11]

Such baptism does not follow the biblical norm nor satisfy the injunction to witness. However, when it is accompanied by such spontaneity as just described, its validity should not be denied.

Initiation Ceremonies

Bar mitzvah is a ceremony in which a thirteen-year-old boy becomes an adult member of the Jewish community. From this age, the boy becomes responsible for his actions and is considered an adult in all respects.[12] He can now publicly read the Torah and wear the tefillin. In actual practice, however, he doesn't lead in adult worship until the age of eighteen or twenty.[13] Following the religious ceremony wherein the young boy reads from the Law, there is a joyous social occasion with a feast for family and friends.[14] This rite of passage has great social and religious significance in the Jewish community.

11. Bilquis Sheikh, *I Dared to Call Him Father* (Waco, TX: Chosen Books, 1978), p. 71.

12. Philip Birnbaum, *A Book of Jewish Concepts* (New York: Hebrew Publishing Company, 1964), p. 94.

13. Harry A. Cohen, *A Basic Jewish Encyclopedia* (Hartford: Hartmore House, 1965), p. 109.

14. *The Encyclopedia of the Jewish Religion*, ed. R. J. Werblowsky and G. Wigoder (New York: Holt, Rinehart and Winston, 1965), p. 57.

Confirmation is practiced in a number of Christian denominations. I was confirmed in the Episcopal Church in 1950 in Tampa, Florida, at the age of twelve. There was a period of instruction and required memorization. On the appointed day, I, along with several other boys, made my public profession of Christ in the cathedral. The bishop, dressed in regal robes, laid his hands on my head and said a prayer for my spiritual well-being. These two somewhat similar services may be regarded as ceremonies of initiation. Both assume commitment, witness, and accountability.

In view of the fact that baptism is so misunderstood in Muslim lands, would it be feasible to construct a functional substitute for baptism that would retain the biblical meaning, but change the form? This ceremony would take place upon one's profession of faith in Jesus Christ. It would be preceded by a time of specific instruction concerning conversion and holiness. This very special service would be attended by believers who would pledge their love and loyalty to the new member of the body. The spiritual leader may or may not lay hands on the one being initiated. (The laying on of hands may cause confusion in regard to other contexts in Scripture where hands are laid on believers.)

Such a ceremony of initiation would retain the scriptural *meaning* of baptism and reduce offense to the onlooking Muslim community. The theological implications of such a departure from the universal biblical practice of water baptism should be thoroughly investigated. While not personally advocating such a position, I would be interested in seeing further research done in this general area.

In 1976, Larry Snider attended an orthodox Muslim mosque in Chicago during the Friday noon worship period. On this occasion a Black American was formally being accepted into the Islamic faith. She had been a Roman Catholic. During the service a Muslim lady read a portion of the Quran which the Catholic convert repeated. Then, in English, she publicly affirmed her faith and commitment to the religion of Islam.[15] A similar service accepting

15. Larry Snider, in a personal interview with the author, 20 November 1978.

Muslim converts into Christianity would perhaps be understood by Muslims as more of a religious experience than an act of social and cultural alienation.

Warren Webster, general director of the Conservative Baptist Foreign Mission Society, comments regarding adaptation of *form:*

> It is the *meaning* of baptism (or its functional substitute) as a "rite of passage" from Islam and initiation into the community of believers who look to Christ rather than to Mohammed for salvation which is the crucial issue. The problem will not be escaped by modifying the rite as long as the meaning remains. Theologically to become a "follower of Isa" in any biblical sense still involves the offense of the incarnation and the offense of the cross and they are not set aside by removing the supposed offense of baptism as an outer symbol of having accepted the other offenses in the process of becoming a new creature in Christ.[16]

Granted, the offense of the cross must remain. This book is dedicated to the formulation of a contextualized Christianity that in no way disturbs basic biblical truth. On the other hand, I am seeking to explore areas where legitimate changes can be introduced to minimize offense to the Muslim. Is it possible for baptism to be one of those areas?

The Imperative of Sensitivity

Baptism, by its nature and practice, has always been in the center of a whirlwind of controversy. The major issues have not been resolved in spite of prolific writers and long-winded expositors! The only reconciliation between divergent views among evangelicals has been humble and loving acceptance of diversity in the body.

It is my view that this loving acceptance can and should extend to the communication of the gospel to Islam; misunderstand-

16. Warren W. Webster, in a personal letter to the author, 17 January 1979.

ings on the part of Muslims must be reduced. We also need to extend that love to new converts who, after prayer, practice baptism in a form that may be personally unacceptable to us. We must trust the Holy Spirit to be active in the lives of the emerging body of Christ. Can we not humbly acknowledge that in all of our sophisticated intellectual prowess, we may not, after all, possess any greater grasp of truth than the unsophisticated illiterate who sincerely quests for Jesus Christ with all his heart?

> We shall know by this that we are of the truth, and shall assure our heart before Him, in whatever our heart condemns us; for God is greater than our heart, and knows all things. Beloved, if our heart does not condemn us, we have confidence before God. (I John 3:19–21)

CHAPTER 9

Muslim
Religious Rituals

Missionaries have generally rejected the convert's continued use of Islamic worship forms, contending that such practices are the external identification of a false religious system. They have strongly advocated a total break with all that is Islamic. This polarized view is now being questioned. An anonymous writer puts forth his opinion rather strongly:

> Very often I felt missionaries in non-Arabic speaking countries working with Muslims were afraid of Arabic forms of worship. I think really they don't understand them and thus it is more of a fear of the unknown. Often, even missionaries working in Arabic countries who speak excellent Arabic, hardly know anything about Arabic worship. They have never studied the Arabic Quran. They have never really sat down and listened to Islamic services. . . . I felt like I had to become more or less incarnate in Islam, not completely, but in a new way for me. I went on and learned the entire Islamic prayer ritual. I found my love towards Muslims greatly increased. I found a new compassion, a new ability to be in their company. A lot of fear that I had about the unknown in the Islamic worship services ceased.

This chapter seeks to explore the possibility of a modified use of Muslim rituals in true and uncompromising worship of Jesus Christ.

Prayer

There is no religion without prayer. From earliest time, man has called upon a superior being. Novalis wrote that "prayer is to religion what thought is to philosophy."[1] Islam has placed prayer in the very center of its theological and practical emphases. Consider these comments on prayer by a Muslim author:

> All sincere prayer brings us nearer to God, which is the ultimate object, and there is an answer, though the answer may not, in God's Wisdom and Mercy, be manifested as we, in our haste and ignorance or in the stress of grief or emotion, may desire. . . . It may be thought that five services daily is a little too much and may become burdensome. In fact that is not so. It is a matter of comparative values. All five services taken together do not take up more than about two hours—no more time than a person in the West is apt to spend watching television. In the eyes of a Muslim, a diversion such as television has little value, whereas participation in congregational worship is nutriment for the soul.[2]

The *salat* or ritual prayer is an essential obligation of Muslim worship. The Quran places maximum importance on this prayer, which is preceded by the call from the minaret of the mosque:

> God is most great. I testify that there is no god but God. I testify that Mohammed is the apostle of God. Come to prayer. Come to prosperity. God is most great. There is no god but God.[3]

1. Quoted in Samuel M. Zwemer, *Taking Hold of God* (Grand Rapids: Zondervan, 1936), p. 13.
2. Muhammad Zafrulla Khan, *Islam: Its Meaning for Modern Man* (New York: Harper and Row, 1962), pp. 101–03.
3. Quoted in Samuel M. Zwemer, *The Moslem World* (Philadelphia: The American Baptist Publication Society, 1907), p. 72.

These five prescribed prayers are to be said daily at dawn, soon after midday, during midafternoon, soon after sunset, and after nightfall. They must be preceded by the necessary ritual ablutions. Surah 5:8–9 describes this act of cleansing: "When ye stand up for prayer, wash your faces and your hands up to the elbows, and wipe your heads and your feet up to the ankles. . . . If ye be sick or on a journey. . .and do not find water, sand your-selves with dry good sand, and rub your faces and your hands with it." The Muslim also must always face toward Mecca when praying.

The prayer ritual consists of seven specific actions: (1) the recitation of the phrase *Allahu akbar* ("God is great") with hands open on each side of the face; (2) a recitation from the Quran while one stands upright; (3) bowing from the hips; (4) standing erect again; (5) sliding to the knees and prostrating with the face to the ground; (6) sitting back on the haunches; (7) a second prostra-tion. At the end of each pair of bowings and at the conclusion of the whole prayer the worshiper recites the *Shahada* and the ritual salutations.[4]

A meaningful time of private intercession may follow the set ritual of the *salat*. The worshiper can then pray for personal needs or can intercede with Allah on behalf of others. A very beautiful gesture marks the conclusion of the prayer. Raising his hands as high as his shoulders with palms upturned to heaven, the wor-shiper offers a final supplication, either in Arabic or in his own words, and then draws his hands over his face and onto his breast as if to convey the blessing received to every part of his body.[5]

One of the concluding prayers is often, "O God! have mercy on Muhammad and on his descendants, as Thou didst have mercy on Abraham and on his descendants. Thou art to be praised and Thou art great."[6]

In light of the centrality of the acts and forms of prayer in

4. G. E. Von Grunebaum, *Islam* (London: Routledge and Kegan Paul, 1909), p. 10.
5. L. Bevan Jones, *The People of the Mosque* (Calcutta: YMCA Publishing House, 1939), p. 118.
6. Ibid., p. 117.

Islam, rethinking their own practices of petition is imperative for Christians who witness to Muslims. Are their prayers biblical? Are they practical? Are they an offense to Muslims?

Prayer in the Old and New Testaments is generally accompanied by some kind of posture or gesture. The usual form was that of bowing down low, as the Oriental does in deference to a superior. The Hebrew words "he prostrated himself" are usually rendered "he worshiped." Ezekiel fell on his face when he saw the glory of the Lord (Ezek. 3:23; 9:8). Jesus took the same position in Gethsemane. Daniel, Stephen, Peter, and Paul knelt in prayer. Only in David's prayer of gratitude (II Sam. 7:18) is sitting mentioned as a biblical posture of prayer. This was an exception.

The contemporary Western Christian sits casually in a chair and listens while someone else leads in prayer. Frequently it seems that a comfortable posture is a prerequisite for talking to God. Often there is little sense of awe or depth of worship in the content of evangelical prayers.

There are great similarities in the prayers of the two religious communities, but there is a basic clash. A great God is the focus of both Muslims and Christians. However, Christ is central for Christians in any approach to God. Muhammad is not as prominent in Muslim prayers, but he is still accorded honor and extreme reverence.

With certain key alterations or substitutions, the Muslim convert can continue in the familiar pattern of prayer which is valued both by him and by his Islamic society. Washing before prayer could be continued, provided that it be explained that the ritual earns no merit. Muhammad would be omitted from prayers. The focus would be on the reality of talking to a personal, loving God reached through the merits of the death and resurrection of the God-man Jesus Christ.

An illustration of contextualized prayer for Muslim converts comes from a description of a meeting conducted by a Coptic pastor in Egypt:

> Many lifted their hands in prayer. Praying was never done sitting down. The pastor had the congregation stand, then he

prayed facing the same way as the people. One felt the congregation united with him by audible expression, and with upraised hands.[7]

In the Old Testament lifting up of the hands toward heaven accompanied kneeling or standing (cf. Exod. 9:29; I Kings 8:22; II Chron. 6:13). This practice was so common that it became a synonym for prayer in Psalm 141:2, "May my prayer be counted as incense before Thee; the lifting up of my hands as the evening offering." We infer that eyes were open during prayer from the statement that the publican would not "lift up his eyes to heaven" (Luke 18:13), and from the practice of Jesus Himself in looking up to heaven as He prayed (Mark 6:41; 7:34). The Bible does not speak of praying with eyes closed.[8]

An example of facing in a certain direction while praying is found in the exhortation of Solomon to the Jews at the time of the dedication of the temple:

> That Thine eyes may be open toward this house night and day, toward the place of which Thou hast said, "My name shall be there," to listen to the prayer which Thy servant shall pray toward this place. And listen to the supplication of Thy servant and of Thy people Israel, when they pray toward this place; hear Thou in heaven Thy dwelling place; hear and forgive. (I Kings 8:29–30)

Another illustration of facing in a certain direction as well as ritually praying three times a day is found in the testimony of Daniel given during his time in captivity:

> Now when Daniel knew that the document was signed, he entered his house (now in his roof chamber he had windows open toward Jerusalem); and he continued kneeling on his

---

7. Bashir Abdol Massih, "The Incarnational Witness to the Muslim Heart," in *The Gospel and Islam: A 1978 Compendium*, ed. Don M. McCurry (Monrovia, CA: MARC, 1979), p. 8.

8. Zwemer, *Taking Hold of God*, pp. 42–45.

knees three times a day, praying and giving thanks before his
God, as he had been doing previously. (Dan. 6:10)

As has been pointed out in earlier chapters, the Islamic
world-view and religious ritual have a close correlation with the
Old Testament and Hebrew way of life. Muslims stand, bow, and
prostrate themselves in prayer. They lift up their hands and leave
their eyes open during intercession. Prayer is performed five times
a day, always in the direction of Mecca. In content, prayer is a
time of worship, praise, adoration, and petition.

An unknown convert from Islam proposed the use of Scripture within the prayer ritual:

> A catechism can be developed where Bible verses are recited
> at appropriate times during prayer. Verses which comment
> on standing, kneeling, bowing and prayer with uplifted
> hands can be spoken by the worshiper as he makes each
> change in position. This would give prayer a biblical flavor
> rather than being a carbon copy of Western cultural forms.

Whatever form is adopted, it is important to emphasize
prayer in the convert church. Muslims must realize that Christians
are serious about prayer. Christians should not be hesitant to be
very public in prayer. If the heart is right with God, then there is
nothing wrong with a high-profile expression of prayer worship.

Religious Chanting and Music

The Quran is a book that Muslims believe should be read,
recited, and chanted. The *Shahada* or creed of Islam is a succinct
statement of belief that reduces the essence of the Quran to a few
brief words. It probably has more power over its adherents than
any other formal creed that has ever been articulated by man.
La-ilaha-illa-'llahu; Muhammadu-Rasulu-'allah, when translated from
Arabic to English, becomes, "There is no god but God; Muhammad is the apostle of God." This creed is the watchword of Islam.
These words are inscribed on banners and doorposts. They appear

on all the early coins of the caliphs. The *Shahada* is heard in the bazaar, in the street, and in the mosque. It is a battle cry and a cradlesong, an exclamation of delight and a funeral dirge. Samuel Zwemer says, "There is no doubt that this continual public repetition of a creed has been a source of strength to Islam for ages, as well as a stimulus to fanaticism."[9]

The chanting of the Arabic Quran is an imperative act of worship for every Muslim. It is generally a group activity.

> Faith is internalized through rhythmic recitation or chanting. For an Arab, the sound of the Quran recited in proper rhythm is like listening to one's own heartbeat. When the Quran is read aloud or recited, whether it be strange syntax or repellent content, the listener is able to incorporate within himself the Word of God and make it an inalienable part of his personality.[10]

Frequently, great emotion accompanies the chanting of the Quran. "It is not surprising, then, that a skilled reciter of the Quran can reduce an Arabic-speaking audience to helpless tears."[11] Geoffrey Parrinder observes that "the ninety-nine Beautiful Names of God are recited on prayer beads and the chanting, with physical movement and breathing techniques, may lead to trance states and ecstasy."[12]

In a Muslim country the people are often observed reciting or reading the Quran as they travel. In sickness, the Quran is the Muslim's comfort. Friends and relatives will enter the patient's room and recite the *Fatiha* and the Throne verse. In Cairo there is a daily radio program that consists of two half-hour recitations of the Quran. The words drift out into the street, home, café, and the

9. Samuel M. Zwemer, *Islam: A Challenge to Faith* (New York: Student Volunteer Movement for Foreign Missions, 1907), p. 102.

10. Krikor Haleblian, "World View and Evangelization: A Case Study on Arab People" (Th.M. thesis, Fuller Theological Seminary, 1979), pp. 87–88.

11. John Alden Williams, ed., *Islam* (New York: George Braziller, 1961), p. 16.

12. Geoffrey Parrinder, *Religion in Africa* (New York: Praeger, 1969), p. 217.

hospital, calling all men to consider the very words of Allah. The faithful Muslim listens with rapt attention, sometimes with loud pious ejaculations.[13] Seyyed Hossein Nasr, a Muslim author, writes of the mysterious blessing derived from the Quran: "The efficacy of canonical prayers, litanies, invocations, etc. is contained not only in the content but also in the very sounds and reverberations of the sacred language."[14]

I have personally observed many of the phenomena just described. Muslims enter into the chanting with great delight and personal satisfaction. At times, I have even heard an entire sermon chanted.

Can this form be utilized by Christians? Should converts retain chanting or should it be discarded as an irrelevant and undesirable component of their new faith in Christ?

> Generally speaking, a Westerner is suspicious of memorization and chanting as a means of effective communication. Since he is trained in coherent and logical thinking, it is difficult for him to accept the possibility that a person can believe without understanding. However, this must not be construed to mean that an Arab is not trained to think in a logical or systematic way. The point is rather brought up to emphasize the fact that these methods are indigenous to Islamic cultures and, therefore, a priori effective.[15]

A plea was made on behalf of evangelistic efforts in the United Arab Emirates for "expressive, poetic translations of Scripture that can be chanted so as to fully communicate to Koran-steeped Arab hearts."[16] It is my view that chanting should be utilized for the glory of God. God's Word can be powerfully communicated to the inquirer or new convert in sessions of chanting, memorization, and recitation. Careful explanation would need to

13. Alfred Guillaume, *Islam* (Baltimore: Penguin Books, 1954), pp. 74–75.
14. Seyyed Hossein Nasr, *Ideals and Realities of Islam* (London: George Allen and Unwin, 1966), p. 47.
15. Haleblian, "World View," p. 88.
16. C. Peter Wagner and Edward Dayton, *Unreached Peoples '79* (Elgin, IL: David C. Cook, 1978), p. 221.

be given in order that the convert fully understands there is no merit connected with the form of communication. It is only as the Word is applied to the heart that spiritual benefits will be reaped.

"Though music is banned, there is in the reading, or rather chanting, of their sacred book something that supplies the place of music for the Muslim."[17] There is no singing nor playing of instruments allowed in the mosque. In some countries, however, songs are sung in praise of Allah and Muhammad outside of the mosque. These same tunes can be used with Christian lyrics. One evening I attended a meeting of Muslim converts. In the first part of the service they were led in the singing of songs in the vernacular but with Western tunes. Most of the men were either off-key or were starting to doze off to sleep. Much later in the evening it was suggested that indigenous tunes be sung with Christian words. All twelve of the men came alive and enthusiastically entered into the singing. It was beautiful! This was followed by the chanting of the Lord's Prayer and other Scripture.

Lest Western Christians consider contemporary Christian music as the scriptural norm, it is well to ponder church history.

> If you lived during the first 1300 years of Christendom, you would have had one choice—a man, never a woman, singing chants in Latin, a language you probably would not have understood. The next two hundred years offered little change except that instead of one man singing, now a group of men sang together forming the church choir. It was not until the 1500's that the masses were able to participate in the service with the singing of hymns in their native tongues.[18]

Still today, one hears chanting in High Episcopal, Roman Catholic, and Orthodox churches. This form can be an instrument to communicate to the heart. Flexibility is called for as this area is explored in the context of Muslim evangelism.

17. Jones, *People of the Mosque*, p. 259.
18. David German, "Church Music Has Come a Long Way," bulletin of the Highland Park Baptist Church (Southfield, Michigan), 6 May 1979.

Fasting

The ninth month of the Islamic year (Ramazan) is observed by a strict fast daily from dawn to sunset. The word *Ramazan* is derived from the word *ramz*, which means "to burn." The month is said to have been so called either because it used to occur (before the change of the calendar) in the hot season, or because the month's fast is supposed to burn away the sins of men.

Surah 2:179–184 outlines the ritual and prohibitions of the fast. An excerpt reads:

> Eat and drink until ye can discern a white thread from a black thread by the daybreak: then fast strictly till night, and go not in unto your wives, but rather pass the time in the mosques. These are the bounds set up by God.

The fast must be kept by every adult Muslim except the sick, pregnant women, and women who are nursing. Young children who have not reached the age of puberty are exempt along with travelers who are on a journey of more than three days. In the instance of a sick person or a traveler, the month's fast must be kept as soon as possible.

The fast is extremely difficult, especially when it falls in the hot summer months. (The Muslim calendar advances ten days each year.) Prohibition of drinking liquid or even of swallowing one's own saliva makes the daily fast of up to fifteen hours almost unbearable where temperatures exceed one hundred degrees.

Many devout Muslims seclude themselves for some time in the mosque during Ramazan. They abstain from all worldly conversation and spend their hours in reciting the Quran. Older men particularly follow this practice.[19]

Surah 2:184 states, "Fasting is prescribed for you as it was prescribed for those before you, so that you may attain to righteousness." Fasting is a physical, moral, and spiritual discipline. Through the experience of the fast the worshiper should be led to

19. Thomas Patrick Hughes, *A Dictionary of Islam* (London: W. H. Allen and Company, 1895), pp. 533–34.

exalt Allah for His goodness. It is definitely an act of merit. The discipline of the fast should assist the devotee to come to know God intimately. The Prophet is said to have commented, "He who abstains from food and drink during the period of fasting, but does not strive to safeguard himself against moral lapses, starves to no purpose."[20]

One other benefit of the fast is cited by Erich Bethmann:

> But whatever the conceptions and arguments are, which are brought forth to defend *Ramazan*, it does not matter. The practical results of *Ramazan* are much more important, and these are undoubtedly a close knitting together of all the followers of Islam, because nothing binds men more strongly together than privations and hardships suffered in common. Many egos with as many wills unite together in one common aim with one common goal, therewith creating a community spirit. This imparts its strength again to the individual ego, gives him a feeling of elation, and creates in him the spirit of fidelity to this community.[21]

A number of missionaries in the Muslim world have kept part or all of the *Ramazan* fast. On September 6, 1977, I decided to participate in the ritual so as to personally evaluate its effects. This twenty-four-hour experiment was totally inadequate, but it gave me at least a feel for the practice.

I was awakened by my host at 3:30 a.m. and offered a large meal of rice and fish curry. I was urged to drink three large glasses of water due to the possible harmful effects of dehydration later in the day. By 4 a.m. we had finished eating "breakfast"—which really wasn't "breaking-the-fast" but commencing it! Following this, and according to Muslim custom, we all went back to bed and slept until 6 a.m.

Around 11 a.m., my colleague and I left in a small boat for a journey of twelve miles, which took six hours. At one point, the boatman, who wasn't fasting, started smoking his pipe and blow-

20. Khan, *Islam*, p. 116.
21. Erich W. Bethman, *Bridge to Islam* (London: George Allen and Unwin, 1953), p. 52.

ing the smoke in our direction. We told him we were fasting. He immediately began to exhale the smoke in the other direction. He then asked us why we weren't praying at the stated times.

Upon arrival at our destination we went to a tin shack we had rented. Soon after 6 p.m. we walked over to a small shop and had a glass of lemon juice and a banana, thus breaking the fast. The shopowner was giving these refreshments free to all who had kept the fast. This earned merit for him. Later in the evening we had another meal of rice and fish curry. We had fasted officially from 4:20 a.m. to 6:23 p.m., a fourteen-hour-period on one of the hottest days of that particular year. That we had been inactive had contributed to making the fast easier for us. I experienced no problem with the absence of food, but abstaining from liquids was difficult. We had continued to swallow our saliva.

Should missionaries and converts keep the fast in the prescribed Muslim manner? There can be no dogmatic answer. I do feel Muslims would appreciate such a gesture of identification. However, the Christian position on fasting should be made clear. Legalism is not biblical. Fasting is not to attain righteousness but rather to create a deeper longing and hunger for God. This must be made explicit. Does becoming like a Muslim in order to win Muslims include the keeping of the fast? The prayerful missionary will research the feelings of the local community in order to discover the correct conclusion for his particular situation.

CHAPTER 10

Muslim Social Practices

Festivals

Festivals (*Ids*) are very central in Muslim society. They are a time of rejoicing which helps bring about social unity. *Qurbani Id* has been explained in Chapter 6. Other *Ids* include *Idu-L-Fitr*, *Maulidu-n-Nabi*, and *Shab-I-Barat*.

Idu-L-Fitr is also called "the festival of the breaking of the fast." It commences as soon as the month's fast of Ramazan is over. There is a significant amount of visiting from home to home.

The *Maulidu-n-Nabi* is the celebration of Prophet Muhammad's birthday. The extent of the celebration will vary among Islamic nations. Generally it is not a public holiday. Religious groups arrange special seminars on the Prophet's life. Poems are read that extol the behavior and accomplishments of Muhammad.

Shab-I-Barat is Persian for "the night of records" and is observed on the fourteenth night of the eighth month, Shaban. Muhammad is alleged to have said that annually on this night God registers in the *barat* (or record) all the actions men are to perform in the ensuing year, and that all the children of men who are to be born and to die in the year are recorded. Muhammad enjoined his followers to stay awake the whole night, to repeat certain prayers, and to fast on the next day. Frequently this night is marked more by feasting and merriment than by fasting—at least on the part of the younger people.[1]

Several observations need to be made concerning these Muslim *Ids:*

1. They are all religious in nature. People performing the rituals identify *Ids* with fasting, feasting, and almsgiving.

2. *Ids* perform a sociological function. These times of celebration are greatly anticipated by the totality of society. Nominal Muslims enter into the ritual with great zest—much as nominal Christians celebrate Christmas.

3. It is difficult for the new convert from Islam not to participate to some measure in these celebrations. There should be understanding toward those believers who feel they must ostensibly follow the dictates of Muslim society during these *Ids.*

4. The foreigner should respect Muslim celebrations. For instance, it is not considerate to eat in public during the month of fasting. It is probably wise to close offices and institutions on the major *Id* days.

5. Christmas, Good Friday, and Easter can serve as functional substitutes for Muslim religious days. These days should be celebrated in a culturally appropriate manner. The converts will want to structure the form of celebration as closely as possible to societal norms. The emphasis must be on the spiritual significance of the particular observance. I have found it rather annoying to see Santa Claus giving out gifts to Christian national children in a predominantly Muslim country.

6. In some Muslim countries, Christians are allowed to put on special Christmas and Easter radio and television programs at government expense. These should be prepared with cultural and spiritual content so as to best communicate Christ to the Muslim heart.

1. L. Bevan Jones, *The People of the Mosque* (Calcutta: YMCA Publishing House, 1939), p. 129.

Birth Customs

There are no special injunctions in the Quran regarding customs to be observed at the birth of an infant. Circumcision is found only in the Traditions.

The following practices are common among Muslims:

1. At the birth of a child he is wrapped in swaddling clothes and presented to a gathering of family and friends. A Muslim priest recites the summons to prayer in the infant's right ear. Alms are distributed to the poor. According to the Traditions, the amount of silver given in alms should be of the same weight as the hair on the child's head. Friends and neighbors visit the home and bring presents for the infant.

2. On the seventh day the sacrifice called *Aqiqa* is performed. In the case of a male, two sheep or a goat is required, but in the case of a female, one sheep or goat is required for the sacrifice. The animals must be without blemish. At the time of the sacrifice the infant's father prays, "O Allah! I offer this in the stead of my son, its blood for his blood, its flesh for his flesh, its bone for his bone, its skin for his skin, its hair for his hair. O God! I make this as a ransom for my son from the fire, in the name of Allah, Allah the Great." The animals are skinned and chopped up into three equal parts. One part is given to the midwife, one part to the poor, and the remaining third is used by the members of the household. The reasons for this ceremony have been listed by Bevan Jones.

> Muhammad is believed to have warned parents that if this ceremony is not performed God will not, at the last day, call up the child by its parent's name. Neglect of it will mean that all through life the child's "hand" will not be "good." Moreover there are positive benefits accruing therefrom. It ensures effective deliverance from all manner of misfortune in this life, and is a safeguard against the influence of Satan. The body is purified by this rite and will be found pure on the day of resurrection. The child that might have otherwise died in infancy will, after the ceremony, certainly live. Yet should it die in childhood, it will go to heaven and though its

parents might go to hell, the child's prayers to God on their behalf will gain entrance to paradise for them also.[2]

3. Considerable importance is attached to the naming of the child. It is common for the child to be given his name on the seventh day. The name may be given by the eldest male member of the family or by some pious man who recites the Quran and then chooses a name from the holy book.

4. As soon as the child is able to talk or when he reaches the age of four years, four months, and four days, he is taught the *Bismillah*, that is, "In the name of God, the Merciful, the Gracious."

5. According to the opinion of Sunni doctors, the circumcision of the child should take place in his seventh year, the operation being generally performed by a barber. But the date of circumcision varies greatly throughout the Muslim world. Not until the child arrives at puberty is he required to observe all of the customs of Muslim law, but it is incumbent on parents to teach the child prayers and the Quran.

Animistic practices sometimes accompany the time of childbirth.

During the first seven days the mother must not strike a cat or she and the child will both die. Candles are lighted on the seventh day and placed in a jug of water near the head of the child to guard it against evil spirits. Before the child is born a special amulet is prepared, consisting of seven grains each of seven different kinds of cereal. These are sewn up in a bag, and when the infant is born, it is made to wear it. The mother also has certain verses of the Koran written with musk water or ink on the inside of a white dish. This is then filled with water, the ink being washed off, and the contents are taken as a potion.[3]

2. Ibid., pp. 411–12.
3. Samuel M. Zwemer, *Across the World of Islam* (New York: Fleming H. Revell, 1929), pp. 127–28.

Animism aside, how should the convert relate to birth ceremonies that have been common to his society for generations? The Muslim birth ceremony should be closely followed. It is a time of joyous celebration. The name of God and Jesus could be whispered in the baby's ear. I know of one missionary who followed this custom with his first-born child.

The *Aqiqa* sacrifice presents more of a problem. Instead of an animal being offered so that God will protect the child from Satan, could not a feast be given for family and friends? During the feast, Scripture verses that speak about the once-and-for-all sacrifice of Jesus could be read. The baby could then be prayed over and dedicated formally to Christ.

The naming of the child with an Old Testament name could be a part of the seventh-day ceremony. This name could be spelled and pronounced as in the Quran.

Circumcision should be carried out on all male children. This is an important part of identification for the convert's children to have with Muslims.

Marriage Customs

Marriage customs and ceremonies vary somewhat throughout the Muslim world. We will attempt to define those practices that are generally representative.

The place of the woman in Islam is in submission to her husband. Muhammad is quoted as saying:

> The best woman is the one who is loved by her husband and her relatives, who is humble in her husband's presence, and who always listens to him, who adorns herself and is cheerful solely to be his joy, and who is virtuous and modest and retiring before others.[4]

4. Bess Donaldson, *The Wild Rue: A Study of Muhammadan Magic and Folklore in Iran* (New York: Arno Press, 1978 reprint of 1938 edition), p. 48.

Almost all Muslim women marry. A single girl past college age is a rarity. The average age of marriage for the girl is approximately fourteen. Muslims are permitted to marry up to four wives. Surah 4:3 states, "Of women who seem good in your eyes, marry two, or three, or four; and if ye still fear that ye shall not act equitably, then one only."

Marriage, according to Muslim law, is simply a civil contract. The consent of both parties in the presence of witnesses is necessary. An *imam* preaches a sermon which enunciates the mutual rights and duties of the husband and the wife. After the sermon the man and woman are asked if they accept the new relationship; and upon an affirmative reply, the marriage ceremony is concluded. A feast follows in the home of the husband's parents.[5]

A Muslim marriage is not conducted in the mosque, but rather in a home or other convenient place. The *imam* injects religious content by having the bridegroom repeat:

1. "I desire forgiveness from God."
2. Four chapters of the Quran. These have nothing to do with marriage, but seem to have been selected because of their brevity.
3. "There is no god but God and Muhammad is His Prophet."
4. A profession of belief in God, the angels, the Quran, the prophets, the resurrection, and the absolute decrees of good and evil.[6]

The marriage customs of Christians (in Muslim lands) and Muslims are similar, but there are a few differences. Christians prefer to have wedding ceremonies in the church. The Christian minister will ask the couple to sit together for their vows, but in the case of the Muslims, the couple will sit in different rooms. The *imam* will go separately to each for the vows. The Muslim bridegroom promises to the bride to give her a certain amount of money if he divorces her. This is not true among Christians—except in isolated instances.[7]

5. Maulana Muhammad Ali, *The Religion of Islam* (Lahore: The Ahmadiyya Anjuman Ishaat Islam, 1936), pp. 628–29.

6. Thomas Patrick Hughes, *A Dictionary of Islam* (London: W. H. Allen and Company, 1895), p. 318.

7. Anwar M. Khan, "Strategy to Evangelize Muslim Jats in Pakistan" (Th.M. thesis, Fuller Theological Seminary, 1976), p. 22.

The Persian wedding ceremony described in Chapter 3 is full of deep and meaningful symbolism. Such ritual can be retained. The Muslim convert should seek to be original in constructing a wedding ceremony that incorporates the best of Muslim culture and also includes Scripture and witness. This will take on varying distinctives from culture to culture. The one thing to be avoided is a ceremony that is full of Western practices that are meaningless and unintelligible to the Muslim community.

Funeral Customs

As a Muslim approaches death, he is encouraged to repeat his affirmation of faith in Allah. If he is unable to do this because of the advanced state of his illness, a friend or relative may do it for him. At the moment of death all those who are nearby begin to wail and recite the Quran. The dead person's feet must then be turned so they face Mecca. The mouth and eyes are closed properly. Perfume is sprinkled on the body.

The washing of the body is extremely important. It may be done by relatives or by specially appointed people. There are customs that regulate which parts of the body must be washed first and how many times the body is to be turned over. All is done very carefully as it is believed that the body is still sensitive to pain in the first hours after death.

The religious service will generally not be held in the mosque. It can be conducted in an open field near the mosque or close to the person's home. Prayers are said on behalf of the departed soul.

When a person dies, the angels come to ask him about his earthly deeds. He must therefore be buried as soon as possible lest they be kept waiting. The grave is dug in accordance with certain specifications concerning direction, length, and depth. Coffins are seldom used. The dead are buried in a white shroud.

After the funeral ceremony the family of the victim is supposed to remain at home for ten days while friends and relatives come to visit them. On the third day, a special service is arranged called KOL. The Quran is read out loud by many people in concert for the benefit of the dead person's soul. Then food is distributed among the children. Then another ritual is held on the tenth day and also on the fortieth day. During these forty days it is necessary to give food to the Muslim Priest. It is believed that the food goes to the dead person.[8]

Several years ago a close friend's mother died very unexpectedly. At Kalid's request, I went and stayed for three days and nights with him. As his father, who had died some years previously, was a high government official, the death of his mother was on the front pages of all the daily newspapers. The elite of the city came to the home to offer condolences.

One of the first acts was to bathe the body. Following this, "professional" priests were hired to come to the home and recite the Quran and say prayers for forty days and nights. There was a time of serious negotiation regarding the price these men demanded for their services. Finally an agreement was reached and they took up their task of praying for the departed soul with intense seriousness.

The funeral was delayed for several days until the older son could arrive from England. Approximately one hundred men lined up in the yard where they faced the coffin and prayed together for the woman's soul. Following this, I drove the coffin in a pick-up truck to the airport where the government had provided a helicopter to fly the body to the village home for burial. On the way to the airport, the two sons exhorted me to drive slowly and to avoid any bumping or jerking.

On the fifth day, the ritual of saying 125,000 prayers for the deceased took place. Over two hundred people came and participated in this special service.

Funeral services for converts should be evaluated in the light of Muslim practices. Simple things (e.g., holding a religious service in an open field close to the person's home) can easily be adopted. Rituals such as saying prayers for the dead will of course be omitted. Perhaps an appropriate substitute can be found. Meetings to

8. Ibid., p. 29.

remember the dead could be held on the days on which Muslims would traditionally hold some ritual. These meetings would be for the purpose of honoring the life and witness of the loved one. If these are not held, the Muslim community will conclude there was no love or respect for the departed person.

This chapter has been intentionally general and brief. Its purpose has been to stimulate thought rather than to offer specific guidelines. The Christian communicator will need to make relevant applications within his particular situation.

PART III

Potential For Contextualization

CHAPTER 11

The Challenge
of Bimbar

Overview

Bimbar is a country that presents a special challenge to Christianity. The people of this land are almost solidly Muslim. The gospel of Christ has made little overt impact in this nation. For this reason I have chosen Bimbar as a representative case-study of the many Muslim countries that continue to be resistant to the Christian message. As in the discussions of Lombaro, I have disguised certain nonessential details in order to protect the identity of the agencies and persons involved.

Bimbar is a nation with a population of twenty million. It has a rainfall of some fifty inches a year which contributes positively to an economy which is based mainly on agriculture. The temperature rises to one hundred degrees in the summer and does not fall below fifty degrees in the winter.

People of Bimbar excel in hospitality. They will always welcome a guest into their home for a cup of tea and a dish of local sweets. Politically, the situation is somewhat fluid. There is a fair amount of maneuvering for power among politicians. Bimbar received independence from colonial rule shortly after World War II. The citizens now pride themselves on their independence. But there is a certain ambivalence in this area caused by an appreciation for Western secular values as over against their own fiercely nationalistic spirit. The literacy rate is 20 percent.

The country has two basic ethnic groups. Each speaks their own distinctive language. Common to both is their firm commitment to Islam. The people are very nearly 100 percent Muslim. As in most countries, there are varying degrees of actual practice, but all would profess their faith in Islam. Almost all would be violently opposed to what they understand to be Christian. Much of their misunderstanding has been derived from their observation of the behavior of colonial rulers and businessmen, in addition to exposure to Western novels and movies.

Prayer is obligatory at the primary and secondary levels of education. The fast of Ramazan is to be observed by all citizens. In one year six hundred Muslims were arrested for violating the fast and were sentenced to two months in prison as punishment. The non-Muslim is not really regarded as a full citizen. To become a Christian is to be a traitor to one's heritage, family, and nation. Almost nothing else could bring greater negative social reaction.

Women can be seen in every kind of lifestyle from the veiled, secluded woman in the home to the student or career woman who has secure and prestigious employment. The vast majority of women tend to be very passive, both in their thinking and behavior. Yet, enigmatically, many of the most courageous of those who have come to Christ are women.

The people of Bimbar are committed to the occult, such as belief in jinn, the evil eye, and fortunetellers. One observer has said, "There are more fetishists than faithful Muslims; thus society is riddled with fear, anxiety, and conflict." Muslims in Bimbar suppose that the Prophet also believed in the evil eye. They avoid looking into the eyes of a person who could cast a spell on them. The means of protection considered most effective against the evil eye is that of stretching out one's right hand and saying, "Five in your eye," which then sends the current of the evil spell back to its source. Many use salt, tar, seeds, shells, and bones to break the power of sorcery. Christians have opposition not only from orthodox Islam but also from these occult influences.

Profile of Christianity

Believers number approximately one hundred fifty. There are seven groups who worship together regularly throughout the country. No organized churches with lay leadership are to be found in Bimbar.

Two evangelical and two cultic Christian missions minister in the country. The evangelical societies have served in Bimbar for ninety years. At present, one mission's staff is down to two, mostly because of government expulsion of their missionaries. There is good cooperation between the two evangelical foreign agencies.

It is speculated that there may be several hundred secret believers who are too intimidated to declare their faith in Christ. Persecution of converts is real. Perhaps nine out of ten who profess faith turn back to Islam under pressure from friends and relatives. Some believers have fled to nearby countries in order to practice their new faith more openly. One missionary has written, "Although the actual attempts on lives of the believers are probably exaggerated, certainly the economic pressures are very real, and the social abuse devastating enough to make secret Christians out of all but a few."

Each of the seven worshiping groups usually meets with a missionary for prayer and the reading of Scriptures. Meeting places are either in a convert's home or a missionary's residence. There is considerable controversy over this practice. Converts are not keen to volunteer their homes because of fear of social reprisal from Muslims. Therefore the assembly will often meet in a different home each week. The missionary dislikes providing a foreign cover for the meeting, but converts frequently will refuse to attend a service held in any other location.

Few, if any, of the groups are even close to becoming indigenous, organized churches with national overseers or pastors taking responsibility to minister spiritually to the believers. The role of leadership most frequently falls on the missionary.

There is a decided difference of opinion concerning what really constitutes a church and also even if such a formalized church should exist. Some regard a church as illegal and capable of bringing retaliation from the authorities. This would in turn destroy the limited freedom the converts now enjoy. Most of the potential elders do not feel they can afford the risk of taking responsibility for a group that is not approved by the state.

Missionaries, for many years, have declared their goal to be the saving of individuals. Presently, there is a change of emphasis. One society has set a goal to establish fifteen new churches in Bimbar.

Many of the present believers are either teen-agers or unmarried young adults. In a few of the groups all the converts are girls or elderly women. Most come from the middle classes and are not only employed, but also educated. Some are now beginning to find Christian spouses, but this continues to be a severe problem. It is recognized that a stable church needs Christian families.

Finances, at present, are basically the responsibility of the missionaries. The missions carry on a literature and radio work that demands a large amount of funding. Nationals have observed that the money flows in from abroad whether they give or not. They have little motivation to contribute to the work of the Lord. A number of young converts have been sent abroad, at mission expense, for theological study. One opinion is that "the Christians have come to view the church treasury as something from which they receive more than as that to which they give."

The worshiping groups are still heavily influenced by the foreign missionaries, who seem to be alternatively appreciated and resented. The believers do not want the missionaries to control them. Yet, they complain of neglect. Missionaries often find themselves unsure as to exactly what actions would be loving and helpful in the long run.

The majority of the converts are at a very immature stage of Christian growth. Most of the believers' minds are still dominated by the desire for material advancement. At least some of the converts have been characterized as susceptible to "suspicion, misunderstandings, questionings, gossip, slander, bitterness, and jealousy."

In terms of church growth, many Christian workers are beginning to see that they have given their time and energy disproportionately to perfecting the few believers, instead of logging hours among Muslims. This has, in turn, provided a poor model for the believers, who, until recently, have not been reaching out to their unsaved friends and relatives. There are some encouraging reports of believers beginning to share their faith with others, but far too many of the believers are defeated to the point that there is not much about their life that would whet the appetite of a Muslim. Among the Christians in Bimbar it is accepted that serving the Lord full-time means working outside the country with one of the foreign missions.

The missionaries have been in some conflict over whether to use the literary or colloquial translation of the Bible and Christian literature. One mission feels that it is degrading to use the colloquial because the Quran and all Islamic writings are in the literary style. They maintain Muslims reject the Bible as an inferior book when they encounter a translation in the language of the man on the street. The other mission uses colloquial translations almost exclusively. They point out that the Greek of the New Testament was not laced with literary fineness but rather geared to the person of average reading skills. This mission feels strongly they must communicate to the masses.

Both evangelical societies are working together on radio projects. Three hours of Christian broadcasting are beamed in from a nearby country each week. A correspondence school, also administered from another nation, has a total enrollment of eighty-five thousand students.

In the last few years, distribution of the Scriptures and other Christian literature within Bimbar has become negligible. The Bible Society stores are either closed or doing minimal business. The one Christian bookshop in all of Bimbar stocks just a handful of titles integrated into a mass of secular books. This is done so the shop can legally keep open. Some believers have begun to give plastic packets containing a Gospel and tracts to interested friends.

A number of nonmissionary Christians have come to Bimbar in secular positions with the aim of witnessing and assisting in church formation. These Western believers do not speak the local language. This causes their contribution to Christian work to be minimal. Also, they are kept very busy in their employment.

With a certain measure of frustration, one Bimbar mission leader has asked hypothetical questions as to who is to blame for the small results that have been reaped after so many decades of faithful witness along with the expenditure of hundreds of thousands of dollars:

1. Is it God's fault? Is there such a thing as "geographical grace"?
2. Is it Satan's fault? Some speak of "strongholds of Satan." If this is a biblical concept, what response does it require?
3. Is it Bimbar's fault? If the people are resistant, does this mean that these millions of Muslims do not want truth or reality? Or, are there pockets of people who, if given a way, would respond to Christ?
4. Is it the missionaries' fault? Are our lives powerless through too little prayer? Or are our methods the obstacle hindering thousands from being baptized in a modern day Pentecost?
5. Is it the fault of the church worldwide? With just a handful of Christian workers in these lands, perhaps there is no mystique to the paltry harvest. Perhaps it is simply the issue of "little sowing—little reaping." Are the Bimbar people resistant or neglected?

A New Strategy

At the risk of being presumptuous, I would like to propose a strategy for the consideration of the two evangelical societies working in Bimbar. These thoughts may have application to other Muslim countries that face a similar set of circumstances.

One cannot help but applaud the tenacious and dedicated labor of this band of missionaries over these past decades. Literally hundreds of Christian workers have left their homes in the West and have sacrificed the prime years of their lives in ministry for the Lord that has brought small returns in the number of people coming to Christ. I share the consternation expressed by the five questions just listed. I'm afraid there is no easy or even single answer to the evangelization of the Bimbar Muslims. Yet, there is one very clear statement that can be made: The methodology of the past years has not been successful in building a church in this needy nation. Perhaps it is time for a new strategy and approach:

1. There must be a continued emphasis on the spiritual dynamic in this outreach. One mission has organized all-day prayer chains for Bimbar. The Christian public in the West should be informed about and motivated to intercede on behalf of new efforts.

2. New missionaries should be recruited and trained in the methodology of effective cross-cultural communication of the gospel. They may be forced to work in secular employment part-time in order to obtain a visa, but their focus must remain heavily on evangelism. They should set the example in outreach efforts. One Bimbar missionary stated, "It takes a national to do the job of evangelism." Indeed, the national will have greater access to his countrymen than will the foreigner, but it is highly unlikely that the converts will be involved in evangelism if their spiritual leaders are not. In I Corinthians 4:16, Paul said, "Be imitators of me."

3. Short-term or "secular" missionaries should not be encouraged. These people may be sincere and dedicated, but it is doubtful if their impact will be commensurate with their vision and effort.

4. The house-church model should be accepted. Homes in Bimbar are centers of social activity and thus can be readily adapted as a church. They provide privacy and require no additional financial expenditure. The expansion process is feasible through new converts' opening up their homes. They must be brought to see this as their responsibility. All meetings in missionary homes should cease.

5. No missionary should contribute more to the local worshiping group than does the average convert. The believers must

be challenged to give more, but this should be along cultural lines. Muslims are motivated to give for specific religious needs; they do not follow the Western pattern of weekly giving. Sending converts out of the country for subsidized Bible training or mission employment should be discouraged and perhaps cut off altogether. Missionaries should, as far as possible, live on a financial standard that is comparable to that of the target group they are seeking to win to Christ.

6. Existing believers should not be overfed. If they are unresponsive, it may be best to minimize efforts with them and press out to new frontiers.

7. Very little experimentation on the pattern of the Lombaro work has been carried out in Bimbar. It is my view that it is time to carefully integrate more Islamic cultural forms into the pattern of Christian worship. This can be carried out in the believers' homes. The converts will have little problem. It is the missionaries who will have to make a rather traumatic adjustment: moving away from Western cultural forms that they have unconsciously identified as Christian.

8. Muslim evangelism will not be successful as long as women, children, and students comprise the convert community. Muslim men must be the target of evangelistic activity. Believers should be encouraged to be discreet in sharing their faith openly until they have brought several others from among their friends and relatives to Christ. "Extraction" must stop. The believers must remain in their culture.

9. Both missions should emphasize the colloquial rather than literary translations of Scripture and other Christian writings. The masses must be kept in focus. The gospel must be made intelligible.

10. Correspondence-school and radio outreach should be continued. Efforts to make contacts with Muslims who have shown interest in the gospel through these ministries should be expanded.

11. There should be an evangelistic focus on meeting the felt needs of the Muslims whose daily lives are heavily influenced by belief in jinn and the spirit world. Exorcism and prayer for healing

(with anointing of oil) can be practiced in a biblical manner. Message content should stress peace and deliverance from fear.

12. Missionaries should expose themselves to emerging missiological data that can assist them in being more effective in their witness for Christ. It may be possible for several to take study furloughs at one of the schools of missions in the States.

Bimbar stands as a direct challenge to the power of the gospel of Christ. The church worldwide should mobilize to see this nation and other Muslim countries like it come under the lordship of our Savior.

CHAPTER 12

Reaction to Contextualization

Uncharted courses of life are not popular with the average person. The unknown causes a measure of apprehension and fear. New initiatives make us vulnerable to failure. Potential loss of face, prestige, and even job security, makes us gravitate toward the safe areas of life rather than launch out into the unexplored. Has this been the case in our approach to Islam? Have we feared adverse reaction from nationals, the mission board, or the home church? How much longer can we continue being "safe" while seeing negligible results for our investment?

Reactions to innovation vary greatly. Caution is the norm. Often the innovator has brickbats thrown at him during his lifetime and then roses are spread over his grave in grateful remembrance of his innovative efforts. But having said this, we recognize that it is still scriptural and proper to count the cost before beginning to build. What are the probable reactions to the contextualization mode of ministry?

Muslim Community

It has been said that a close identification in lifestyle on the part of the Western missionary could be regarded by the Muslim as an act of hypocrisy and ridicule. Also, the Muslim could lose respect for a foreigner who adopts a simple lifestyle when in reality he is known to have significant financial resources. Living in a bamboo hut would be inconsistent with possessing expensive cameras and a motorcycle, along with making annual trips out of the country for vacations.

It has been my experience, however, that Muslims do appreciate whatever sincere gestures are made toward cultural identification. They realize that total assimilation is impossible. But, as the missionary seeks to learn the vernacular, adopts national dress, enjoys local food, and generally has a comparable lifestyle, the Muslim becomes extremely appreciative.

How would an American feel if, in a small town in the Bible Belt, an orthodox Egyptian Muslim priest with a long black beard and dressed in a flowing white robe moved into a mansion and began to propagate Islam? Suppose that his lifestyle is superior to that of the local people, his dress is distinctive, he eats Egyptian food, he speaks English with a heavy accent, and all of his literature was originally written in Arabic and then translated into awkward English. The priest worships on Friday and passes out Islamic literature on the doorstep of the Christian church on Sunday. Inquirers at his weekly service are made to sit on the floor and to go through unusual (and unappreciated) ritual that is totally alien to the American way of life. How popular would such a propagator of a foreign religion be with the local population? We, as Americans, would expect a Muslim missionary to this country to minimize the social and cultural distance between himself and those to whom he desires to propagate his message.

A current illustration relates to the Hare Krishna movement in America. In the initial years, the American converts to this Eastern Hindu religion dressed in long saffron-colored robes and cut almost all of their hair, with the exception of a pigtail. They then moved out on the streets and to the airline terminals to distribute their literature and preach their message. Their appearance repelled and in some cases frightened the people they accosted in public places. Recently, however, the Hare Krishna movement has ordered that all evangelizers wear regular American clothes when out on propagation assignments.

As to the usage of Islamic cultural forms within Christian worship, this is no problem to Muslims. When this happens they see Christianity in a new light. It no longer looks so foreign and strange. They are then willing to consider the content of the biblical message.

Convert Church

If the Muslim-convert church is basically homogeneous and has had minimal contact with a Western type of Christianity, then it will have little or no problem with contextualized worship. The convert is just following ritual he has known all his life. He appreciates the familiar. The church is then set up to draw and accommodate the Muslim inquirer. No new believer needs to feel culturally ashamed to invite a Muslim friend or relative to attend a service of worship.

There is a danger that converts who retain some Muslim worship forms may look askance at their Christian brothers who they consider have adopted forms that either belong to another local religion or are culturally Western. They may become proud, feeling that they are superior in their expression of Christian worship. This pride can be deadly in terms of spiritual growth. We cannot ignore this danger. But neither can we turn back simply because of it.

It is wonderful when the Christians of any culture think of Jesus Christ as indigenous to their own race and society. I have sought to illustrate this truth in a poem:

I Had a Dream...
There standing before me on a dusty path
   in a remote village of India
      stood Jesus.

His ganji and lungi were soiled,
    His brow filled with sparkling beads
        of perspiration.
Hands of labor radiated a message
    of dignity.
Calloused feet spoke of hours behind
    a plow.
His brown, golden skin communicated a
    startling truth.
God had become a Bengali!

I fell upon the hot blistering earth
    in awe and reverence.
His hands of love tenderly embraced me
    and drew me to His breast.
His voice spoke with the tenderness
    of the flow of a small rippling brook,
Yet with the authority of the roaring Ganges,
    "Come, my child,
    Come and follow Me."

My conquered will could only respond with
    words of brokenness,
        "My Lord and My God."
Slowly rising to my feet, I found myself struggling
    for composure.
        "What new thing was this?"

My heart was as joyous as the dancing of the
    newborn lamb;
My tattered clothing seemed as regal as that of the
    wealthy landowner;
My aching limbs became as refreshed as if I had just
    bathed in the cool waters of the nearby pond;
The gnawing pangs of hunger subsided as if I
    had just eaten a most sumptuous meal of rice and curry.

Yes, now I understand, I have just accepted
    Jesus of Bengal
        as my Lord . . .
            My God.

Established Church

The problem of the relationship between the established church and the convert church was explored in Chapter 7. The traditional churches sometimes make such unreasonable cultural demands on the inquirer that all but a hardy few will totally reject them. This does not mean I support alienation and distance between the two churches. Homogeneity and autonomy do not exclude close links of fellowship, love, and mutual esteem.

A recent convert wrote anonymously of the turmoil he experienced by being rejected by Muslim society and not being fully accepted by the traditional church:

> My friends never ask me anything except the formal, "How do you do?" But this is just a formal courtesy that social scientists believe to be usually no more meaningful than mere wagging of the tail of one bird to another. The answer has to be, "Fine, thank you." They do not try to know what is going on in your mind. . . . My life is critical and uncertain in that my old friends have rejected me, and new friends have not yet accepted me.

How much better would it have been if this believer could have been brought into a warm, accepting community of converts who had been experiencing similar trauma in coming to faith in Christ! They could have empathetically entered into his life and given him the social and spiritual support that he so desperately needed.

It is my hope that through prayerful consultation the established church can come to accept the homogeneous convert church.

Missionary Society

Missionary societies have a variety of structures. Some allow for maximum field autonomy. Others require clearance from a headquarters, many miles distant, for even the most mundane of decisions. This latter type of organization is very unwieldy and often is an insult to the spiritual and administrative capabilities of field missionaries. It is frequently impossible for executives sitting in an air-conditioned office in a major Western city thousands of miles from the scene of action to even begin to enter into the intricacies of a problem that may demand a decision more quickly than a telegram exchange allows. On the other hand, missionary leadership from the home end is a balance to the overall program of the society. Executives may see issues more clearly from a distance than do those who are emotionally involved in a given situation.

The key word is *balance.* Home and field have complementary roles and functions. They should extend themselves to the maximum to seek to understand each other. Both have experience and perspectives that are invaluable to the other.

A strategy such as the one being proposed in this book needs to be carefully examined by field and home staffs. There will be the "go-getters" who can't wait to get started, and there also will be the "supercautious" who will put up every roadblock possible in order that the status quo not be disturbed. Both extremes should be carefully listened to. In the end, the mission needs to pull toward middle ground—avoiding being bogged down in the mire of safe traditionalism and also avoiding the foolhardy excesses of activism that has not seriously thought through all possible consequences.

As mentioned earlier, the North American Conference on Muslim Evangelization took place in late 1978. The conference was preceded by the distribution of forty foundational papers written by experienced people who are knowledgeable in many areas of Islam. It was very gratifying to see the warm response on the part of those who attended to the various proposals of new approaches to Islamic evangelism. The follow-up to the conference has been the establishment of the Samuel Zwemer Institute*, a nerve center for research, teaching, and information dissemination. Don McCurry, former missionary to Pakistan, is the founder-director of this new and unique center. Various missionary

*Samuel Zwemer Institute, Box 365, Altadena, California 91001.

societies are anxious to use the facilities of this institute and thus to open themselves to the fresh ideas that are being advanced in these days.

Western Church

The layman in the average Western church knows little concerning Muslim evangelism. His information is likely limited to a yearly visit from some missionary when Islam may be referred to for ten or fifteen minutes in a message from the pulpit. This situation is being changed by contemporary political events in the Middle East as well as the oil crisis. However, few Western Christians ever read a book or see a film that centers on Muslim evangelism.

I have visited a considerable number of churches and have sought to explain the necessity and *modus operandi* of the contextualized approach to Muslim evangelism. The response has been overwhelmingly positive and even enthusiastic. Many have come up to me after the service and said, "Hey, what you are talking about is applicable right here in America among the various groups of people in our society." What an exciting response, for this is precisely what contextualization is all about! It is my conviction that there will be a great deal of support from the Western church when it explores and grapples with the issues of a contextualized approach to Muslim evangelism.

CHAPTER **13**

Spiritual
Considerations

One of the components of missiology might be termed "spiritual dynamics." Other segments of this discipline include research, anthropology, study of non-Christian religions, historical survey of missions, an emphasis on the church, social concerns, and general biblical theology. One can easily see a potential danger here. Emphasis on spiritual dynamics can easily be lost in the excitement of an academic exploration of new, fresh, and stretching missiological pursuits. After all, prayer and Bible study are "taken for granted" in any mission strategy. How can a person be a missionary and not concern himself with intercession and daily personal encounter with the living Word of God?

My experience leads me to observe that neglect of prayer and Bible study occurs all too readily. Professionalism is a constant temptation to a full-time Christian worker. It must be recognized that such an attitude is in contrast to what is described in the Bible as a "man of God." Consider what J. Herbert Kane, a respected missiologist, had to say in response to a series of eight articles on the contemporary state of missions which was published in a leading evangelical magazine:

We are told that missions "are doing as much damage as good." And how do we propose to remedy the situation? By harder work, better tools, and more effective methods! "The current explosion in missiological knowledge and training will raise the level of skill and efficiency in carrying out the task" and the "new breed of missionaries," we are assured, will be "smarter" than their predecessors.

The greatest danger with modern missiology is its almost total preoccupation with the horizontal dimension. We have not yet learned that it is "Not by might, nor by power, but by my spirit, saith the Lord of hosts" (Zech. 4:6). Robert Hall Glover, of a former generation, said: "Christian missions are no human undertaking, but a supernatural and divine enterprise for which God has provided supernatural power and leadership." Is it not strange that not one of these essays makes even a passing reference to the ministry of the Holy Spirit, the executive member of the Godhead, who is supposed to be in charge of the whole operation? (Acts 1:8; Rom. 15:19)[1]

All concerned with Muslim evangelism must strive for balance. Disregarding the missiological data would be to our loss. These cultural insights need to have a prominent place in our strategy and methodological approach. But missiology should not be a threat to an emphasis on spiritual considerations! Can not the two be complementary? A balanced view will lead to a greater impact for Christ in the Muslim world.

Scripture

Without the Bible, we have no Christianity. The mission imperative is based wholly on what we find in Holy Scripture. Man's lost condition is revealed in the Word. God's concern for man and His love gift to the world are portrayed for us between Genesis,

---

1. J. Herbert Kane, letter to the editor, *World Vision Magazine* 23.3 (1979): 19.

the book of beginnings, and Revelation, the book of endings. The Bible cannot be regarded as just a volume of literature filled with distortions and inaccuracies. A prerequisite for any building project is the determination of the reliability of the foundation. Samuel Zwemer clearly stated his position on the authority of Scripture:

> The effect of thinking in gray is inevitable on the messenger as well as on his message. Twilight of life is not conducive to spiritual health. We need the full blaze of the light of the glory of God in the face of Jesus Christ. His authority must be supreme in the intellectual sphere. His belief in the Old Testament scriptures and His statement that "they cannot be broken" leaves only one alternative; if we reject them, we reject Him also. It is not hard to accept the miracles of the Old and New Testament if we accept the miracle in the first chapter of Genesis and the greater miracle in the first chapter of John's Gospel. . . . A mutilated gospel can only mean a mutilated spiritual life.[2]

The Bible is not to be handled just as a cognitive tool. I have met nominal Christians who know more about the Bible than I do. It is inadequate merely to fill the mind with memorized words. The heart must be warm and responsive as it feasts on the Word. Only this process will lead on to both holiness and meaningful evangelistic activity for Christ.

Holy Spirit

Malcolm Martin writes powerfully concerning the proper relationship between the missionary and the Holy Spirit:

> We can say that the missionary lives in the Spirit, but we must also say that the Spirit lives in the missionary. How does

2. Samuel M. Zwemer, *Dynamic Christianity and the World Today* (London: The Intervarsity Fellowship of Evangelical Unions, 1939), pp. 32–33.

the missionary have an interior awareness of the Spirit? What is the relationship, the communion, between the missionary and the Spirit? As the Spirit dwells in the depths of the soul of a person, it acts like a furnace that warms the whole being, just as the sun which energizes the earth gives it light and life. The missionary looks in meditatively upon this power burning within. He or she penetrates the secret recesses of the soul, boring through the crusts of attachments and failings, ripping away at them. Baring the self, recognizing weaknesses, and egoism, the missionary stumbles naked before the Creator, the Father, the source of all love. Once this has been discovered in the very marrow of one's being, the missionary is moved with an insatiable yearning for the God who lives within and in others as well. Now the missioner cannot help but love God since he or she knows that God is love and loves the missionary especially.[3]

The doctrine of the Holy Spirit is very controversial among evangelical believers. Many denominations treat the Holy Spirit as just a minor theological teaching that should be avoided lest emotional excesses occur. These Christians have cut a major biblical truth out of their personal lives and ministry. I conclude that this is one of the reasons for much of the nominal Christianity that exists in the West. When the Holy Spirit is given from God for the purpose of creating holiness and power in the lives of believers, how can such a gift be denied?

One must admit there are excesses and false teaching which do bring embarrassment to believers. This should be no reason to disregard one of the central teachings of the New Testament. The missionary to Islam stands in particular need of the empowering and encouraging ministry of the Holy Spirit. "The true evangelist needs not only intellectual preparation by possessing all his heritage and his resources, he needs also the baptism of fire. The

3. Malcolm Martin, "The Missionary and the Holy Spirit," *Missiology* 5.2 (April 1977): 225.

Holy Spirit alone can confer this grace, even as He did at Pentecost on the Apostolic Church."[4]

Romans 8 is the great chapter of the New Testament on the Spirit of God. One derives from this powerful passage the conviction that the Lord will give grace to overcome the spiritually debilitating power of the flesh. The Holy Spirit desires to give victory to His children.

A number of years ago my wife and I were living in a small town where we had neither electricity nor running water. One day was particularly hot with high humidity and a temperature in excess of one hundred degrees. The previous night I had slept little due to the overwhelming heat and absence of a fan. In the morning I was walking quickly to the marketplace to try to get the mundane task of purchasing groceries out of the way as quickly as possible so I could get on with the "more important aspects of the Lord's work." The sun was blazing down, causing a great deal of sweating and general discomfort. A scowl covered my face.

Hundreds of people were pushing and shoving along the dusty path. As usual, scores of men looked my way with expressions of wonderment that a tall, white-faced stranger was in their midst. Children emitted their words of gleeful disrespect. All in all, it was a rather miserable experience for me, particularly in light of my intense dislike for marketing, which was distinctly a man's function in that town. My face clearly indicated the depth of my misery.

Suddenly, the Lord spoke to me about my testimony. Almost no one in that huge crowd could read the Bible. Few had ever been presented with the message of the Word of God. They did, however, know that the miserable white man they were observing was a representative of the Christian religion. Perhaps, for hundreds of people, this countenance of mine was as close as they would come to a Christian witness. The Holy Spirit deeply convicted me. As I was jostling along that dusty road, I cried out

4. Samuel M. Zwemer, *Evangelism Today* (New York: Fleming H. Revell, 1954), p. 115.

to Him for the grace and strength to portray the reality of the Christian faith in my face and actions—as well as in my formal message.

Edwin Orr sees the ministry of the Holy Spirit as being crucial in any breakthrough in Islamic evangelism.

> Undoubtedly, there is more responsiveness among Muslims today than hitherto. The movement of the Spirit has given the Christian constituency more sympathy and less antipathy for Islam. But expectation of an outpouring of the Spirit on Christian witnesses and on Muslim hearers has a low priority, just as such revival had a deplorably low priority at the Lausanne Congress on Evangelism, despite its excellence. . . . What cannot God do in Islam, which recognizes the God of the patriarchs and the prophets and reveres the person of Jesus? Many of us have engaged in the hard work of scraping the frost off a car, after a hard freeze, a tedious job; but, when the sun arises, hard work becomes a pleasure as the frost is melted into moisture. There will be an outpouring of the Spirit to prepare the way of the Lord.[5]

Prayer

Prayer is the most talked about and least used resource of the Christian faith. We regard it as our "spiritual" duty to act upon prayer requests and to give casual assurances of our intercession to friends who may be in some particular state of need. But is there any real seriousness in our prayer ministry? Is there a vibrant faith that believes prayer will really change lives and circumstances? If so, proof is hard to come by! How many missionary conferences place prayer in a central place on the program? How well attended are meetings which are devoted exclusively to prayer?

A few winds of change are blowing among evangelicals. Asbury Seminary has hired a professor of prayer and has students who are majoring in prayer. Campus Crusade for Christ (C.C.C.)

5. J. Edwin Orr, "The Call to Spiritual Renewal," in *The Gospel and Islam: A 1978 Compendium,* ed. Don M. McCurry (Monrovia, CA: MARC, 1979), p. 425.

has assigned the oversight of their program of prayer to the president's wife, Vonette Bright. C.C.C. has eight full-time staff members in their Prayer-Care ministry who go to work daily at the prayer chapel in Arrowhead Springs, California, and pray for eight hours. This is their only assigned task. In 1976, a new emphasis on prayer was introduced into the ministry of the Evangelism Explosion (E.E.) outreach of the Coral Ridge Presbyterian Church in Fort Lauderdale, Florida. Two church members who are not on the E.E. team are asked to volunteer to pray for each E.E. worker on a regular basis but especially on Tuesday nights when the workers are out witnessing. The lay evangelist is responsible to get in touch with the two intercessors each week to report the results and give prayer requests. When this process started, the number of professions of faith immediately went up 100 percent.[6] Operation Mobilization is another organization that places a very high priority on prayer.

That prayer is not a passive exercise is pointed out by Zwemer:

> The ministry of intercession is a great battlefield. We need the whole armour of God, for we wrestle in the trenches against all the powers of darkness. On our knees we are kings and priests in God's universe. Napoleon or Alexander never had such an empire. George Mueller and Hudson Taylor were ambassadors plenipotentiary of their King.[7]

Prayer is a refuge for the troubled heart. Possibly every Christian worker has felt like leaving the battle at some point in his career. The following excerpt from a veteran missionary's recent letter displays an honesty unusual among the servants of Christ:

> How can I tell you that there are many times when I want to take the next plane out of here? Since Christmas when I

6. C. Peter Wagner, *Your Spiritual Gifts* (Glendale, CA: Regal Books, 1979), pp. 75–76.

7. Samuel M. Zwemer, *Taking Hold of God* (Grand Rapids: Zondervan, 1936), p. 32.

became very tired physically, I've been fighting to stay on top of things. I haven't written many letters because of fatigue but mostly because of depression. Our work load is impossible. Jim works from 70 to 80 hours a week. But the thing that tires us more than anything is the criticism and accusations of others.... Our family has suffered and our relationships with each other have become strained. We are all "pressed down but not crushed." Sometimes when difficulties come and the very existence of our work is at stake, we pray together into the night. We minister to each other. How can I convey to you our need of your intercessions? Believe with us that the Lord will protect us from the enemy. Believe that He will not only protect us but give us a victorious and fruitful ministry here that will influence all of Africa and the entire world. Is this too much to ask?

The spirit of this call to prayer clothed in the garb of honesty parallels David's cry to the Lord in Psalm 28:

To Thee, O Lord, I call; My rock, do not be deaf to me, lest, if Thou be silent to me, I become like those who go down to the pit. Hear the voice of my supplications when I cry to Thee for help, when I lift up my hands toward Thy holy sanctuary. (vv. 1–2)

Many a servant of God in the Muslim world knows what it is like to experience the loneliness and the frustrations of the pit! But there can come bountiful release through an encounter with God in dynamic and effectual prayer. Prayer is a catalyst between God and us.

> Prayer effectuates ministry.
> Prayer enlightens understanding.
> Prayer animates love.
> Prayer encourages patience.
> Prayer strengthens faith.[8]

8. Phil Parshall, *The Fortress and the Fire* (Bombay: Gospel Literature Service, 1976), p. 27.

Patience

In II Corinthians 6, Paul informs the believers that he has done nothing that would discredit the ministry. Verse 4 commences a list of the afflictions he has endured. The sixth verse mentions that the hardships, beatings, imprisonments, and tumults have all been endured in a spirit of patience. The flesh would naturally cry out in impatience during such unnatural ordeals. Only the Spirit could fill the restless heart with patience.

"Strengthened with all power, according to His glorious might, for the attaining of all steadfastness and patience" (Col. 1:11). It is interesting to note that the power of God is directed toward helping the believer to attain patience. God's Spirit is the agent of making an impatient person patient.

"Preach the word; be ready in season and out of season; reprove, rebuke, exhort, with great patience" (II Tim. 4:2). This is a special word from the Lord to those who are engaged in Muslim evangelism. The ministry of outreach must be performed with a holy patience. Even if results seem negligible, the faithful reaper will continue on in tenacious faith that "faithful is He who calls you, and He also will bring it to pass" (I Thess. 5:24). My calling in missions has been to win Muslims to Christ. The first thirteen years of my ministry saw minimal fruit. At times, it was very hard to hold on in patience to the belief that God would do the improbable—if not the impossible—and bring Muslims to Himself. There were temptations to quit and go seek a more fruitful ministry. One such incident centered around a brief preaching opportunity I had in India among nominal Christians. A number of young people accepted Christ. One of those converts went on to become an outstanding staff member of Evangelical Students of India. Other opportunities for fruitful ministry have opened up in America. I can only thank the Lord for giving me the patience to remain working among Muslims. My small part in seeing the fruit of these past few years would seem to verify the wisdom of "hanging in" even when there was so little in the way of encouragement.

Raymond Lull faithfully ministered among Muslims while

the horrible Inquisition was taking place. He preached incessantly, wrote hundreds of books, and was imprisoned, reviled, and cast out of cities. For a year before his death he labored among a small group of Muslim converts that he had won to Christ. Finally, on June 30, 1315, he was stoned to death by an angry mob outside the city gate of Bugia, North Africa, while he was preaching about the love of Christ. At any point in his long life, he could have moved into a revered and comfortable position in academia. Instead, he chose to press on patiently, with little tangible fruit, in the great task of Muslim evangelism.[9]

Over a half century ago the following words were penned by the "Apostle to Islam":

> The Alpine climber who is trying to reach a summit can "on the upward path" scarcely see his goal except at certain fortunate moments. What he does see is the stony path that must be trodden, the rocks and precipices to be avoided, the unending slope that gets ever steeper; he feels the growing weakness, the solitude and the burden; and yet the inspiration of the climber is the sight of the goal. Because of it all the hardships of the journey count for naught. The evangelization of the Muslim world is a task so great, so difficult and so discouraging at times that only the upward look can reassure the climbers. The evangelization of that world is not a phrase to be bandied about easily; it is a deep life-purpose, a work of faith, a labor of love, a patience of hope long deferred but undying.[10]

The "patience of hope" will be well rewarded in the future heavenly presence of Jesus Christ.

Faith

Faith and patience are closely related to one another. It is faith in a loving God, whose will it is that no one perish, which

9. Samuel M. Zwemer, *The Cross Above the Crescent* (Grand Rapids: Zondervan, 1941), p. 268.

10. Samuel M. Zwemer, *Call to Prayer* (London: Marshall Brothers, 1924), p. 70.

causes the communicator of the gospel to Muslims to press on with patience and forbearance. Faith is not simply a psychological exercise. Rather, it is firmly rooted in biblical truth. Hebrews 11 depicts men who endured the crucibles of life because they saw Him who was invisible.

Noah's message seemed ludicrous. Consider the emotionally draining taunts and ridicule of the onlooking crowd. Noah never swerved from his divinely appointed task. Nothing could detract him from that which he knew to be truth. The rejecting nonbelievers of Noah's day remind me of the Muslims who hear the message but refuse to heed its warning.

Abraham went forth into an adventure of faith with God. At times he must have wondered about God's timetable. Yet he refused to turn aside onto easier paths.

Moses needed only to have given consent and he would have immediately been secure as a member of Pharaoh's family. Never would he have known the meaning of want or deprivation. But by faith Moses refused.

> All these died in faith, without receiving the promises, but having seen them and having welcomed them from a distance, and having confessed that they were strangers and exiles on the earth.... But as it is, they desire a better country, that is a heavenly one.... And all these, having gained approval through their faith, did not receive what was promised. (Heb. 11:13, 16, 39)

God's special approval will be extended to those who, through their ministry to Muslims, could easily be included in the Hebrews 11 roll call of the faithful.

Love

Love is a word so often used in general terms that it is stripped of any depth of meaning. In a cross-cultural context, the anthropological concept of "cultural validity" has a particular relevance and assists the missionary in considering what it means to "love" those of another ethnic and linguistic background.

Cultural validity maintains that an observer should first evaluate a culture in terms of its own values and goals before comparing it, either positively or negatively, with another culture. This approach helps overcome the natural ethnocentric tendency to evaluate other cultures to their disadvantage by always starting from the perspective of emphasizing the strengths of one's own culture. Westerners have tended to speak derogatorily of so-called primitive societies that have not attained the same measure of technological sophistication that they have. The cultural-validity model recognizes that each culture may reach high levels of development in certain areas, such as social structures in much of the East, and technology in the West. Without a proper recognition of cultural validity, comparisons of various cultures will often be made on the basis of whatever criteria the one who does the comparing deems to be of most value.[11]

Love can be most functional as it works itself out from a humble heart. A national becomes relaxed and appreciative when he feels the Westerner is an accepting rather than an attacking person. A humble recognition of the faults of one's own culture disarms the defensive national. Charles Kraft overviews some of the weaknesses of Western culture.

> Our quest for freedom and individualism mitigates against the development of close friendships, neighborliness, and stable marriages. Our extreme competitiveness, expressed interpersonally, intergenerationally, economically, vocationally, politically, and even between churches, is ripping our society apart. The naturalistic worldview at the center of our culture, the depersonalization of our people, the uncontrolled competitiveness between the various segments of our society, the choice usually to value the unknown and untried above the known but imperfect—these and so many other features of our society point not to its superiority but to its sickness.[12]

11. Charles H. Kraft, *Christianity in Culture* (Maryknoll, NY: Orbis Books, 1979), p. 49.
12. Ibid., p. 51.

David Barrett, in *Schism and Renewal in Africa*, works through some of the deep conflicts that exist between Western missionaries and the practitioners of the more indigenous expressions of African Christianity. He points out that, in many instances, missionaries have failed to convey real brotherly love to the Africans. Schism and hurt have been the natural consequence:

> In regard to this one small facet only—love as close contact with others involving listening, sharing, sympathizing and sensitive understanding in depth as between equals—missions in many tribes had failed; there was, so it appeared, no contact, no dialogue, no comprehension, no sympathy extended to traditional society or religion.[13]

Barrett sees an emphasis on *philadelphia* or brotherly love as the corrective. Otherwise, the perception of Christianity will continue to be extremely negative.

In one Muslim country in 1974, an insensitive convert used a loudspeaker to give his testimony in public. He spoke in very negative terms of his former religion. Muslims with guns came in large numbers from neighboring villages. They barricaded the Christians in their homes. Only the timely arrival of the police prevented a great deal of bloodshed. Real love would have prevented the convert from openly attacking that which was most precious to his former friends and relatives.[14]

One evening I was returning home from a distant city. I had taken the overnight launch and was sharing a small cabin with a highly schooled Muslim engineer. After drinking tea together, I, with open Bible, began to witness to this gentleman about the Christian faith. He was very responsive and gracious. Suddenly, the door flew open and another Muslim barged into the cabin. This man had been listening to my conversation through the thin cabin walls. He looked at me and assured me that I, along with all other Christians, was going to hell. Later, he calmed down and we

---

13. David Barrett, *Schism and Renewal in Africa* (London: Oxford University Press, 1968), p. 155.
14. Anwar M. Khan, "Strategy to Evangelize Muslim Jats in Pakistan" (Th.M. thesis, Fuller Theological Seminary, 1976), p. 61.

ended up drinking tea together in a spirit of peace and friendliness.

It hurt me deeply to be told I was going to hell. I tried to turn that situation around and realize how Muslims feel when a Christian tells them they are lost, without God, and will spend eternity in hell. A parallel in mission history occurred when Spanish missionaries, in their preaching in China, proclaimed that the long line of emperors was burning in hell.[15] Love will not speak of hell without a broken heart.

Frank Khair-Ullah decries a cold, logical approach to Muslim evangelism:

> The intellectual, the social, the emotional barriers may be overcome but unless by the grace of God we touch another heart with love, it may never really come to know the much greater and wonderful love of God for him. A recent convert who was struggling with the social and intellectual barriers, while still a Muslim wrote these words, "It is stimulating to think that cases of conversion through sheer reasoning between dogmas of two religions are very rare, perhaps nonexistent. In cases of conversion where prosperity, social status, security, vengeance against native society, emotional experimentation and the like, are not the motives, the change of faith is motivated perhaps infinitely more frequently by love for charming virtues of a magnetic person, or love for a group of lovable associates than by cold religious arithmetic."[16]

Zwemer adds his testimony: "After forty years' experience, I am convinced that the nearest way to the Muslim heart is the way of God's love, the way of the Cross."[17] David Hesselgrave sees a uniqueness about witnessing to Muslims: "To a degree unparal-

15. Vincent Cronin, *The Wise Man from the West* (New York: E. P. Dutton, 1955), p. 280.

16. Frank Khair-Ullah, "Evangelism Among Muslims," in *Let the Earth Hear His Voice*, ed. J. D. Douglas (Minneapolis: World Wide Publications, 1975), pp. 823–24.

17. Zwemer, *Cross Above the Crescent*, p. 246.

leled in other parts of the world, the missionary to Jews and Muslims must win a hearing by demonstrating Christlike qualities of integrity and love. Only then can he begin to communicate the God of the Bible who is truth and love personified."[18] As one earthy statement puts it, "The Muslims and other non-Christians can only be won with love not by force. Flies come to honey, not to vinegar."[19]

Jesus Christ contextualized love—for Jews, for Muslims, and for the world. His ambassadors will have a goal no less exalted or lofty. Only then will this book and its emphasis on contextualized methodology have any validity.

The following missionary version of I Corinthians 13 adequately sums up my feelings concerning the relationship of contextualization to the highest of all Christian virtues:

> I may be able to speak fluently the language of my chosen
>   field and even understand its culture,
>   but if I have no love, the impact of my speech is no
>   more for Christ than that of a businessman who
>   comes to exploit the people.
> I may have the gift of contextualizing God's word when I
>   deliver it to my hearers.
>   I may have all knowledge about their customs,
>   I may have the faith needed to combat witchcraft,
>   but if I have no love, I am nothing.
> I may give everything that I have to the poor, to the
>   hungry in the favelas,
>   I may even give my life for them,
>   but if I have no love, this does no good.
>
> Love is . . .
>   thinking in their thought patterns,
>   caring enough to understand their world view,
>   listening to their questions,
>   feeling their burdens,

18. David J. Hesselgrave, *Communicating Christ Cross-Culturally* (Grand Rapids: Zondervan, 1978), p. 188.

19. Khan, "Strategy to Evangelize," p. 62.

respecting them,
    identifying with them in their need,
        belonging to them.

Love is eternal.
    Cultures pass away.
        Dynamic equivalents will change because cultures
        change.
            Patterns of worship and church administration will
            need revision.
                Languages will be altered over time.
                Institutions will be replaced.
                    . . . Because these are not reality.

Since I am finite, I can only study how to express the
    Message cross-culturally, trying to free it from my
    cultural bias.
I am able to do this only in a limited way,
    but I pray that the Spirit will use my life to show Christ
    to those with whom I work.

Meanwhile these remain . . .
    Identification,
        Contextualization
            and
                Love,
                    BUT THE GREATEST OF THESE IS LOVE.[20]

20. Jean McCracken, "First Corinthians 13," *Evangelical Missions Quarterly* 15 (1979): 151. Reprinted with permission from the July 1979 *Evangelical Missions Quarterly* published by the Evangelical Missions Information Service, Box 794, Wheaton, Illinois 60187.

The author invites correspondence at the following address:

Dr. Phil Parshall
5930 S.W. 112th Avenue
Miami, FL 33173
U.S.A.

Questionnaire on Contextualized Baptism

Many of us who are attending this conference on Islam have struggled with the problem of the Muslim interpretation of Christian baptism. To the grassroots Muslim whom I serve, baptism is synonymous with the denial of one's cultural, social, political, economic, and religious value systems. Alienation from one's heritage is considered to be subsumed within the act of Christian baptism. I am presently writing a book which deals with the subject of possible adaptations of Islamic forms to Christianity. One of the most important areas to be considered will be baptism. Would you please help me out by filling in this questionnaire and returning it to me by the end of this conference? It will greatly enhance the value of this research if I can have access to your experience on the subject.

With sincere appreciation,
(signed) Phil Parshall

1. Name of mission, country, and years served on the field.
2. Describe briefly the problem (if any) you feel in regard to Christian baptism on your field.
3. What do you think of the following for Muslim converts:
   A. Secret baptism with only a few Christians present.
   B. Baptism in a distant place.
   C. Self-baptism.
   D. No baptism.
4. Baptism includes both form and meaning. A number of people are proposing that, with respect to meaning, baptism be viewed as an *initiation rite.* They feel that any relevant cultural *form* is acceptable to convey the meaning of this "rite of passage." The form in the New Testament was water, while the meaning was initiation or identification. The proposal being presented by this group is that in a culture where the form is misunderstood, it must be changed, with the expectation that a change in the form of baptism could be compared to substituting leavened bread and Kool-Aid for unleavened bread and wine in the observance of the Lord's Supper.
   A. What is your opinion of this proposal?
   B. What alternative forms could you suggest as culturally relevant to Muslim society?
   C. Could a specific period of prior training which culminates in the laying on of hands by the church leaders— and which linguistically is termed "initiation"—serve as a functional substitute for our present mode of Christian baptism? This would roughly correspond to the Jewish bar mitzvah or the Christian rite of confirmation.

Bibliography

Abbott, Freeland. *Islam and Pakistan*. Ithaca, NY: Cornell University Press, 1968.

Accad, Fuad. "The Qur'an: A Bridge to Christian Faith." *Missiology* 4.3 (1976): 331–42.

_____. "Words in Perspective—Christ in Culture." In *Conference on Media in Islamic Culture Report*, edited by C. Richard Shumaker, pp. 62–64. Marseilles: Evangelical Literature Overseas, 1974.

Addison, James. *The Christian Approach to the Moslem*. New York: Columbia University Press, 1942.

"Agapao." In *Theological Dictionary of the New Testament*, edited by Gerhard Kittel, translated by G. W. Bromiley, vol. 1, pp. 35–55. Grand Rapids: Wm. B. Eerdmans, 1964.

Ahmad, Aziz. *Studies in Islamic Culture in the Indian Environment*. Oxford: Clarendon Press, 1964.

Ahmed, Sufia. *Muslim Community in Bengal 1884–1912*. Dacca: Oxford University Press, 1974.

Ali, Abdullah Yusuf. *The Holy Quran*. Lahore: Shaikh Muhammad Ashraf, 1934.

Ali, Maulana Muhammad. *The Religion of Islam*. Lahore: The Ahmadiyya Ishaat Islam, 1936.

Ali, Zaki. *Islam in the World*. Lahore: Muhammad Ashraf, 1947.

Allen, Roland. *The Ministry of the Spirit: Selected Writings of Roland Allen*. Edited by David Paton. Grand Rapids: Wm. B. Eerdmans, 1962.

_____. *Missionary Methods: St. Paul's or Ours?* Grand Rapids: Wm. B. Eerdmans, 1962.

Almquist, Arden. *Missionary, Come Back!* New York: World Publishing Company, 1970.

Anderson, John D. C. "The Missionary Approach to Islam." *Missiology* 4.3 (1976): 285–300.

Arensberg, Conrad M., and Arthur H. Nichoff. *Introducing Social Change*. Chicago: Aldine, 1971.

Avery, George. *The Baptismal Sacrifice*. London: S.C.M. Press, 1959.

Azariah, Vedanayakam. "The Church and Its Mission." In *Addresses and Other Records*, vol. 7, Tambaram series.

_____. "The Place of the Church in Evangelism." In *Evangelism*, vol. 3, Tambaram series.

Banks, Donald. "Causes of Friction Between Missionaries and Nationals." *Evangelical Missions Quarterly* 12 (July 1976): 149–54.

Barclay, Harold B. "The Perpetuation of Muslim Tradition in the Canadian North." *The Muslim World* 59 (1969): 64–69.

Barclay, William. *The Letters to Timothy, Titus, Philemon*. Edinburgh: St. Andrew Press, 1962.

Barnouw, Victor. *Culture and Personality*. Homewood, IL: Dorsey, 1973.

Barrett, David. *Schism and Renewal in Africa*. London: Oxford University Press, 1968.

Bethman, Erich W. *Bridge to Islam*. London: George Allen and Unwin, 1953.

Birnbaum, Philip. *A Book of Jewish Concepts*. New York: Hebrew Publishing Company, 1964.

Braun, Neil. *Laity Mobilized*. Grand Rapids: Wm. B. Eerdmans, 1971.

Brewster, E. Thomas, and Elizabeth S. Brewster. *Language Acquisition Made Practical*. Colorado Springs: Lingua House, 1976.

_____. "What It Takes to Learn a Language and Get Involved with People." *Evangelical Missions Quarterly* 14 (April 1978): 101–05.

Brown, Arthur Judson. *The Foreign Missionary*. New York: Fleming H. Revell, 1907.

Burns, Robert Ignatius. *Islam Under the Crusaders*. Princeton, NJ: Princeton University Press, 1973.

Buswell, James O., III. "Contextualization: Theory, Tradition and Method." In *Theology and Mission*, edited by David J. Hesselgrave, pp. 87–111. Grand Rapids: Baker Book House, 1978.

Cailliet, Emile. *The Christian Approach to Culture*. New York: Abingdon-Cokesbury Press, 1953.

Calverley, Edwin E. "Christian Theology and the Qur'an." *The Muslim World* 47 (1957): 283–89.

_____. *Worship in Islam*. London: Luzac and Company, 1957.

Chaney, Charles. "The Apostolate of the Church in the Second Century." *Missiology* 5.4 (1977): 434.

Chowdhury, D. A. "The Bengal Church and the Convert." *The Moslem World* 29 (1939): 346–47.

Christensen, Jens. *The Practical Approach to Muslims*. Marseilles: North Africa Mission, 1977.

Chun, Chaeok. "An Exploration of the Community Model for Muslim Missionary Outreach by Asian Women." D.Miss. dissertation, Fuller Theological Seminary, 1977.

Clarkson, Thomas. *A Portraiture of Quakerism*. Indianapolis: Merrill and Field, 1870.

Cohen, Harry A. *A Basic Jewish Encyclopedia*. Hartford: Hartmore House, 1965.

Conference on Media in Islamic Culture Report. Edited by C. Richard Shumaker. Marseilles: Evangelical Literature Overseas, 1974.

Conn, Harvie M. "Contextualization." *Partnership* 12. Abington, PA: Partnership in Mission, 23 October 1978.

_____. "Contextualization: Where Do We Begin?" In *Evangelicals and Libera-tion*, edited by Carl E. Armerding, pp. 90–119. Nutley, NJ: Presbyterian and Reformed, 1977.

_____. "The Muslim Convert and His Culture." In *The Gospel and Islam: A 1978 Compendium*, edited by Don M. McCurry, pp. 97–111. Monrovia, CA: MARC, 1979.

Cook, Harold R. *Historic Patterns of Church Growth*. Chicago: Moody Press, 1971.

_____. *Missionary Life and Work*. Chicago: Moody Press, 1959.

Cooper, Elizabeth. *The Harim and the Purdah*. New York: The Century Company, 1877.

Corbin, Don. "Attempts to Penetrate the Culture." In *Conference on Media in Islamic Culture Report*, edited by C. Richard Shumaker. Marseilles: Evangelical Literature Overseas, 1974.

Covell, Ralph R. "The Extension Seminary and Church Growth." In *Crucial Dimensions in World Evangelization*, edited by Arthur F. Glasser, pp. 453–58. Pasadena: William Carey Library, 1976.

Cragg, Kenneth. *The Call of the Minaret*. New York: Oxford University Press, 1956.

_____. *The Wisdom of the Sufis*. New York: New Directions Books, 1976.

Cronin, Vincent. *The Wise Man from the West*. New York: E. P. Dutton, 1955.

Dale, James Wilkinson. *Judaic Baptism*. Philadelphia: Wm. Rutter and Co., 1871.

Daniel, Norman. *Islam and the West*. Edinburgh: Edinburgh University Press, 1960.

DeVries, Ad. *Dictionary of Symbols and Imagery*. Amsterdam: North-Holland Publishing Company, 1976.

DeWaard, Hank. "Transforming Supernaturalism in a Javanese Worldview." Paper presented to Charles H. Kraft, Fuller Theological Seminary, 1979.

Dictionary of the Bible. Edited by James Hastings. New York: Charles Scribner's Sons, 1951.

Documents of Vatican II. Edited by Austin Flannery. Grand Rapids: Wm. B. Eerdmans, 1975.

Donaldson, Bess. *The Wild Rue: A Study of Muhammadan Magic and Folklore in Iran*. New York: Arno Press, 1978 reprint of 1938 edition.

Dorsey, Barbara Belle. "Christ's Plan of Training Disciples Applied to Youth Leadership Today." M.R.E. thesis, Fuller Theological Seminary, 1956.

Douglas, Robert Cristy. "Strategic Components in Proposed Experimental Approach to Evangelization of Muslims." Project presented to the School of World Mission, Fuller Theological Seminary, 1977.

Dretke, James Paul. "Opening a New Door to Dialogue Between Christians and Muslims in Ghana." D.Miss. dissertation, Fuller Theological Seminary, 1974.

Dyck, Peter. "A Theology of Service." *Mennonite Quarterly Review* 44.3 (July 1970): 262–80.

Dyrness, William A. "Contextualization and the Christian Communicator." *ACCF Journal* 1 (1978): 5–8.

Ehat, Donald M. "Towards a Personal Philosophy of Leadership Development." M.R.E. thesis, Fuller Theological Seminary, 1960.

Elder, Earl E. "Crucifixion in the Koran." *The Moslem World* 13 (1923): 242–58.

Ellickson, Jean. "A Believer Among Believers: The Religious Beliefs, Practices and Meanings in a Village in Bangladesh." Ph.D. dissertation, Michigan State University, 1972.

Ellis, William T. *Men and Missions.* Philadelphia: The Sunday School Times, 1909.

Encyclopedia of the Jewish Religion. Edited by R. J. Werblowsky and G. Wigoder. New York: Holt, Rinehart and Winston, 1965.

Engstrom, Ted W. *The Making of a Christian Leader.* Grand Rapids: Zondervan, 1978.

Ericson, Norman R. "Implications from the New Testament for Contextualization." In *Theology and Mission,* edited by David J. Hesselgrave, pp. 71–85. Grand Rapids: Baker Book House, 1978.

Farah, Caesar E. *Islam: Beliefs and Observances.* Woodbury, NY: Barron's Education Series, 1968.

Fatemi, Nasrollah S. *Sufism.* New York: A. S. Barnes, 1976.

Fernea, Elizabeth Warnock, and Basima Qattan Bezirgan, eds. *Middle Eastern Muslim Women Speak.* Austin: University of Texas Press, 1977.

Fisher, J. D. C. *Christian Initiation: Baptism in the Medieval West.* London: S.P.C.K., 1965.

Gardner, John W. *Excellence.* New York: Harper and Row, 1961.

Gatje, Helmut. *The Qur'an and Its Exegesis.* Berkeley: University of California Press, 1976.

Gaudefroy-Demombynes, Maurice. *Muslim Institutions.* London: George Allen and Unwin, 1961.

German, David. "Church Music Has Come a Long Way." Bulletin of Highland Park Baptist Church (Southfield, Michigan), 6 May 1979.

Gibb, H. A. R., and J. H. Kramers. *Shorter Encyclopedia of Islam.* Ithaca, NY: Cornell University Press, 1965.

Gilliland, Dean Stewart. *African Traditional Religions in Transition.* Hartford: The Hartford Seminary Foundation, 1972.

Glasser, Arthur F. "Power Encounter in Conversion from Islam." In *The Gospel and Islam: A 1978 Compendium,* edited by Don M. McCurry, pp. 129–39. Monrovia, CA: MARC, 1979.

_____, ed. *Crucial Dimensions in World Evangelization.* Pasadena: William Carey Library, 1976.

Goldsack, W. *Christ in Islam.* London: The Christian Literature Society, 1905.

Goldsmith, Martin. "Community and Controversy." *Missiology* 4.3 (1976): 320–23.

Gowing, Peter G. *Mosque and Moro.* Manila: Philippine Federation of Christian Churches, 1964.

Gray, Richard. *The Cambridge History of Africa.* Volume 4. Cambridge: Cambridge University Press, 1975.

Greenleaf, Robert K. *The Servant as Leader.* New York: Paulist Press, 1977.

Grewal, J. S. *Muslim Rule in India.* Calcutta: Oxford University Press, 1970.

Guillaume, Alfred. *Islam.* Baltimore: Penguin Books, 1954.

Gurney, Joseph John. *Observations on the Distinguishing Views and Practices of the Society of Friends.* New York: Samuel S. and William Wood, 1856.

Hahn, Ernest. *Jesus in Islam: A Christian View.* Hyderabad: Henry Martyn Institute of Islamic Studies, 1978.

Hakim, Khalifa Abdul. *The Islamic Ideology.* N.p., 1953.

Haleblian, Krikor. "World View and Evangelization: A Case Study on Arab People." Th.M. thesis, Fuller Theological Seminary, 1979.

Haqq, Akbar Abdul. "Inaugural Address: Samuel Zwemer Institute." Pasadena, 31 March 1979.

Harman, S. *Plight of Muslims in India*. London: DL Publications, 1977.

Hassan, Hassan Ibrahim. "Aspects of Shi'ah History." *The Muslim World* 47 (1957): 271.

Hay, Ian M. "Missions and the Future." In *Evangelical Missions Tomorrow*, edited by Wade T. Coggins and E. L. Frizen, Jr., pp. 119–31. Pasadena: William Carey Library, 1977.

Hefley, James C. *The New Jews*. Wheaton, IL: Tyndale House, 1971.

Hesselgrave, David J. *Communicating Christ Cross-Culturally*. Grand Rapids: Zondervan, 1978.

_____, ed. *Theology and Mission*. Grand Rapids: Baker Book House, 1978.

Hiebert, Paul. *Cultural Anthropology*. New York: J. B. Lippincott, 1976.

_____. "Culture and Cross-Cultural Differences." In *Crucial Dimensions in World Evangelization*, edited by Arthur F. Glasser, pp. 45–60. Pasadena: William Carey Library, 1976.

_____. "Social Structure and Church Growth." In *Crucial Dimensions in World Evangelization*, edited by Arthur F. Glasser, pp. 61–74. Pasadena: William Carey Library, 1976.

Hoffman, Valerie. "The Christian Approach to the Muslim Woman and Family." In *The Gospel and Islam: A 1978 Compendium*, edited by Don M. McCurry, pp. 581–93. Monrovia, CA: MARC, 1979.

Hopewell, James F. "Preparing the Candidate for Mission." In *Theological Education by Extension*, edited by Ralph D. Winter, pp. 36–53. Pasadena: William Carey Library, 1969.

Hughes, Thomas Patrick. *A Dictionary of Islam*. London: W. H. Allen and Company, 1895.

Husayni, Ishaq Musa al. "Christ in the Qur'an and in Modern Arabic Literature." *The Muslim World* 50 (1960): 297–302.

Inniger, Merlin W. "Getting to Know Their 'Heart Hunger' Is a Key to Reaching Muslims." *Evangelical Missions Quarterly* 15 (January 1979): 35.

"Islam." *Encyclopaedia Britannica, Macropaedia*, 1974 edition, vol. 9, pp. 911–26.

"Islamic Mysticism." *Encyclopaedia Britannica, Macropaedia*, 1974 edition, vol. 9, pp. 943–48.

Jeffery, Arthur, ed. *Islam: Muhammad and His Religion*. New York: Liberal Arts Press, 1958.

Jenkinson, E. J. "Jesus in Moslem Tradition." *The Moslem World* 18 (1928): 263–69.

Jobes, Gertrude. *Dictionary of Mythology Folklore and Symbols*. New York: Scarecrow Press, 1961.

Johnson, Robert, ed. *The Church and Its Changing Ministry*. N.p.: General Assembly of the Presbyterian Church in the U.S.A., 1961.

"John the Baptist." In *The New Bible Dictionary*, edited by J. D. Douglas, pp. 641–42. Grand Rapids: Wm. B. Eerdmans, 1962.

Jones, L. Bevan. "How Not to Use the Koran." *The Moslem World* 30 (1940): 280–91.

_____. *The People of the Mosque.* Calcutta: YMCA Publishing House, 1939.

_____, and Violet Rhoda Jones. *The Life of Muslim Women.* London: Fellowship of Faith for the Muslims, n.d.

July, Robert W. *A History of the African People.* London: Faber and Faber, 1970.

Just, Sister Mary. *Digest of Catholic Mission History.* Maryknoll, NY: Maryknoll Publications, 1957.

Kane, J. Herbert. Letter to the editor. *World Vision Magazine* 23.3 (1979): 19.

Kearney, Michael. "World View Theory and Study." *Annual Review of Anthropology* 4 (1975).

Keesing, Roger. "World View and Cultural Integration." In *Cultural Anthropology*, pp. 406–25. New York: Holt, Rinehart and Winston, 1976.

Kennedy, D. James. *Evangelism Explosion.* Wheaton, IL: Tyndale House, 1970.

Khair-Ullah, Frank. "Evangelism Among Muslims." In *Let the Earth Hear His Voice*, edited by J. D. Douglas, pp. 816–27. Minneapolis: World Wide Publications, 1975.

_____. "The Role of Local Churches in God's Redemptive Plan for the Muslim World." In *The Gospel and Islam: A 1978 Compendium*, edited by Don M. McCurry, pp. 566–77. Monrovia, CA: MARC, 1979.

Khan, Anwar M. "Strategy to Evangelize Muslim Jats in Pakistan." Th.M. thesis, Fuller Theological Seminary, 1976.

Khan, Muhammad Zafrulla. *Islam: Its Meanings for Modern Man.* New York: Harper and Row, 1962.

Kietzman, Dale W. "Conversion and Culture Change." In *Readings in Missionary Anthropology*, edited by William A. Smalley, pp. 124–31. Tarrytown, NY: Practical Anthropology, 1967.

_____. "The Missionary's Role in Culture Change." In *Readings in Missionary Anthropology*, edited by William A. Smalley, pp. 276–81. Tarrytown, NY: Practical Anthropology, 1967.

Kinsler, F. Ross. *The Extension Movement in Theological Education.* Pasadena: William Carey Library, 1978.

Kluckhohn, Florence R., and Fred L. Strodtbeck. *Variations in Value Orientations.* Westport, CT: Greenwood Press, 1961.

Kraemer, Hendrik. *Religion and the Christian Faith.* Philadelphia: Westminster Press, 1956.

_____. *A Theology of the Laity.* Philadelphia: Westminster Press, 1958.

Kraft, Charles H. *Christianity in Culture.* Maryknoll, NY: Orbis Books, 1979.

_____. "The Cultural and the Supra-Cultural." Paper at Fuller Theological Seminary, 1971.

_____. "Cultural Conversion." In *Conference on Media in Islamic Culture Report*, edited by C. Richard Shumaker. Marseilles: Evangelical Literature Overseas, 1974.

_____. "Dynamic Equivalence Churches." In *Conference on Media in Islamic Culture Report*, edited by C. Richard Shumaker. Marseilles: Evangelical Literature Overseas, 1974.

_____. "Dynamic Equivalence Churches: An Ethnotheological Approach to Indigeneity." Paper at Fuller Theological Seminary, n.d.

_____. "Dynamic Equivalence Churches in Muslim Society." In *The Gospel and*

Islam: A 1978 Compendium, edited by Don M. McCurry, pp. 114–22. Monrovia, CA: MARC, 1979.

_____. "God, Man, Culture and the Cross-Cultural Communication of the Gospel." Paper at Fuller Theological Seminary, 1972.

_____. "God's Model for Cross-Cultural Communication—The Incarnation." *Evangelical Missions Quarterly* 9 (Summer 1973): 208–10.

_____. "Ideological Factors in Intercultural Communication." *Missiology* 2.3 (1974): 295–313.

_____. "Intercultural Communication and Worldview Change." Paper at Fuller Theological Seminary, 1976.

_____. "A Survey of Islam in Nigeria." B.D. thesis, Ashland Theological Seminary, 1957.

_____. "What Is God Trying to Do?" *Theology News and Notes,* Fuller Theological Seminary, March 1977.

_____. "The Younger Churches: Missionaries and Indigeneity." Paper at Fuller Theological Seminary, 1971.

_____, and Ralph D. Winter. "Basic Questions That Need to be Researched with Respect to Communicating the Gospel to Muslims." Paper at Fuller Theological Seminary, 1975.

Latourette, Kenneth. *A History of the Expansion of Christianity.* Volume 2. New York: Harper and Brothers, 1939.

Leaney, A. R. C. *The Rule of Qumran and Its Meaning.* London: S.C.M. Press, 1966.

Let the Earth Hear His Voice. Edited by J. D. Douglas. Minneapolis: World Wide Publications, 1975.

Levy, Reuben. *The Social Structure of Islam.* Cambridge: Cambridge University Press, 1957.

Lewin, Leonard, ed. "The Elephant in the Dark." In *Christianity, Islam, and the Sufis.* New York: E. P. Dutton, 1976.

Lewis, Barbara Anne. "Pakistan Mosaic: The Interaction of Animist, Islamic and Western Cultures." Unpublished paper, 1972.

Lindsell, Harold. *Missionary Principles and Practice.* Westwood, NJ: Fleming H. Revell, 1955.

_____, ed. *The Church's Worldwide Mission.* Waco, TX: Word Books, 1966.

Lings, Martin. *What Is Sufism?* Berkeley: University of California Press, 1975.

Loewen, Jacob A. "Toward Contextualization—An Analysis of Factors Motivating or Inhibiting Syncretism." Unpublished paper, Emory University, 1979.

McCoy, Joseph A. *Advice from the Field.* Baltimore: Helicon Press, 1962.

McCracken, Jean. "First Corinthians 13." *Evangelical Missions Quarterly* 15 (1979): 151.

McCurry, Don M. "Cross-Cultural Models for Muslim Evangelism." *Missiology* 4.3 (1976): 280.

_____, ed. *The Gospel and Islam: A 1978 Compendium.* Monrovia, CA: MARC, 1979.

McEwan, P. J. M., ed. *Africa from Early Times to 1800.* London: Oxford University Press, 1969.

McGavran, Donald A. "The Adaptation-Syncretism Axis." In *Christopaganism* or *Indigenous Christianity*, edited by Tetsunao Yamamori and Charles R. Taber, pp. 225–43. Pasadena: William Carey Library, 1975.

_____. "Basic Policy in Evangelism." Paper at Fuller Theological Seminary, 1964.

_____. *The Clash Between Christianity and Culture*. Washington, DC: Canon Press, 1974.

_____. *The Conciliar-Evangelical Debate: The Crucial Documents, 1964–1976*. Pasadena: William Carey Library, 1977.

_____. "The Entrepreneur in Modern Missions." Paper at Fuller Theological Seminary, 1978.

_____. *Ethnic Realities and the Church*. Pasadena: William Carey Library, 1979.

_____. *How Churches Grow*. London: World Dominion Press, 1959.

_____. "Social Justice and Evangelism." *World Vision Magazine*, June 1965.

_____. *Understanding Church Growth*. Grand Rapids: Wm. B. Eerdmans, 1970.

Mallick, Azizur Rahman. *British Policy and the Muslims in Bengal*. Dacca: Bangla Academy, 1977.

Martin, Malcolm. "The Missionary and the Holy Spirit." *Missiology* 5.2 (April 1977): 223–40.

Massih, Bashir Abdol. "The Incarnational Witness to the Muslim Heart." In *The Gospel and Islam: A 1978 Compendium*, edited by Don M. McCurry, pp. 85–92. Monrovia, CA: MARC, 1979.

Mathews, Shailer, and Gerald Birney Smith. *A Dictionary of Religion and Ethics*. New York: Macmillan, 1923.

Mennonite Central Committee. "MCC: A Christian Resource for Meeting Human Need." Public relations material, 1979.

Mernissi, Fatima. *Beyond the Veil*. New York: Schenkman, 1975.

Merrill, John E. "Friends of the Muslims." *The Moslem World* 30 (1940): 138.

Miller, William McElwee. *A Christian's Response to Islam*. Nutley, NJ: Presbyterian and Reformed, 1977.

_____. *Ten Muslims Meet Christ*. Grand Rapids: Wm. B. Eerdmans, 1969.

Morrison, S. A. "Thoughts on Evangelism." *The Moslem World* 34 (1944): 199–208.

"The Mosque Should Be Used as the Centre of Community Service." *Dainik Bangla*, 1 August 1977.

Muldrow, William F. "Identification and the Role of the Missionary." *Practical Anthropology* 18 (1971): 208–21.

Murdock, George Peter. *Africa: Its Peoples and Their Culture*. New York: McGraw-Hill, 1959.

Musk, Bill. "Popular Islam: The Hunger of the Heart." In *The Gospel and Islam: A 1978 Compendium*, edited by Don M. McCurry, pp. 208–21. Monrovia, CA: MARC, 1979.

_____. "Roles: God, Communicator, Muslim." Special project for Dean Gilliland, Fuller Theological Seminary, 1978.

Nakhosteen, A. "The Bible in Moslem Hands." *The Moslem World* 35 (1945): 300–03.

Nasr, Seyyed Hossein. *Ideals and Realities of Islam*. London: George Allen and Unwin, 1966.

Neill, Stephen. *Christian Faith and Other Faiths*. London: Oxford University Press, 1977.

_____. *Christian Missions*. Baltimore: Penguin Books, 1964.

_____. *Salvation Tomorrow*. Nashville: Abingdon, 1976.

Newbigin, Lesslie. *The Open Secret*. London: S.P.C.K., 1978.

Nicholls, Bruce J. "A Living Theology for Asian Churches." Paper presented to the Asia Theological Association Consultation, Singapore, 10-15 November 1978.

Nida, Eugene. *Message and Mission*. New York: Harper and Brothers, 1960.

Niebuhr, H. Richard. *Christ and Culture*. New York: Harper and Brothers, 1951.

Nomani, Mohammad Manzoor. *Islamic Faith and Practice*. Lucknow: Academy of Islamic Research Publications, 1962.

Nyrop, Richard F. *Area Handbook for Bangladesh*. Washington, DC: U.S. Government Printing Office, 1975.

Obeng-Abyemang, Nicholas. "Rooting the Church in West African Soil." *Christianity Today* 23.14, 20 April 1979, pp. 51-53.

Oliver, Roland, ed. *The Cambridge History of Africa*. Volume 3. Cambridge: Cambridge University Press, 1977.

Orr, J. Edwin. "The Call to Spiritual Renewal." In *The Gospel and Islam: A 1978 Compendium*, edited by Don M. McCurry, pp. 419-25. Monrovia, CA: MARC, 1979.

Padwick, Constance E. "The Language of Muslim Devotion." *The Muslim World* 47 (1957): 5-21, 98-110, 194-209, 299-317.

Parratt, J. K., and A. R. I. Doi. "Syncretism in Yorubaland: A Religious or a Sociological Phenomenon?" *Practical Anthropology* 16 (1969): 109-13.

Parrinder, Geoffrey. *Jesus in the Quran*. London: Faber and Faber, 1965.

_____. *Religion in Africa*. New York: Praeger, 1969.

Parshall, Phil. "Evangelizing Muslims: Are There Ways?" *Christianity Today* 23.7, 5 January 1979, pp. 28-31.

_____. *The Fortress and the Fire*. Bombay: Gospel Literature Service, 1976.

Paul VI, Pope. *On Evangelization in the Modern World*. Washington, DC: U.S. Catholic Conference, 1975.

Peters, George W. "Issues Confronting Evangelical Missions." In *Evangelical Missions Tomorrow*, edited by Wade T. Coggins and E. L. Frizen, Jr., pp. 156-71. Pasadena: William Carey Library, 1977.

Pfander, C. G. *The Mizanu'l Haqq ("Balance of Truth")*. London: The Religious Tract Society, 1910.

Pickett, Robert C., and Rufino L. Macagba, Jr. "Food and Health as Partners of Muslim Evangelism." In *The Gospel and Islam: A 1978 Compendium*, edited by Don M. McCurry, pp. 553-63. Monrovia, CA: MARC, 1979.

Pickthall, Mohammed Marmaduke. *The Meaning of the Glorious Koran*. New York: New American Library, n.d.

Pike, Kenneth L. *With Heart and Mind*. Grand Rapids: Wm. B. Eerdmans, 1962.

Rahim, Ataur Muhammad. *Jesus Prophet of Islam*. Norfolk, England: Diwan Press, 1977.

Read, Herbert. *To Hell with Culture*. New York: Schocken Books, 1963.

Redfield, Robert. *The Primitive World and Its Transformations*. Ithaca, NY: Cornell University Press, 1953.

Reyburn, William D. "The Current Status of Bible Translations in Muslim Languages." In *The Gospel and Islam: A 1978 Compendium*, edited by Don M. McCurry, pp. 362-73. Monrovia, CA: MARC, 1979.

Rich, John A. "Religious Acculturation in the Philippines." *Practical Anthropology* 17 (1970): 196-209.

Rickards, Donald. "Development of New Tools to Aid Muslim Evangelization." In *The Gospel and Islam: A 1978 Compendium*, edited by Don M. McCurry, pp. 429-38. Monrovia, CA: MARC, 1979.

Riggs, Henry H. "Unbeaten Paths in Work for Moslems." *The Moslem World* 31 (1941): 116-26.

Rigors, Paul. "Leadership and Domination Among Children." *Sociologus* 9 (June 1933).

Robinson, Robert. *History of Baptism*. Boston: Press of Lincoln and Edmands, 1817.

Robson, James. "Muhammadan Teaching About Jesus." *The Moslem World* 29 (1939): 37-54.

Rogers, Everett M., and L. Floyd Shoemaker. *Communication of Innovations*. 2nd edition. New York: Free Press, 1971.

Ryan, Patrick J. *Imale: Yoruba Participation in the Muslim Tradition*. Missoula, MT: Scholars Press, 1978.

Saeed, Ibrahim. "Why Am I a Christian?" *The Moslem World* 18 (1928): 66-72.

Salvation Army Book of Doctrine. London: International Headquarters, The Salvation Army, 1935.

Scherer, James A. *Missionary, Go Home!* Englewood Cliffs, NJ: Prentice-Hall, 1964.

Schimmel, Annemarie. *Mystical Dimensions of Islam*. Chapel Hill: University of North Carolina Press, 1975.

Sell, Edward. *Sufism*. London: The Christian Literature Society for India, 1910.

Sheikh, Bilquis. *I Dared to Call Him Father*. Waco, TX: Chosen Books, 1978.

Siddiqi, Md. Mazheruddin. *Women in Islam*. Lahore: The Institute of Islamic Culture, 1959.

Silvernale, Lynn. "Study of Bengali Culture." Unpublished paper, 1975.

Sire, James. *The Universe Next Door*. Downers Grove, IL: Inter-Varsity Press, 1976.

Smalley, William A. "Cultural Implications of an Indigenous Church." *Practical Anthropology* 5 (1958): 51-65.

_____. "Proximity or Neighborliness?" In *Readings in Missionary Anthropology*, pp. 302-04. Tarrytown, NY: Practical Anthropology, 1967.

_____. "Respect and Ethnocentrism." In *Readings in Missionary Anthropology*, pp. 255-57. Tarrytown, NY: Practical Anthropology, 1967.

Smith, Edwin W. *The Golden Stool*. Garden City, NY: Doubleday, Doran and Co., 1928.

Smith, Margaret. "Transmigration and the Sufis." *The Moslem World* 30 (1940): 351-57.

Smith, Montgomery W. "Homogeneity and American Church Growth." D.Miss. dissertation, Fuller Theological Seminary, 1976.

Smith, Wilfred Cantwell. *Modern Islam in India*. London: Victor Gollancz, 1946.

_____. *Pakistan as an Islamic State*. Lahore: Shaikh Muhammad Ashraf, 1916.

Soltau, T. Stanley. *Missions at the Crossroads.* Grand Rapids: Baker Book House, 1955.

Sommer, Annie Van, and Samuel M. Zwemer, eds. *Our Moslem Sisters.* London: Fleming H. Revell, 1907.

Spradley, James P., and David W. McCurdy. *Anthropology: The Cultural Perspective.* New York: John Wiley and Sons, 1975.

Stacey, Vivienne. "Levels, Styles and Locations of Training Programs." In *The Gospel and Islam: A 1978 Compendium,* edited by Don M. McCurry, pp. 442–51. Monrovia, CA: MARC, 1979.

Stendahl, Krister. *Paul Among Jews and Gentiles and Other Essays.* Philadelphia: Fortress Press, 1976.

Steward, Julian H. *Theory of Culture Change.* Urbana: University of Illinois Press, 1955.

Stock, Frederick E. *People Movements in the Punjab.* Pasadena: William Carey Library, 1975.

Stott, John R. W. "Christians and Muslims." *Christianity Today* 23.5, 1 December 1978, pp. 34–35.

Swank, Gerald O. "General Description of Fulani Evangelism for West Africa." Paper for the Sudan Interior Mission, 1978.

Sweetman, J. W. "A Muslim's View of Christianity." *The Moslem World* 34 (1944): 278–84.

Symonds, Richard. *The Making of Pakistan.* London: Faber and Faber, 1952.

Taber, Charles R. "Contextualization: Indigenization and/or Transformation." In *The Gospel and Islam: A 1978 Compendium,* edited by Don M. McCurry, pp. 143–50. Monrovia, CA: MARC, 1979.

Thomson, William. "An Introduction to the History of Sufism." *The Moslem World* 35 (1945): 63–66.

Toliver, Ralph. "Syncretism: A Specter Among Philippine Protestants." *Practical Anthropology* 17 (1970): 210–19.

Trimingham, J. Spencer. *The Christian Church and Islam in West Africa.* London: SCM Press, 1955.

————. *The Influence of Islam upon Africa.* London: Longmans, Green and Company, 1968.

————. *Islam in East Africa.* London: Edinburgh House Press, 1962.

————. *Islam in West Africa.* Oxford: Clarendon Press, 1959.

Tritton, A. S. *Islam Belief and Practices.* London: Hutchinson University Library, 1962.

Turner, Nathan W. *Effective Leadership in Small Groups.* Valley Forge, PA: Judson Press, 1977.

Van Akkeren, Philip. *Sri and Christ: A Study of the Indigenous Church in East Java.* Translated by Annebeth Mackie. London: Lutterworth Press, 1970.

VanTil, Henry R. *The Calvinistic Concept of Culture.* Grand Rapids: Baker Book House, 1959.

Verkuyl, Johannes. *Contemporary Missiology: An Introduction.* Translated by Dale Cooper. Grand Rapids: Wm. B. Eerdmans, 1978.

Vidyarthi, L. P. *Leadership in India.* Bombay: Asia Publishing House, 1967.

Visser 't Hooft, W. A. *None Other Gods.* London: Student Christian Movement Press, 1937.

Von Grunebaum, G. E. *Islam*. London: Routledge and Kegan Paul, 1909.

_____. *Muhammadan Festivals*. New York: Henry Schuman, 1909.

Voobus, Arthur. *Early Versions of the New Testament*. Stockholm: Estonian Theological Society in Exile, 1954.

Wagner, C. Peter. "The Birth of the Extension Seminary." In *Crucial Dimensions in World Evangelization*, edited by Arthur F. Glasser, pp. 438-44. Pasadena: William Carey Library, 1976.

_____. "Changing Patterns of Ministerial Training." In *Crucial Dimensions in World Evangelization*, edited by Arthur F. Glasser, pp. 399-411. Pasadena: William Carey Library, 1976.

_____. "How God Makes Ministers." In *Crucial Dimensions in World Evangelization*, edited by Arthur F. Glasser, pp. 412-19. Pasadena: William Carey Library, 1976.

_____. *Your Spiritual Gifts*. Glendale: Regal Books, 1979.

_____, and Edward Dayton. *Unreached Peoples '79*. Elgin, IL: David C. Cook, 1978.

Wakatama, Pius. *Independence for the Third World Church*. Downers Grove, IL: Inter-Varsity Press, 1976.

Watt, W. Montgomery. *Islam and the Integration of Society*. London: Routledge and Kegan Paul, 1966.

_____. "Thoughts on Muslim Christian Dialogue." *Hamdard Islamicus* 1.1 (1978).

_____. *What Is Islam?* London: Longmans, Green and Company, 1968.

Wedeck, H. E., and Wade Baskin. *Dictionary of Pagan Religions*. New York: Philosophical Library, 1971.

Weld, Wayne C. *The World Directory of Theological Education by Extension*. Pasadena: William Carey Library, 1973.

White, R. E. O. *The Biblical Doctrine of Initiation*. Grand Rapids: Wm. B. Eerdmans, 1960.

Whitehouse, Aubrey. *The Qur'an Says . . . .* Birmingham: The Fellowship of Faith for the Muslims, n.d.

Williams, John Alden, ed. *Islam*. New York: George Braziller, 1961.

Williams, Thomas. "Ideology and Socialization." In *Introduction to Socialization*. St. Louis: Mosby, 1972.

Willowbank Report. A report of the Lausanne-sponsored Consultation on Gospel and Culture. *Partnership* 12. Abington, PA: Partnership in Mission, 23 October 1978.

Wilson, J. Christy, Sr. "The Bible and Moslems." *The Moslem World* 27 (1937): 237-50.

_____. "Moslem Converts." *The Moslem World* 34 (1944): 171-84.

Wink, Walter. *John the Baptist in the Gospel Tradition*. Cambridge: Cambridge University Press, 1968.

Winter, Ralph D. "The Highest Priority: Cross-Cultural Evangelism." In *Crucial Dimensions in World Evangelization*, edited by Arthur F. Glasser, pp. 105-31. Pasadena: William Carey Library, 1976.

Wismar, Adolph. *A Study in Tolerance*. New York: AMS Press, 1966.

Wong, James. *The Third World Missions*. Pasadena: William Carey Library, 1973.

_____, Peter Larson, and Edward Pentecost. "Missions from the Third

World." In *Crucial Dimensions in World Evangelization*, edited by Arthur F. Glasser, pp. 345–96. Pasadena: William Carey Library, 1976.

Woodsmall, Ruth Frances. *Eastern Women Today and Tomorrow*. Boston: The Central Committee on the United Study of Foreign Missions, 1933.

Wysham, William N., trans. "From Islam to Christ." *The Moslem World* 18 (1928): 49–60.

Yancey, Philip. "Lessons from the Camps: Isolating the Human Spirit." *Christianity Today* 23.15, 4 May 1979, pp. 25–29.

Young, Frank. *Initiation Ceremonies*. New York: Bobbs-Merrill, 1965.

Youssef, Michael A. "Theology and Methodology for Muslim Evangelism in Egypt." M.A. thesis, Fuller Theological Seminary, 1978.

Zwemer, Samuel M. *Across the World of Islam*. New York: Fleming H. Revell, 1929.

_____. "Atonement by Blood Sacrifice in Islam." *The Moslem World* 36 (1946): 189–92.

_____. *Call to Prayer*. London: Marshall Brothers, 1924.

_____. *The Cross Above the Crescent*. Grand Rapids: Zondervan, 1941.

_____. *Dynamic Christianity and the World Today*. London: Intervarsity Fellowship of Evangelical Unions, 1939.

_____. *Evangelism Today*. New York: Fleming H. Revell, 1954.

_____. *The Influence of Animism on Islam*. New York: Macmillan, 1920.

_____. *Islam: A Challenge to Faith*. New York: Student Volunteer Movement for Foreign Missions, 1907.

_____. "Islam's Allah and the Christian God." *The Moslem World* 36 (1946): 306–18.

_____. *The Moslem World*. Philadelphia: American Baptist Publication Society, 1907.

_____. *Taking Hold of God*. Grand Rapids: Zondervan, 1936.

_____, and A. E. Zwemer. *Moslem Women*. West Medford, MA: Central Committee on the United Study of Foreign Missions, 1926.

Subject Index

Scripture Index